BUILDING A SUCCESSFUL

NETWORK MARKETING COMPANY

BUILDING A SUCCESSFUL

NETWORK MARKETING COMPANY

The Systems, the Products, and the
Know-How You Need to Launch or
Enhance a Successful MLM Company

Angela L. Moore

PRIMA PUBLISHING

PRIMA PUBLISHING and colophon are registered trademarks of Prima Communications, Inc.

Library of Congress Cataloging-in-Publication Data

Moore, Angela L.
  Building a successful network marketing company : the systems, the products, and the know-how you need to launch or enhance a successful MLM company/Angela L. Moore.
    p.   cm.
  Includes index.
  ISBN 0-7615-1273-X
  1. Multilevel marketing.   I. Title.
HF5415.126.M66 1998 658.84
658.8'4—DC21   98-9245
                                                                                        CIP

98 99 00 01 HH 10 9 8 7 6 5 4 3 2 1
Printed in the United States of America

How to Order
Single copies may be ordered from Prima Publishing, P.O. Box 1260BK, Rocklin, CA 95677; telephone (916) 632-4400. Quantity discounts are also available. On your letterhead, include information concerning the intended use of the books and the number of books you wish to purchase.

Visit us online at www.primapublishing.com

*This book is dedicated to my son Jimmy Moore,
the ultimate performer and musician who brings
joy to my life through his talent and love.*

Contents

Contents

MY GOAL IN writing this book is to generate a *Success Formula* that defines the ingredients, or *success factors*, of a successful network marketing company, from an owner's or corporate executive's perspective. I also want to provide you with the opportunity to see how other executives and educators view specific aspects of network marketing.

More and more people are looking for a road map to begin the journey of starting their own company, or to help them learn how to grow their existing business by distributing new and different product lines through this popular channel. In my consulting business I am constantly challenged to answer such questions as, "Where do I begin?"; "What compensation plan should I use?"; "How do I find leaders who will develop the field?"; "My business is not growing fast enough; what's going wrong?" Owners and investors need answers to those and other questions, but until now there has been no reference book of answers. Scarier than scarce answers are the questions that do not get asked because people entering the arena don't know what it is that they don't know.

This book is written for intrigued investors, entrepreneurs, and company owners or potential owners who are asking themselves, "How can I start my own network

marketing/multilevel marketing (MLM) company?";
"How can I get into this apparently lucrative business?";
or "'How can I take my existing company to the next sales
level?" Even large companies that currently operate in another distribution channel such as retail, direct mail, and
the infomercial market want to test the waters to see how
the network marketing channel can support or supplement their mainstream distribution. Other entrepreneurs
in the international arena are also looking to enter this
channel. Not only do they see the success of numerous
U.S.-based companies, but they look to the ease of entry
and lack of need for bricks and mortar in the form of
storefronts to get their products to market.

The intent of this book is to satisfy their curiosity and
answer their questions. It will also help people currently
in the business to reevaluate their strategy against the
unique Success Formula provided in this book. It will also
serve as a guide through the legal maze associated with
starting a legitimate company that is in it for the long
term.

Richard Poe created quite a stir and developed widespread interest in the field with his *Success* magazine article "Network Marketing: The Most Powerful Way to
Reach Consumers in the '90s." Following that, he published the now best-selling book entitled *Wave 3: The New
Era in Network Marketing*, which examines this process
called network marketing. While that book primarily
targeted distributors in the field, it also began to define

what a "Wave 3" or *good* network marketing company would look like.

Craig Bradley (who has helped to grow a major network marketing company from the inside out) approached me with the idea of writing a book about network marketing and MLM companies from an insider's, or corporate executive's, viewpoint. Craig suggested I author a book sharing guidelines for a start-up company's success. I have been an "insider" (meaning I have experienced things from the owner's perspective) and executive in various successful companies for more than twenty years, and I love to share my insights with others. Creating a book on the subject seemed not only appropriate but also exciting. With Craig's urging, I set out to write a book that outlines the steps to starting and building a successful Network Marketing/MLM company; one that could be used as a tool for start-ups and help existing companies reevaluate their businesses.

The formula I developed is a combination of factors I've observed and learned. People in the industry will both agree and disagree with some of the success factors, since entrepreneurs as a group generally have vivid opinions. And as the first person to chronicle the set of key success components for a network marketing venture, I hope to pave the way for others to say more on the subject in the future. I do believe this book will give you valuable ideas that will offer extensive payback as you start your own network marketing company or upgrade your existing business. That's what will make my writing and your reading of this book worthwhile.

Some of the Success Factors are generic to the start-up of any business, such as appropriate products, or servicing and satisfying customers. Others are more specific to the network marketing industry. Creating a unique culture, offering consumable products, and giving priority to recognition of people are more precisely related to the success of a network marketing company. My own theory is that many non-MLM companies would do well to adopt some of the cultural and emotional aspects of our industry in order to reconnect with their employees and customers. After all, corporations' impersonal cutbacks and lack of connection and loyalty to their employees is fueling the growth of our industry, as former members of Corporate America's top management join the ranks of our field leadership and distributors. You can only repress human expression for so long before people find another outlet for creativity and recognition, and network marketing has become that Mecca.

As you read the chapters (especially Chapters 13 through 16) you will be treated to input and observations from some of the industry's top authorities. At the end of the book, there is a resource list that references places for you to go to get specific help to make your venture into network marketing all that it can be.

Because I want to educate and not confuse the reader, I have also provided a glossary at the back of the book. Network marketing has many words that appear to belong to a language all its own. Because so many terms are uniquely defined or used interchangeably (such as network marketing, direct selling, and multilevel marketing), it's necessary to define them and provide explanations of how the industry uses them.

Many books have been written about network marketing, MLM, and direct selling companies—nearly all from the perspective of the field sales force. They focus on why network marketing is the career of choice, or how to choose a company with which to be associated. They provide ideas about various topics such as how to recruit, train, and motivate a sales force. If you are a distributor or a prospective distributor, by all means read those books too. They fill a need and reach a huge audience, as the latest statistics show that more than eight million people distribute products through direct selling and network marketing.[1]

Distributors and prospects can also find useful information in this book to determine how a company measures up to the Success Formula. This formula will help distributors or investors determine if a company they are considering is ethical and in business for the long term, and it will also help them understand why tough decisions often need to be made in the short run to help keep the company around in the long run—especially decisions relating to the conduct of its independent distributors in the field.

---

1. *1996 Direct Selling Industry Guide: Growth and Outlook Survey,* Washington D.C., Direct Selling Association, 1996.

As the book unfolds, Success Formula components should become evident, and I feel honored to be able to share the resulting equation with you. My hope is that this formula will serve as a checklist for start-ups that need a guide, for existing companies to see how they measure up, and for distributors and prospective distributors to see how a company they represent or are considering fills the bill. Ultimately, only you can be the judge to determine if my goals are met.

Thank you for embarking on this journey with me.

Acknowledgments

THERE WERE NUMEROUS pleasurable moments in the process of writing this book. Some came through the recollection of many days gone by working with various network marketing companies. I have fond memories of the many people who educated me and enabled me to undertake the writing of this book.

The most rewarding aspect of writing the book was the connection with others and the teamwork that was required to finish the job. Many, many people undertook the effort with me to transform the work into an educational piece for you to learn from. Others helped by checking in and continually motivating me to keep moving forward.

I would like to thank the many executives in the industry who joined me in the effort to write the book. First, I would like to thank Craig Bradley for suggesting the idea for the book that is now a reality. Thanks are due to contributors Spencer Reese, Kevin Grimes, Dan Jensen, Buddy LaForge, Kirsten Park, Bill Spears, Kenny Troutt, Dallin Larsen, Craig Keeland, Al Wakefield, and Keith Harding. They all shared their knowledge so that others interested in participating in this great industry can succeed. Marlene Futterman from the Direct Selling Education Foundation and Liz Dogherty from the Direct Selling Association were also very helpful in providing materials and edits needed for information about those organizations. All of these individuals were wonderful to work with, and each sacrificed their already precious time to contribute. For this, I will always be grateful.

Another individual who unselfishly reviewed and edited my materials was Beth Fitz Gibbon. She came to my rescue and did a terrific job, with little notice, reworking the original manuscript into something much easier to read and understand. My heartfelt thanks to Beth. Going into the home stretch, Julie Dean joined the team to rekey in all of Beth's suggestions, allowing me to meet the deadline.

It was a great pleasure to work with Susan Silva and Leslie Eschen from Prima Publishing. Since this is my first book, I did not know what to expect. Susan directed my efforts and supported my various "change requests" all along the way. I always felt she was a partner, pulling for me to produce a winner. Leslie, as well as the copy editor, Leslie Ayers, enhanced the readability of the work through their efforts. Many thanks to Kerry Tassopoulos and Sharon Holman from Excel Communications for connecting me with Prima.

Writing is a challenge for me, mainly because it requires too much sitting down. I am a roll-up-your-sleeves, jump-into-the-middle-of-the-action kind of person, and it's next to torture for me to sit down and focus on only one thing at a time. Because I am blessed with more energy than most, and need to be operating on twelve or more cylinders at a time to be happy, writing this book was a real test of character.

My specialty is synergizing things that already exist, and taking them to the next level, not looking back on the past. The patience required for writing and teaching what one already knows through the written word astounds me. I will forever have a great deal more admiration for those who do it on a regular basis.

Because of my ability to be distracted, I could not have completed the book without the emotional support provided to me by my friends and family. I truly appreciate the support provided by Lisa Stringfellow, a talented writer who shared her secrets (and many delicious dinners) with me. My brother Mel and my niece Shari kept sending me encouragement via e-mail. My brother Ferd and my sisters-in-law Tabby and Betty kept me laughing with their computer-generated certificates and much appreciated "Author's Tool Kit." My other siblings, Pat, Sylvia, and Tony, also lent their support.

My mom and dad, Syl and Clara Lindauer, kept praying for me, and now I can tell them their prayers are answered, because at least I finished the book. I am very grateful to Tom Landis, who has always been my mentor and friend and the person who gave me courage to explore all life has to offer. Thank God for my son Jimmy who encourages me to lighten up and inspires me by his example and kindness. I appreciate this group of people and others too numerous to mention.

Other friends provided much needed encouragement and often material resources to accelerate my timeline. They include Spencer and Maryann Reese, Kevin Grimes, and Jan Wood. Thanks also to my clients for their understanding of my need to schedule engagements around my timeline.

BACKGROUND AND HISTORY

Objective

THE PURPOSE OF this chapter is to give some background and familiarize you with the historical roots of network marketing as we know it today. This industry is more than one hundred years old. It has evolved from simple door-to-door selling into a complex combination of high-tech and "high touch" support and complex compensation plans. According to the Direct Selling Association's 1997 Growth and Outlook Survey, the industry generated estimated sales in 1996 of more than $20.8 billion with an estimated 8.5 million salespeople in the United States alone, and many millions more worldwide (see Figure 1.1).

This chapter also offers a comparison to franchising to help you understand network marketing from a knowledge base you may be familiar with. The principles of integrity and partnership outlined here explain why companies entering this

1997 Direct Selling Growth and Outlook Survey

Estimated 1996 U.S. Retail Sales   **$20.84 Billion**

Percent of Sales by Major Product Groups

    Home/family care products (cleaning products, cookware, cutlery, etc.)   33.6

    Personal care products (cosmetics, jewelry, skin care, etc.)   29.2

    Services/miscellaneous/other   18.3

    Wellness products (weight loss products, vitamins, etc.)   13.1

    Leisure/educational products (books, encyclopedias, toys/games, etc.)   5.8

Location of Sales (reported as a percent of sales dollars)

    In the home   70.9

    In a workplace   14.3

    Over the phone (in follow-up to a face-to-face solicitation)   8.4

    At a temporary location (fair, exhibition, shopping mall, etc.)   3.6

    Other locations   2.8

Sales Strategies (method used to generate sales, reported as a percent of sales dollars)

    Individual/one-to-one selling   77.7

    Party plan/group selling   20.7

    Customer placing order directly with firm (in follow-up to a face-to-face solicitation)   0.7

    Other   0.9

Compensation Structure (multilevel vs. single level)

    Percent of firms   77.3/22.7

    Percent of sales dollars   64.9/35.1

    Percent of salespeople   79.8/20.2

Estimated 1996 U.S. Salespeople   **8.5 million**

Demographics of Salespeople

    Independent contractors/employees   99.9%/0.1%

    Female/male/couples and two-person teams   59.3%/23.4%/17.3%

    Part-time/full-time (30+ hours per week)   85.6%/14.4%

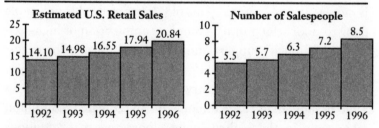

For further information contact Liz Doherty, Director of Communications, or Tonya Johnson, Member Services Coordinator.

NOTE: With the exception of estimated retail sales & number of salespeople, this fact sheet is not comparable to previous years.

Figure 1.1 1997 Directing Selling Growth and Outlook Survey
Reprinted with permission from the Direct Selling Association, Washington, D.C.

field must act responsibly and earn their position of trust and honor as legitimate businesses.

What Is Network Marketing?

Network marketing (often referred to as multilevel marketing, which more appropriately defines the payment structure) has its roots in direct selling. Let me first clarify that the substance of the direct selling/network marketing channel of distribution lies in the person-to-person (high touch/personal endorsement/testimonial) aspects of the selling process, and the promotion of a product line or service. I like to think of it as QVC up close and personal. The term "multilevel" actually describes the various levels tagged for pay-out on a sales organization created by an individual distributor.

Distributors are compensated for introducing new customers to a particular product line, and for recruiting potential distributors to continue the process, so that product is moved through to consumers. Compensation is distributed throughout the multilevel pay-out chain, as opposed to a single-level commission plan. In other words, up-line individuals earn income on the efforts of others in the lower levels of the sales organization they have created, even though they are not directly involved in every sale of the product. Another interesting concept in this multilevel pay plan is that distributors don't merely get an initial reward for enticing a customer to buy a company's product. Each time that customer reorders—even if he or she orders directly from the company—the distributor receives additional income, known as residuals, over and over again. This is what attracts distributors to the industry.

The concept of residual income is not new. Insurance agents have enjoyed its benefits for many years. The concept there is to sell a life insurance policy that will be renewed annually. For this sale an agent receives a commission on the first year. Each year customers pay their renewal fees, the selling agent receives another residual check (even though the customers may never see the agent again). It's a great concept—one that got better with the introduction of multilevel participation.

Every time a customer or distributor purchases another product or uses a service provided by the network marketing company, that distributor's *up-line distributor* (the person who introduced him or her to the company, also known as their *sponsor*) earns a portion of the marketing pay-out pool—as does everyone else in the up-line who produces enough volume to qualify.

These pay-outs simply represent a different way to distribute money, which, in retail, normally makes its way through the marketing chain in the form of markups to wholesalers, salespeople, middle men, and retailers. So, actually, both retail and MLM methods pay out on multiple levels. The difference in MLM companies is that their distribution chain is a number of independent individuals who reap rewards over and over again, in the form of residual income, each time a product or service is moved to a customer. It gives the "little guy" an opportunity to actively participate in big earnings.

The Pathfinders

Avon, Watkins, Mary Kay, and Amway are household names. They are the pioneers of the direct selling industry, with hundreds of years of combined experience from which to learn. While all those companies have contributed to the success of the direct selling/network marketing industry, I will share some of my insights about Avon because of my familiarity with the company. I held various management and executive positions within Avon for more than thirteen years.

Avon's core U.S. business is not an MLM company, but it is one of the first direct selling companies, and a lot can and has been taken forward from the concepts ingrained there. It is not considered MLM because its pay structure is generally a one-level commission plan, and it does not provide for residual income throughout an organizational chain. All representatives buy from the company at wholesale and mark up products to retail customers, producing their commission. Representatives' customers can also buy directly from the company at retail price, via direct mail, and the company provides commission checks to its representatives.

Nevertheless, Avon has many of the warm features needed to be a successful direct selling company. It offers equal opportunity to everyone, there are strong recognition and incentive programs, and it offers consumable products, which gives its sales force a reason to keep contacting customers. Avon also hosts annual conferences to launch new products; and, recruiting is the lifeblood of the business. Additionally, Avon has set the stage for storytelling, and created a strongly ingrained and highly regarded culture that is reflected in a statement called "The Principles That Guide Avon." Those principles are presented on a plaque to each individual inside the company as soon as they enter the management ranks.

Second-generation companies have coupled many of Avon's basic features with advanced technology to make direct-to-customer distribution easier. Add to that the strength of a multilevel compensation structure, and tremendously successful network marketing companies began to emerge. In addition to attracting mostly women like Avon does, these second-generation companies also attract high-powered business people—men, women, and couples—by offering a highly viable business opportunity, a gateway to financial freedom and a way to escape the corporate world.

As a matter of fact, many executives in other top direct selling and network marketing companies around the world today are Avon corporate alumni. Many others hail from other first-generation direct selling companies. Our gratitude will always be with these pathfinder companies who have given birth to an entire industry.

As we move forward, just a word of caution. There are many MLM companies that start up and fail. Every failure can be attributed to: insufficient funding, greediness at the company level, lack of integrity, poor product choices, inability to deliver service (initially, or at a large growth phase), failure to comply with legal requirements, false claims, and even computer malfunctions. Inevitably the founders or management have failed to consider and implement one or more of the critical ingredients needed for success, which are outlined in the following chapters.

Even if you do not agree with The Formula—the recipe developed by many "master chefs" at successful companies (and observed and reiterated herein)—at least consider the ramifications of *not* adding all the ingredients to your creation. Otherwise your venture will not be all that it can be.

The Franchise Comparison

Before we go on, it might be helpful to compare the responsibilities of a network marketing company's home office to that of a franchiser. (Note: This comparison has no relevance to the legal definition of franchises.) The comparison may help clarify what responsibilities anyone setting out to start a network marketing company should expect. In addition to the usual elements of a franchise, it is important to note that trust is key. Just as franchisees need to trust and "buy in" to what the franchiser has developed, so must the field sales organization.

When a franchiser develops a concept, he or she puts together a formula that a franchisee can replicate—all but guaranteeing success. It is imperative that network marketing companies do the same. Network marketing has been called "The People's Franchise"; it is up to companies to deliver on the promise of a formula for success to the people who choose to represent us.

Think of any fast food chain, and you will see the analogy come into focus. Each franchise has a unique product, concept, or formula that sometimes includes a secret ingredient, and always has a proven delivery system. All of these components are tested in the beginning stages of the company's life. Usually, it is done in one or more stores, and because the formula works, it is then rolled out and made available to other investors who want to make money by using the tried and true concept.

Franchisees who sign up and start their own stores have certain expectations. These include such things as trusting that the company is legal and ethical, that vendors have been tried and are reliable, that products are safe and exceptional, that the home office will provide sufficient support to help them get started, and that the company will be around for the long term. It is also expected that the franchiser wants to create a win-win situation for both himself and the franchisee.

Individuals who sign up with "The People's Franchise," or your network marketing opportunity, have a right to expect the same. Each time they bring someone else into the business, they are putting their reputation on the line, and you must honor that trust.

A successful network marketing company ties together product, opportunity, an easy-to-duplicate recruiting process, an attractive compensation plan, and systems that make it all work together. In the case of network marketing companies, there is also a secret ingredient, often referred to as the "magic." This magic should comprise several factors. First, there needs to be a company mission, or a stated higher purpose that attracts masses of followers. Second, there must be sufficient recognition, an ingredient that fills a void sadly missing in many people's lives. Third, there needs to be a *sales personality*, or a highly visible person from the home office to whom people are attracted and want to be inspired by.

Additionally, it is expected that companies recognize a fiduciary responsibility to their distributors. Companies must be honest, run a legal operation, offer products that work and are fairly priced, have high integrity, ship product when it is ordered, make decisions in the best interest of the distributors, and not be greedy. Further, network marketing companies have an obligation to train their distributors in the do's and don'ts of product and earnings claims, and, in general, to abide by self-imposed rules similar to the Direct Selling Association's Code of Ethics.

Any time a new or existing company doesn't play fair or operate legally, or doesn't abide by the implied expectations as outlined in this book, it hurts the reputation of the entire industry. Often companies operating outside the rules draw unfavorable attention from the Food and Drug Administration, attorneys general, or other regulators. Worse yet, failed expectations leave a bad taste in the mouths of former distributors and customers who were drawn into the fold. Because their expectations were not met, they assume the industry as a whole is likewise disappointing. They are let down, and not likely to return to other "good" companies, making it harder for all the legitimate companies in the business to succeed. It is up to us in the industry to ensure that we are delivering on the implied promises to our distributors and meeting the needs of our field sales force.

Distributors also have obligations and implied promises to deliver on. Similar to expectations in a franchise, it is the duty of the distributor (like a franchisee) to bring new customers into the store, or in our case the product catalog. Franchisees and distributors both need to "staff" their organizations with reliable, hard-working people. If a franchise owner just opens his door and puts up the sign, but does not advertise for and recruit employees and customers, the Success Formula will do him or her no good. On the other hand, if the franchisee recruits talented staff, trains them adequately, offers them opportunities to be promoted, and recognizes and rewards their efforts, the store will most likely be successful. If sufficient numbers of customers are also recruited and appreciated for their role and contribution to success, the business will thrive.

As with franchise opportunities, it is important to recognize that network marketing companies sell two things: the Product and the Opportunity. One must also realize that franchisees and customers are both important to ultimate success. If all franchisees just ordered product for their store without soliciting any ultimate consumers, their ventures would flop. Likewise, having willing customers without additional franchisees or locations to service that demand would limit the long-term growth of the franchise.

In network marketing, we must teach our distributors to value both distributors and customers. In the same way that not all customers want to buy a franchise, but love and want to buy the product the franchise offers, not all network marketing customers want to become distributors. Actually, many are scared off because they are made to feel if they do not become a distributor (that is, buy a franchise store, in the language of the franchise example), they are not valued. Both distributors and customers must be made to feel valued, so the company will grow with a good balance of distributors and customers, each happy with his or her choice.

Ultimately, a strong, healthy, successfully growing company is what the company owners and their distributors desire. Those in the home office are wise to remember that they owe it to themselves and their distributors to deliver on the promise of success.

The Success Formula

The Success Formula requires that each company involved in network marketing take responsibility for delivering on the promise of success to its distributors. Components of the formula include: unique, safe, quality products; an attractive opportunity and compensation plan; an easy-to-replicate recruiting process; and systems that make it all work together. Additionally, some of the "magic" ingredients include a company mission or higher purpose, recognition that makes people feel good, and strong personal relationships between the company leadership and the field sales force.

PRELIMINARY CONSIDERATIONS

Objective

THE PURPOSE OF this chapter is to review the need for a distinct name, mission, look, image, and culture for your network marketing company. It will become an important ingredient in your success by portraying who you are and what you stand for. The brand for your products and your company or opportunity are important preliminary considerations.

Background

One of the first things to consider as you decide who you are as a network marketing/MLM company revolves around what you are selling and how you want that image to be portrayed, both to the public at large and more specifically to your potential distributors.

It really doesn't matter whether you are marketing a product or service, because in both cases you offer a financial opportunity. A franchise can offer products or services that appeal to customers, but there is a totally different marketing effort needed to attract franchisees to open stores and distribute products. In network marketing/MLM the franchise is known as the financial opportunity, or simply as "the Opportunity," which I'll discuss later. But first, I want to focus on other considerations that should addressed at start-up and reviewed throughout the life span of your business.

Your Name

Every network marketing company needs a distinct look, name, feel, mission, and culture that should revolve around its product offering and Opportunity. As you probably already know, many of the names chosen for MLM companies would be laughed out of the boardrooms of traditional retail channel companies. Some names are chosen to represent a key ingredient in a product (such as Melaleuca for the oil), or to project the desired results of a company's products (such as Youngevity or ShapeRite Concepts).

Others are chosen to reflect their impact on the entrepreneur, such as Excel. It's amazing how you can build on a great name like this: It translates into special events (*Excel*ebration), TV broadcasts (*Excel*TV), then into the *Excel*erator Business Kit, and a whole array of other motivational concepts. These types of names and their spin-off lingo are standard "inside" the industry. When I worked at Avon we used so many internal words that had no equivalent in the "outside" world that a group of us put together a "deck" (a presentation document) that was a glossary of Avon terms, known as "Avonese." To an outsider, these inside terms would appear to be a foreign language.

Likewise, the name you choose will create spin-offs and an internal lingo that will become part of your culture, so consider the possibilities when choosing an appropriate name. You will be surprised at how many different ways it will be twisted and molded to fit a situation. How else could you have an AmaGram or a MelaGram (publications of Amway and Melaleuca respectively)? In fact, many, many words I keyed in for this book come up as errors on spell check, and when I review the options, I find no suggestions for corrections. That is telling about how much internal industry lingo is used.

As you select your company's name, give some thought to how it will be used, not only in conjunction with product promotions, but also from a motivational standpoint. How can your people in the field use it to aid in recruiting because of the interesting nature or catchy image it conjures up? Be sure the name reflects your company's mission, too.

Your Mission

In addition to your product or service, it is necessary to have a greater good, or mission, that your company focuses on in addition to your product or service. It can be a better environment, healthier lifestyles, an upscale lifestyle based on the financial opportunity, etc. It gives your company a reason for being, and distributors become attached to the cause. Whatever greater good you choose should lead you to develop your mission statement, which in turn helps you develop an overall look and feel for the company; and it should be considered when choosing the company and product brand names.

Your Look

Your look should fit your image. If it's upscale, you need to use clean lines and lifestyle pictures for your brochures, magazines, and on your product labels. On the other hand, if you want to portray a scientific message, the look should be more angular, be laced with photos of your scientific team, and include charts and graphs to dazzle onlookers with your expertise. Other companies may choose a natural, environmentally friendly image, which suggests an entirely different set of design criteria.

Often, there are teams of physicians or other experts who support the theory behind your product and make your product literature look very official. Another approach for nutritional products is the endorsement of athletes, many sponsored by the company. If this is the case, your materials and product labels should look more sports and fitness oriented, with people participating in fitness activities. You may include scenes at the gym or outdoors portraying a particularly popular athletic activity of the day. Many companies even support Olympic athletes, and use their names, photos, and testimonials freely in the literature about related products.

Part of your image should also reflect your culture, and vice versa. If you are a very conservative company, with a businesslike approach versus a totally warm or rah-rah motivational approach, this should come through, too. The look of the models in your literature, magazine, or on your labels should always reflect your company's culture. If you are very conservative, and have attracted conservative distributors, be sure your art department knows the boundaries of what is considered in good taste from a conservative standpoint. If you are upscale and have attracted upwardly mobile people, be sure you are putting that message out there, and that your literature and products look as expensive and high-quality as they are.

One of the more recent start-up companies reflects its upscale high-tech image in its literature, but also shows its balanced, personal, touchable, approachable side by including photos and personal information about the CEO and president, along with his and her personal voice mail numbers. That says a lot about the company culture.

Your Logo

Your image or look should immediately give the observer a feel for your quality, stability, seriousness, or sense of fun. Your logo can do this if it is properly designed. You can get help at start-up from companies whose primary business is designing logos and company images. If you can't afford outside help at first, here are a few things to keep in mind.

When designing your logo, be sure it works in many media. For instance, you will have print pieces, magazines, product packaging, audio- and videotapes, training manuals, planners, and so on. For this reason, a clean and simple yet versatile logo is best. Logos that have incomplete shapes, shading, and lines through them can be hard for your art department to translate to all media.

Your color scheme is also very important. Certain colors, like dark green and blue, or bold red and burgundy, create a sense of expensive and powerful items. Black, gold and silver, and many metallic colors can create a classy feel, whereas some colors, such as yellow, light pink, pale blue, and other less intense colors, may give a poor impression. Additionally if you choose one color for your logo, be sure it will match nicely with many other colors to offer variety throughout your various pieces over time.

Another way your logo will be used is on promotional items and wearables. It will most likely show up on buttons, or even glitter pins that your distributors create themselves. A word of caution here: You will spend a lot of time and money on your logo, so it is in your best interest to protect it, as well as your trademark. While it may seem harsh not to allow distributors to create their own promotional items, my advice is to control this through the home office. Only items worthy of and in keeping with the look you are trying to achieve should be approved, so your image does not get undermined. There

15

are various legal reasons you do not want distributors to produce homemade literature or other items, the most important being that they could be construed as labeling or product claims.

Another consideration is whether you want your look to be busy or simple. My vote is simple, even if you are trying to achieve a scientific message. Many companies overkill on details in their literature, and too many charts and graphs are not impressive, but rather a tune-out vehicle. Keep your message, literature, brochures, and labels clean, simple, and succinct. This works best with *all* consumers. Now and again you will have some distributors who need to know every sordid detail and scientific fact about your products or services. In my experience, this only creates analysis paralysis rather than sales growth. You may want to have one detailed piece for this sort of person, but your mainstream distributor is more interested in your overall mission and motivation. Remember, most successful people in this business operate from the heart, not the head, so the simpler and more fun and motivational you can keep things, the more your sales will grow.

Your "Feel"

Distributors often expect that when they go to a company-sponsored event, they will be able to see and talk to, or at least shake hands with, the CEO, president, and other corporate officials. Some very successful companies follow this approach. One huge MLM company whose event I attended had the CEO and vice president of sales on hand in the lobby long before the event started for the express purpose of giving new and potential recruits the opportunity to meet them and ask questions. I applaud them for this accessibility; it adds a lot of credibility to their message.

One company president I know always takes a suite in the meeting hotel, not because he wants something so ostentatious, but because he wants to let people who can't afford their own room sleep in his. He would never have told me this, because he always did it discreetly; but when I called his room on numerous occasions to finalize meeting agendas, different people kept answering, so I finally figured out what was going on.

At another meeting I attended, I heard a distributor say from the stage that when she was just beginning her business and went to a distant town for a company meeting, the CEO invited her to take a free ride home on the corporate jet. It so motivated and impressed her to be treated so specially, even though she felt she was a "nobody," that she reset her goals and dreams. She is now a very high-ranking distributor with that company and has aspirations to own her own plane someday. This type of treatment and accessibility to high-ranking company officials has untold payback on an ongoing basis. It's just what was missing from the lives of those distributors when they were in the corporate world.

In more formal companies, the CEO, and sometimes even the president, stay in the background, and are not very accessible. In this case, you will usually see them show up at events at the last minute, and dash off back stage when breaks occur. Generally the "sales personality" (described in Chapter 6) is sent to soothe the masses. This does not mean these company executives like their distributors less; it usually reflects their need for privacy, or their need to delegate the show of warmth to someone for whom it comes more naturally. Some individuals operate from the head, while others operate from the heart (see Chapter 6 for more on this topic).

While this is very much an issue of personal preference, and in many cases a style one has grown comfortable with, if I were advising you which way to be, I would suggest the more informal, accessible approach. The more you can touch the

17

people, the more real you become, and the more loyal your followers will be. If it is not in your disposition to expose yourself in this way, partner up with someone who is warm, loving, and very visible in the company and the field. If these roles are defined early on, there are no withdrawals later as the organization grows.

Your Culture

All of these "feels" define the culture of the company. It is what makes some companies attractive to one person, while others go elsewhere. Some people love the high-energy frenzy at rallies that are very emotional, while others are attracted by a more sedate, businesslike atmosphere. All companies must create a motivational atmosphere, but how they do it can be quite different. You can tell what a company's appeal is by attending any large event it sponsors. You can tell by watching who is attracted to the meeting (attendees/distributors); what they wear, whether it's business attire or casual garb; and what paraphernalia they don, such as buttons, flashing pins, homemade-looking items, or simply businesslike lapel pins. You can also tell by what happens at the meeting. Are there people standing on chairs, yelling as a result of hype or other contrived motivation? Is it a more formal business meeting where recognition is tastefully done, and people are made to feel welcomed, but not encouraged to do anything that makes them uncomfortable?

Before you start a company, and even after you are going for a while, I encourage you to step back and see how people perceive its culture. It is a good idea to look to other companies—both those you admire, and those you don't—for a fresh perspective of your own company. Attend another company's event as an observer to see how you stack up. Take off your own company's hat, put on your objective one, and you will learn a lot.

Your Story

One consideration that helps define the culture of your business and who you are is what I call your *story*. Storytelling is a well-developed art in all network marketing companies. Each person has a story to tell about the impact a product had on his or her life, or how the economic opportunity led to a turnaround in a family's success, or even how meeting new people and sharing the Opportunity gave that person the stage on which to grow and develop personally.

Likewise, most companies have a story about why they came into being. Stories range from developing specific products to address a family member's ailment to feeling compelled to make the world a better place with environmentally safe or unique product discoveries to offering an alternative way to achieve financial independence. These stories are compelling; often, when people hear the story (which should be repeated often in presentation books, from the stage at gatherings, and to leaders in various forums), they are reenergized and recommitted to the mission and purpose of belonging to that organization.

Founders are sometimes the best storytellers about the founding days and mission of a company, along with the handful of original distributors. They don't describe it as "the good old days," however, because years later, when they are recalling events for new distributors, things have generally gotten much, much better: The company's look has improved, with four-color literature replacing the photocopied material originally used for promotion. Often, even the compensation plan has added features that make it different—and probably more lucrative—from when it started.

Regardless of what your company's beginnings are, the story should be kept alive and handed down through generations of down-lines. So be sure you recognize and embellish what got your business started in the first place, because that will become your story.

Integrity of the Product Line

Another area where you should start out right, to save time and changes later, is to clearly define who you are, and what umbrella, or theme, will encompass your group of products or service offerings. Some companies just keep adding products and lines that veer way off-base from who and what they are. The lines look different from one another, there is no overall theme or thread that ties the offerings together, and as such, these companies look strange to new customers. Product line reviews show the need for major changes.

Once you have decided what direction to take, gather all your proposed products and communication pieces in one room for review. Include in this session information on your mission, the look and culture you are trying to create, and the theme that ties your offerings together. This review should create some instant feedback: Any product or communication piece that doesn't fit will stand out like a sore thumb.

Existing companies should do these marketing reviews at least once a year—or, even better, twice a year. I also recommend that you do a communications audit annually to ensure that your company's message is consistent and reinforced in accordance with your initial intent.

You will be surprised at how easily your product line can get out of whack because you introduced some hot new product whose look and feel are totally different from those of your existing line. Existing companies should review their products by setting up a physical display of all products and promotional and communication materials. Everything should have a similar look and feel, even if you have different brand lines. Somehow the products need to have an identity that says they are yours. This is a good time to determine if the look and feel is still what you want, or if it needs some modification and relabeling to become more contemporary and congruent. In some cases, a complete makeover is necessary or desirable.

Because of inventory cost considerations, a change in the look of your product line will probably need to be phased in over time. This can be translated into your strategic plan, and be used for motivational purposes in your new product launch strategy.

Product Mix and Contribution

Another review you should do at start-up and annually is to examine the composition of your sales volume and profits. Many companies are unaware that a small number of products make up the majority of their sales and profits. You should do an annual "source of sales review" that lists your product sales by sales volume and unit movement from top to bottom. From this exercise you can also determine what percentage of sales each product represents and, depending on how much you order at a time, your inventory turns.

You should also list the profitability of each item both in terms of real dollars and percent of margin. You can then identify your most to least profitable items and the total contribution of each product and product line to your company's bottom line. If you have some items that just aren't moving, you should look at whether they have been properly promoted. If they have, recognize their limited value, sell them off, and move on. But be prepared for those two users of the discontinued products to send you many letters begging you to keep them!

As you are starting up your business, you should project what volume and percentage of sales each item will represent. In order to meet your projections it will be necessary to properly price and promote the items, and ensure the story surrounding the products' benefits substantiates their price. And remember, communication and promotion are not a one-time event! With the turnover in this business, all products are new to new distributors, so be sure they know the features, advantages, and benefits of each. The key is to keep promoting each product as long as you want to sell it.

If you have a commodity—long-distance phone service, for example—it is important that you are competitive and that you offer value-added services. Every consumer knows (or thinks he or she knows) the cost of long distance, because it has been hawked on TV so much. But there are many distinctions that make one service's cost different than another's. You must be sure your distributors are equipped to handle questions and objections, and to educate the consumer. As a result of misleading commercials—with print so small that goes by so fast at the bottom of the screen—you have to change perceptions with realistic explanations.

Product or Opportunity Lead?

The question often arises of whether distributors should lead with the product or the Opportunity to attract new people into the business. Attracting new distributors or representatives into the fold should always be a priority, but there are many legal, logical, and financial reasons to endorse a balanced approach that meets both potential customers' and distributors' needs. Chapter 5 explores these reasons in-depth.

The logical and financial reason to lead with the product is that not everyone wants to own one of your franchises. If you have great products, you expand your audience for consumption if you allow everyone to buy and try them. Those who just want to continue purchasing your products should not only be allowed to do so, but be openly welcomed as important members of your business family. Additionally, as a general rule, consumers would like to have at least tried the products before they "buy" a franchise. Companies that are product driven and market great products are also more likely to stay in business for the long term. Distributors may come and go, depending on their motivation, but if you offer a truly outstanding product, even those who leave will continue to seek you out to get it. Once a consumer has tried and is hooked on the product, they are more likely to be open to becoming a distributor because they believe in its value and know they can count on its results.

There are a number of companies that stress selling *only* the Opportunity. They imply—and often, unfortunately, it's true—that the product is just a means to an end. Individuals who only want to buy the product are made to feel like outcasts or a bother because the company's main goal is to get them into the business. Balancing the positioning of both the product and the Opportunity works best because different people will want different choices. Putting this equation out of balance is dangerous.

Pushing only the Opportunity is risky. If the product will not stand on its own regardless of the channel, it will not support the business in the long run. It may be inferior or marginal, and it may be overpriced in order to support the compensation plan—so no real ultimate consumers would consider buying at the retail price. This approach creates a chain of buying distributors, sets up limitations on growth, and creates a legal challenge known as the personal consumption dilemma. (MLM attorney Spencer M. Reese reviews this issue in Chapter 16, in the legal section "The Personal Consumption Dilemma.") Even without this problem, selling to as many customers as possible is always a good business practice. Don't inhibit your business's growth by promoting only the Opportunity at the expense of the product. Balance is the key.

The Success Formula

To create and maintain a successful company, you must know who you are, what you sell, and what you stand for. The Success Formula prescribes that once you establish your mission, your story, your culture, and your image, you must maintain its integrity. The best way to build your brand and franchise is by sending a consistent message through product line choices, your logo, your literature, the look and feel developed at events, and the warmth your executives show distributors and customers.

You must also be vigilant about maintaining a balance of emphasis on both your product line and your Opportunity. If emphasis is placed strictly on product, your "franchise" of stores or distributor count will not grow as fast as you would like. If the emphasis is strictly on the Opportunity, with no demand being created for the product, the chances for long-term success are minimal. The best approach is to maintain a balance between the two, respecting the source of sales from each effort. You can't have product sales without distributors, and you won't keep distributors without excellent products.

PRODUCT
SELECTION

Objective

THERE ARE VERY specific guidelines to follow when choosing an appropriate product or service to sell via the network marketing channel. In this chapter, I will lead you through the basic process of selecting items that have the best chance for success. I will also discuss how product selection is important if you want to offer an autoship or backup order program.

As you will see, it is not only the product but the product's greater goal as it relates to an enhanced lifestyle that is important in attracting distributors to sell and customers to buy. While it is easiest to choose a product line about which the public is already informed and to which it is already receptive, network marketing alone allows the opportunity to introduce revolutionary products that can best be presented one-on-one to capture the unique story behind them.

Choosing a Product Line

Because of the large pay-outs desired, the residual aspects of the compensation plan, and the ability to tell the product's story one-on-one and demonstrate its benefits firsthand—think of it as QVC up-close and personal—certain product lines are best suited to network marketing. When considering a product, service, or group of products to distribute through the network marketing channel, there are several points to keep in mind.

To be successful in MLM, a product or service must be consumable. In other words, the product or service will be used up and reordered. The faster it is consumed, the better suited the product. For example, durable goods such as a water filter system or medical magnets are comparatively high ticket items to start with, and they create the need for continuous new contacts and sales because the original purchaser will not use them up and reorder replacements. For this reason, these are not the best product choices. While some of these companies may succeed, it takes much more dedicated salespeople skilled in traditional selling techniques than you generally find because the sales force must pitch the products over and over to new customers due to their low reorder rate. However, if certain components with a high reorder rate are needed to keep them functional, or service contracts are used to keep them running, these products become more viable.

Much better choices are items such as personal care items—toothpaste, for example—which are used every day (we hope) by all family members; nutritional supplements; or long-distance telephone services, which are consumed and must be repurchased month after month. Once consumers choose your essentially exclusive brand and formula, the sale is made, and from then on, it's an almost unconscious decision to replace it each time they run out. This works well for network marketing because it has the potential to create residual income for distributors on customer reorders.

In Chapter 10 the autoship/backup order concept is explored in depth. As you will learn, there are specific advantages to both companies and distributors that make these programs desirable. However, in order to support these programs, appropriate consumable products must be offered to avoid inventory buildup at distributors' homes.

With an autoship or backup order program, goods are generally shipped every month, similar to a book of the month or record club. Often, the selection offered by network marketing companies is the same predetermined group of products (either selected by the company, or customized by the distributor), or a quarterly rotation of products. Because of the repetitive nature of shipments, the grouping should be such that a distributor can use or sell all these products in a thirty-day time span. Nutritional supplements (vitamins), daily needs (toothpaste, soap, etc.), and some household products (laundry detergent) make good choices to support these programs. Other more durable items are less apt to be attractive choices if you want to offer these programs.

Also, products whose purchase is simply trading dollars that consumers already spend on similar products have an appeal in network marketing. If the item is already known and widely accepted by the public, the job of convincing people that they need it is easy. At that point, it merely becomes a choice of which brand they will use. Using our examples, it is much easier to get potential customers to see that they need toothpaste than it is to convince them to purchase a water filter; their parents already did the pro-toothpaste training for you. Long-distance telephone service is used virtually every day in many households, so the decision to buy is inherent; the only question is from whom. However, in the case of the water filter, the distributor has to create the need and it is a more consultative sale—not to mention a greater investment is required of the consumer.

Even items whose need has to be demonstrated or whose story must be told can be successful. For instance, once a customer is educated about the specific benefits of some nutritional supplements, new topical ointments, or advanced personal care products and he or she makes an initial purchase, these products' consumability creates a much greater probability of a reorder from your "store."

One of the major benefits of this channel is its person-to-person aspects: the ability to demonstrate, give testimonials, and endorse a company's products. For this reason, unique or exclusive products do well in network marketing. Storytelling has a rich history in this industry. Appealing stories are told about the company and the product, including testimonials of how products have affected people's lives, and how the income earned through the marketing plan has enhanced lifestyles and created debt-free financial freedom for participants. If your product or line has a story behind it and there is a need to educate consumers on why they need it, the one-on-one approach used in direct selling/network marketing is a good choice.

It is important to choose a product line that reflects the company's greater goals and higher purpose. For instance, if you desire a health and fitness mission and message, there are a lot of internally consumed or externally applied product line choices available. Nutritional supplements, weight loss products, and fitness or energy bars that work internally complement a health-promoting message. For external applications, personal care items that go toward keeping people's skin, hair, and body looking better and healthier make for good line extensions.

On the other hand, if your image is natural and environmentally conscious, it would not be wise to introduce products that do not perpetuate that image. It is also unwise to use lots of nonbiodegradable containers or to ship your products in non-environmentally sensitive packaging. Instead, you would choose recycling programs and refillable containers to continue to project your company's desired image and purpose.

Distinguishing the Line

A product's uniqueness will also make it a star long into the company's maturity. The best products are those whose unique composition, or the methodologies of deriving benefits from them, allow them patent protection. Having a patent is a great selling point, and it reassures distributors and customers that the product cannot be copied. This offers protection from other companies duplicating a product and selling it in the same or another channel at a lower price or in a retail environment to reach potential customers. Lately, for example, retail and mail order have picked up on the vast array of education provided by network marketers in the area of nutritional products and herbs, and turned it into a profitable business for themselves.

If it's impossible to patent your product, then clearly distinguishing it or its delivery system as unique and proprietary is extremely important. The story you develop to keep this mystery and loyalty alive may be your only road to survival with a product that can be copied or promoted in a similar manner. Take this threat to your future seriously, and do all you can up front to distinguish your product from all existing and future competition. If it is a great product, other "me too" products will follow. Spin your tale wisely, and it will pay off in the long run. It should go without saying that your products must do what you say they will and be of exceptional quality.

When deciding on the width and breath of your product line, there are numerous considerations. First, it is important

29

to have enough products so distributors can easily purchase and sell their required monthly quota to qualify for compensation. The product fuels your compensation plan. The sales requirement should be in consumable products, so distributors can meet it month after month without filling their garage with excess product. The products must be attractive and exhibit value and appeal to consumers at the retail level. It is best to start with the smallest number of products (often referred to as SKUs, or Stock Keeping Units). That allows distributors to comfortably meet their quota—and lets you keep a manageable investment level. It also allows distributors to use and have firsthand knowledge of all products in the line.

One way many companies allow their distributors to try a large part or all of the product line is to offer a special package available only for a short time after people join as distributors. It can be called a "Distributor Product Pack," a "Career Pack," or any name that creates the appropriate marketing spin needed to move it. These packs are product assortments packaged as a unit, containing a large variety of products for a value price. Generally, companies offset the limited revenue on these packages at the lower price point by reducing the base or bonus points given, allowing for the most attractive price to the purchaser. Often, there may be a flat commission paid on these packs as an incentive for the sponsor to encourage the new distributor to purchase one. Of course, the long-term benefit is getting new distributors to try and gain belief in the product line. It allows them to quickly obtain true experience with and testimonials for the various products.

Another tactic for allowing the sales organization to test products is to offer special prices on specific products or a line of products that the company wants to promote. This can be monthly or seasonally. It is best to use high-margin products, which will give you the short-term leverage to reduce the price (or you can adjust volume points), and it gets more people using the high-margin product. As you introduce new items into the line, it is wise to offer a package special that includes all the new items at an attractive price, which gets new products into the hands of your distributors quickly. Also, at gift-giving occasions, simply putting together an assortment in an attractive gift package can stimulate sales.

As your company grows, there should be plenty of room to announce new products once or twice a year; these products should be a natural extension of the existing line. It is important to do an annual (or more frequent) product line review to determine which SKUs are moving, which ones need to be promoted, and which ones need to be repositioned, repackaged, or even discontinued. By the way, discontinuing an item is sometimes a surprisingly novel way to move or give new life to a product in this industry. (Perhaps it's the New Coke syndrome.) As soon as you decide to discontinue something, everyone (or so it will seem when the two vocal people keep calling and writing) wants and cannot live without it. It may be an undiscovered way to relaunch a product.

Impact Products

During the start-up phase of your business, it is important to plan ahead. You will need one or two *impact products* that allow your sales force to pull prospective customers into the product line immediately. An impact product is one that can be demonstrated or tried to achieve an immediate noticeable result. An example would be a spot remover that can work in front of a potential customer who has spilled something on an article of clothing, or has a spot on the carpet that nothing else would work on. Voilà! Your product does the trick. When you have such products, it is important to support them in an easy-to-sample package or low-cost sample size.

Speaking of samples, there are generally two philosophies taken by companies with regard to providing samples to the sales organization. Some companies see samples as a profitable item and they charge higher prices to make up for higher costs incurred in the production of the samples, knowing that the sales organization will need them. Another much more palatable approach from the field's point of view is that samples will lead to full-size product sales, so they are made available at a close-to-cost price to allow the sales organization inexpensive access to door-openers. With this approach, distributors can afford to purchase large quantities of samples at a relatively low cost. And since company executives have faith in their product, they know putting out these samples will allow potential customers to try the product and become valuable and loyal customers of the full-size product. They expect to see their investment return on a long-term, big-picture basis.

Back to impact products. Another example of an impact product may be a pain cream that takes effect quickly when applied, or a diet pill that gives people an immediate burst of energy. Examples could go on and on, but I think you get my drift. Impact products are like the products on the end of the aisles in a grocery store, or those irresistible items at the checkout lane that you have to pick up while you wait your turn. They make people spend money now, to gratify their needs. Products like these can make up the core of your product line. They are important sample products to equip new distributors with because they are door-openers and quick income producers.

Profitability and Sourcing

For products to be considered viable in the network marketing arena, profit margin must be high. There must be a healthy profit margin to cover the expenses of the marketing plan (which is sometimes as high as 50 percent of wholesale price), plus other incentive and recognition programs, special offers, the normal cost of goods, distribution, and overhead expenses. Many companies have to price product at six to eight times cost or more. If a product cannot move at this price point, it doesn't make the line.

Services also need to have an acceptable margin to support the compensation plan. If they cannot stand alone to do so, perceived added value must exist so that higher than normal prices can be substantiated. Alternatively, other components of the compensation plan such as high residual usage of the service (such as long distance or electricity) must make up the shortfall of margin. When the margin on any one item may not be high enough to sustain a viable business and income opportunity, another tactic is to offer enough services in tandem to build the average order to an acceptable level of profit. Services such as long-distance telephone, cable TV, or other utilities can be bundled for this purpose.

One last thought on profitability. Generally, companies relate pay-out of the compensation plan to product profitability. Often, the relationship between wholesale price and bonus points is one to one, or some other constant ratio. My thought is that it is better to have a variable relationship between price and bonus points on different products right from the start. This allows you more flexibility to choose a wider variety of exciting products with varying profit margins. If you start out with a static ratio, and only offer products that meet that criteria, you can create headaches for yourself later.

For instance, at a future date, you may want to add a hot new product that would add value to the line, but it would require that you reduce the ratio to be more competitive at the retail level. However, even though it may be good for the overall business, your distributors will resist the change because it will feel like a take-away. By planning ahead, you can avoid this issue.

Another consideration is whether to produce your own product or have a third party manufacture it. There are pros and cons to both options.

The pros to manufacturing your own product include: protection of your secret formulas or processes; potential for better margins because you cut out a middleman; the in-house control of quality assurance; and, the ability to always be first in line to produce exactly what you need, instead of being only one of many customers (and, at first, probably only a small customer) of a third party. Cons of producing your own products are the potential need for large sums of capital and a manufacturing facility, which may not be an option, especially at start up.

Suffice it to say that if capital is not an issue, and since proprietary manufacturing processes and unique formulas are key to success, producing your products in house is the better way to protect your secrets, and react to your inventory needs. If you do go outside, be sure to take appropriate steps to protect your formulas with trade secret agreements, and have alternative vendors identified in the event your first choice fails. Your business depends on it.

Services

Recently there has been a migration toward offering services with residual potential via network marketing. You only need to look to companies such as Excel Communications to know that it made MLM and services work together. Excel started selling long-distance telephone services through network marketing in 1988. Since long distance is a service familiar to most everyone, it is an easily understood product in terms of consumer knowledge and training (everyone knows how to dial 1 plus), it has enormous potential for reorder (everyone uses it on a monthly basis), and it is consumable (it is used up each time you hang up). It is a great match for this distribution channel. One other advantage of long distance is that because it is a service and not a physical product, no inventory investment or buildup is required of the distributors. The only drawback is the declining profit margin on this now commodity-priced service.

Excel truly has made the formula work for them. They have nearly one million representatives, and in 1997, their revenues exceeded $1 billion. What's more, at this writing the company is reviewing the local market and other utilities, which should be a big boon to its distributors because they can overlay an almost instant increase in the average order by converting all their long-distance customers into local customers.

Other services that are beginning to emerge are travel services, legal services, security services, cable or satellite TV, Internet services, and anything that has start-up and subscription charges. These are not proven home runs yet, but other services come to mind that have the potential of Excel. For instance, gas fuel has been deregulated at the consumer level, and somewhere around the year 2000 electricity will be deregulated nationwide. Some states have chosen to accelerate their schedule, and are now offering the consumer options for where to purchase electricity. As soon as the operational and government issues are settled, this could be a wide open market for network marketers, either as a stand-alone product, or as an add-on for existing network marketing companies (see Chapter 12, "Capitalizing on the Channel").

An Exception to the Rule

There are a few exceptions to the consumable product that have been a huge success. The most notable that comes to mind is

Longaberger Baskets. These baskets are not consumable, but they are handmade and make unique gifts and presentation vehicles for other beautiful things. Every company in the industry envies Longaberger's success. The company has a small group of salespeople who sell via the party plan, but each distributor has a huge average order. Other companies envy this equation because shipping and overhead is lower when you only have to manage a small group of orders and distributors. In 1996, Longaberger's sales topped $500 million with only thirty-three thousand salespeople. That is more than $15,000 in sales per person per year.

Another unique aspect about Longaberger is that turnaround on orders defies the norm. Generally a network marketing company has to turn orders around in twenty-four to forty-eight hours to give the impression of good customer service. At the opposite end is Longaberger, which custom-makes its baskets, so each order goes though a creative process that can take weeks. But its customers are apparently more than happy to wait patiently and get what they want. In order to accommodate the production process, Longaberger employs more than five thousand individuals at its site.

As we have seen, there is an exception to every rule. If you have an idea for something so unique and exquisite that it is worth paying a premium price and waiting for, it can work. Just drive by the Longaberger's building in Newark, Ohio, and you will see what I mean. You shouldn't need any more detailed directions: It's the only basket-shaped building you're likely to come across there or anywhere else!

Product Consideration Checklist

The following checklist recaps important characteristics of products that work in a network marketing environment. Use it to see how your ideas stack up.

Product checklist:

o Does the product have emotional appeal?

o Is it consumable?

o Is it unique and exclusive (patented if possible) so that you are the only source?

o If it is not totally unique, can you create a unique selling proposition to distinguish it from the competition?

o Does the price point offer value and appeal at the retail/consumer level?

o Are the margins high enough to make them profitable, yet competitively priced?

o Are you confident enough in its quality to offer a money-back guarantee?

o Does it lend itself to economical packaging and shipping?

o Does it have a good story that can be told over and over?

o Does it tie in to the company mission, image, and focus?

o Does it have potential as an impact product?

If you have answered "yes" to most of these questions, you probably have a winner. If most of your answers are "no," or if the answer to the profitability question is "no," go back to the drawing board. As a thought-starter, here are some product categories that have met with success in network marketing and direct selling companies:

Nutritional supplements
Vitamins
Antiaging products

Chapter Three

Topical ointments
Personal care products
Daily needs
Weight loss and management
Food/meal replacements or snacks
Skin care
Makeup and beauty products
Pharmaceuticals
Health, fitness, and performance products
Household cleaning products
Candles
Telecommunications services
Self-improvement services

There are many more untapped categories that can fit the bill. Just be sure the one you choose fits a consumer niche where you can be king, and that it is not just a fad, but a category that responds to an enduring trend. This will service your business best over the long term.

The Success Formula

The product you select and offer for sale is a crucial ingredient in the Success Formula. It will mean the difference between success and failure for your company in the long run. The products in your line must be unique and consumable, have a compelling story behind them, offer a value to customers, and be of the highest quality to support a money-back guarantee. If you can also offer one or two high-impact products to make distributors' jobs of approaching prospects easier and more successful, you are one step ahead on the road to success.

COMPENSATION PLANS

Objective

OMPENSATION PLANS ARE complex and important ingredients in the Success Formula. This chapter pre-´ sents an overview of related considerations. The compensation plan is a large portion of your cost of sales expense, so proper design and planning is essential.

This chapter also features a series of articles written by Dan Jensen, chairman of Jenkon International. These articles give an overview of what behavior you want to encourage through your compensation plan and some frank, realistic insights into proper strategic planning. Later, in Chapter 16, you will have a chance to review legal considerations.

Choosing a Plan

First, let me acknowledge that I am *not* a compensation plan expert. As you start your company, the best thing you can do is acknowledge that you are not an expert in this area either. In general, my advice is to beware of most people who call themselves experts in this area. Many field people appoint themselves experts, but they have not lived on the corporate side of the business, so their views may not be in your best interest. Instead, seek out someone who has a corporate perspective, and check his or her references.

Assuredly there are many who consider themselves experts, and others who truly are, but I challenge anyone to get a panel of these people to agree on the best compensation plan in the industry today. Opinions on this topic vary widely. Variations on the compensation plan theme are conceived and introduced frequently; sometimes it's the flavor of the day that gets the most attention. However, there are many successful MLM companies, each with very different compensation plans. The fact that people cannot agree on one single plan is probably a good thing.

The compensation plan is a major, but not the overwhelming, factor in attracting potential distributors to join your organization. A poor plan without proper rewards will not get off the ground, but almost any plan that pays out an appropriate share of the dollars generated can be sold in the field. Does it have to be fair? Absolutely! Do distributors have to be able to make money? Of course! However, don't delude yourself by thinking the perfect compensation plan, absent other important factors, will draw the masses to your company. It is merely one of the factors.

Instead, the overall attractiveness of your product, the sales personality (see Chapter 6, "Structuring the Sales Organization"), your company's stability, and the relationship recruits have with the person who approaches them to join will win in the end. My guess is that well over 75 percent of active distributors in any organization who are currently receiving a check could not even accurately explain in detail their own plan, much less any other plan in the industry. All of the plans are duly complicated, and far too complex for anyone to comprehend on his or her first look at the business opportunity. This points out an exception to the keep-it-simple rule; simplicity is not always the most successful plan in this industry. It also points out that the compensation plan is hardly the magic ingredient in your network marketing company's success.

Trying to understand the entire compensation plan and explaining it to a new prospect or recruit can be compared to attempting to explain to an entry-level person the complexities of a corporation's pay plan, stock options, deferred compensation, and perks for the CEO before telling that person what his or her own starting wage will be. You can't take a drink of water from a fire hose; it's just too much to swallow at once. While it is important to know that things get better up the chain, it is better to wait until one has it in his or her sights to explain it. Initially focusing on the details of what's currently available to a new person makes the most sense; painting the dream of what's to come later with broad strokes may make the novice feel more comfortable.

Keep in mind that the compensation plan is a vital consideration from the company's and ultimately the distributor's perspective. It has a significant impact on the profitability, and thus the long-term viability, of the company. All distributors want to know that they are part of something that will be around for the long term. Their work and anticipation of residual income involves the placement of trust that falls like a fiduciary responsibility on the company's owners. Management must respect that and take it seriously.

Instead of proposing the best plan, or even reviewing all the details of various plans in-depth, I'll leave it to the true experts. At the end of this chapter I have included an article and guidelines provided by Jenkon International Chairman Dan Jensen. Dan has great insights and a corporate perspective on the subject.

He will cover the details of various compensation plans; I will discuss the philosophic and strategic considerations. Why would you want to choose a particular compensation plan? Why might you want to wait and not put everything out at the beginning, when your internal investments will be significant? Why might you want to hold back some dollars to use for minor tweaking to the plan at a later time since no one starts out with a perfect plan? And why would you want to add leadership enhancements once your plan is maximized or approaching that position? You need to reserve a pool of money to keep the leaders motivated when they reach "saturation" of the plan, or to be used for short-term incentives when your business's growth curve stalls at a plateau.

A significant part of the formula to establish up front is what percentage you can afford to pay out in your plan. This number is generally stated as a percent of sales—actual wholesale dollars to the company, not including retail commissions—or some other figure that is commonly used when promoting the plan to the field. In other words, review your plan from a strictly financial perspective as it relates to product sales dollars (wholesale price) paid to the company. As mentioned in the last chapter, it is important to select products with significant margins to allow for a generous pay-out, as well as a healthy profit.

The percentage that you can afford to pay out will also be the basis of the value attributed to bonus points as it relates to wholesale price. It can be a 1-to-1 or smaller ratio (see Chapter 3, "Product Selection" for suggestions). Many companies allow for between 30 and 50 percent pay-out of wholesale price when the plan is *fully compressed*. A plan is fully compressed when all available amounts and levels of the compensation are paid out and no breakage occurs (see the article at the end of this chapter entitled "Compensation Plan Breakage: Why and How," for more information on breakage). Sometimes companies promote that they are paying out 55 percent or more, but that is just marketing hype and financially unrealistic. They get their percentages by manipulating the calculation, using an artificial percent of retail commission combined with the backside of the compensation plan, which is calculated on wholesale dollars.

For this calculation, you should use a percent of wholesale, which will reflect your true sales income and expense. It's unlikely that any company could operate on a margin of less than 50 percent of wholesale and still make a decent profit. Generally, somewhere between 35 and 45 percent is realistic. If you can afford to pay out more because you have high-dollar margin products, go for it. If not, don't make the mistake of overextending your funds. Remember, you must pay all operating expenses and company overhead out of the remaining balance. That includes cost of goods, distribution operations, all home office personnel and administration, and don't forget Uncle Sam. Your marketing plan pay-out is a similar trade-off to other channels' normal distribution costs such as marketing, warehousing, middlemen, redistribution, catalogs, sales commission, and advertising.

In the early stages of your business, you probably will not be paying out the full amount, especially if the percentage includes leadership bonuses, because no one, or at most very few distributors, will be at that level. Also, at first, people in the sales organization will not capture all roll-ups. Because there will be gaps in the structure, unpaid dollars will roll up to the company.

Now let's talk about the philosophy behind your compensation plan. There are so many plans out there: the binary, the matrix, the stair-step/breakaway, and the unilevel, along with hybrids of all those plus the latest and hottest coded and training bonuses. And, with more and more variations being designed every day, it's easy to get confused about which one to choose. The best way to determine how to split up the percentage you will pay out is to look down the road at what you want your company to look like in three to five years and beyond.

Based on your vision, you will be able to choose a plan that best fits your needs. There are companies, such as Jenkon, that offer this service. They have you fill out a questionnaire to help you through this process. They run a computer model of the plan you selected to show you the pay-outs at various points in the business growth cycle. They can help you estimate what percentage of distributors will actually reach each level in the plan, and predict total company compensation plan pay-out costs utilizing various scenarios. This helps you predict average income at various levels within the plan. Basically, it's a virtual "what if?" game with predictive powers. I recommend you take this road and invest in this type of service, or, at the very least, complete this exercise some other way to determine your plan, to ensure that it will fit your vision and fall within economically feasible boundaries.

If you fail to do any analysis or modeling, you could be in for an unpleasant surprise. Even if you do modeling and analysis, you may overlook or underestimate changes in behavior your field sales force will make that compresses your plan earlier or requires pay-outs higher than you expect. For this reason, when running your models and doing your analysis, plan conservatively to protect your bottom line. An error of only 2 or 3 percent can be very costly.

If after launching a new or enhanced plan you find out you did make a mistake and underestimated the impact of the plan, be sure to take corrective action quickly. Having to recall a newly introduced or enhanced plan is not a fun place to be, but be honest with your field leaders, and do what is needed for the long-term survival of the company.

Pay-out Structure and Timing

In addition to determining what level of pay-out you can afford, you should know how you would like to structure your pay-out. For instance, is your philosophy to pay out most in the front, middle, or back end of the program? Do you want to have a large number of people making a small income? Or do you want a few distributors earning a huge income? Or would you prefer some middle ground, where a significant number can earn a respectable income, while the number of people earning the highs and lows is smaller? Your pay-out strata will change based on the type of plan you select. By running a "what if?" scenario against various plans and populations, you can determine how many will achieve top-level earner status and what their earnings will be versus the next two to three levels down, as well as what percentages distributors will earn at the lower levels.

Frequency of pay-out should also be considered. Many companies pay out to their distributors only once a month, while others generate as many as ten checks a month. Some pay out weekly, others at month's end. While both methods work, the weekly pay-out wins the vote of the sales force. But some companies with weekly pay-outs are realizing the negative cost effect of administration, check production, and mailing. This will become an even greater factor as they approach international expansion, especially if they plan to have worldwide down-lines. Imagine the complications of weekly calculations, exchange rates, reporting, and mailing hundreds of thousands of checks a week worldwide!

One final thought on pay-outs: A new standard is being set in the industry to allow quick accessibility of funds for distributors. Excel Communications announced this year the establishment of FirstExcel Bank, which will facilitate direct deposit for distributors who establish accounts there. I am sure this practice will increase in popularity. It certainly gives Excel, which led the way, a competitive advantage in this arena.

Plan for the Future

To recap, all different types of plans have worked for various companies, and no one plan is the best, so select one that most closely fits your company's personality and overall marketing message. Prepare your plan for the future by not putting all the money out at first. Save something to go back to the well for, as needed, but don't be cheap. Later, your economies of scale in manufacturing and distribution will help improve your profitability and provide additional funds for fueling your marketing plan.

One last reminder: When selecting your compensation plan, be sure to consider your audience of potential distributors. By knowing the *target recruit* you wish to attract to your compensation plan—just as you should know the target consumer for your product—and *your own vision* for the future, you will be in the best position to select the most appealing plan. Good luck on this journey . . . it's not an easy process.

The Success Formula

Indeed, the compensation plan plays a major role in the Success Formula. It is, however, not the end-all ingredient many make it out to be. As long as it is fair, competitive, and legal, it will serve you well. If you can make it simple, too, that will be a miracle.

The attractiveness of the entire "franchise package" is what's the most important. You can have a great product and a fair compensation plan and have great success. On the other hand, if you have a marginal or poor product, even with a great compensation plan, you will not succeed.

Compensation Plans 101

As promised, following is a compilation of educational materials provided by an individual who has a great deal of knowledge on the subject of multilevel marketing compensation.

Dan Jensen founded Jenkon International in 1978. Jenkon, a computer software firm specializing in solutions for direct selling/network marketing clients, serves more than six hundred industry clients. By working with many of the industry's leaders, Dan has acquired a unique level of experience and knowledge about what makes a compensation plan successful. His company helps many start-ups through the process of compensation plan development.

Dan will cover *Principles of a Successful Compensation Plan*, *Compensation Plan Types*, *Compensation Plan Breakage: Why and How*, *Roll-up and Compression: To Do or Not to Do*, and *Are You Wasting Your Hard-Earned Commission Dollars?*

Each section has stand-alone value, and, in combination, all of these sections offer a basic education about compensation plans. Equipped with this foundation, you will be better positioned to process strategic considerations about your own plan, and in general, become familiar with many of the terms and rationales behind various types of plans. I am very grateful, as you will be, to Dan for his expert contributions on this complex subject matter.

Principles of a Successful Compensation Plan

By Dan Jensen, *Chairman, Jenkon International, Inc.*

Introduction

A compensation plan that fails to motivate distributors can stagnate a company as fast as any other factor. While there are many factors that contribute to the success or failure of direct selling companies, the compensation plan is one of the biggest. There are many who ask us, "What's the best compensation plan out there?" Unfortunately, there is no answer to this question, but there are proven principles of success common to virtually all successful plans. What makes a compensation plan great? This article may help to identify the real success factors of a compensation plan.

Always follow these golden rules:

o   Always provide incentive dollars for an expected behavior. Don't waste incentive dollars on behavior that provides little value to you or the distributor. Question each *type* of compensation and verify that it will provide the expected return on investment.

o   Leverage the principle of *relationships*. Most people recruit others they already know. They want to work *with* them. Be sure your plan builds on these relationships. A plan where a new recruit is trained or mentored by a person other than the sponsor usually results in poor recruitment and weak relationships.

o   Recognition is as important as compensation.

As Jim Adams has said, "Distributors will work for money, but they'll kill for a cause."

Five Objectives for Success

1. Sell product to end consumers

Retailing products to end consumers is key to moving products from garages to customers. Corporate failure is inevitable if people stop buying product which they do not (or cannot) sell.

Have a motivating retail/wholesale profit—a minimum of 25 percent discount from retail or 33 percent markup over wholesale. This retail profit is the basis on which people are motivated to sell retail products. Other motivations are usually artificial and will not withstand the test of time.

Have a realistic retail price or people won't be able to sell product to end consumers. Don't sell products whose wholesale price is *really* the market retail value and then add an artificial retail price even higher.

Require heavy emphasis on retailing from field leaders, training, and in marketing materials.

Retailing products based on the hope of future rewards will never result in movement of product to retail consumers. If distributors are selling product by promoting the dream that buyers will earn future commissions when they, in turn, sell the product to others, you'll eventually be sitting on a "time bomb" of unhappy distributors with lots of inventory stacking up in their garages. Companies that do this always fail. Proper retailing moves the product from distributor to end user in volumes justified by natural consumption.

2. Build organizations (recruit)

This is achieved by placing incentives on building group volume. Recruits must easily see that it is easier to have others do the selling to build their business *in addition* to their own selling.

Recognition and reward should be built in to the plan, especially for the new recruit. Most recruits are lost in the first sixty days because they lose confidence that they will succeed in the long term. Rewarding them early on maintains their interest and excitement.

Lack of rewards for new recruits results in sales leaders promoting "buy-in" organization building. They pitch people that a "buy-in" is an investment in their future. The new recruits have greater "equity" (inventory) to keep them in longer, but quickly become disillusioned. They are quick to complain to regulatory officers that "they were taken." Regulators are always on the watch for "investment schemes" of this nature.

You can reward people early by building a series of goals and rewards. As they reach each goal, they are recognized and compensated. It builds their confidence that they can achieve their future dreams.

This process builds the initial skills required to eventually become managers. Lack of early incentives builds ineffective field managers who do not have the skill to sell and recruit based on product viability.

3. Build managers (people who train others to sell and recruit)

This must follow Step 2 or the field force will have many ineffective managers who do little to earn their compensation.

You can build managers by teaching them the basic skills of success for distributors: product retailing and recruiting. Once they learn these skills, they become managers as they teach others (those they recruit) to do the same. Successful managers learn the power of *duplication.*

Incentives are placed on group activities: group volume and recruiting. Group volume incentives usually reward both those selling and those recruiting.

4. Build sales leaders (people who train others to manage)

Incentives must exist to motivate and reward managers who build other managers. Avoid disincentives that penalize a manager when a new manager is created; otherwise managers will work hard to suppress their own star performers from reaching their full potential, for fear of losing significant compensation in the future.

Provide incentives that reward managers for several generations of other down-line managers, so they will want to train their managers to build other managers as well.

Avoid making it too easy to become a sales leader. Distributors who don't know how to build other managers or train other managers to succeed should not be entitled to become sales leaders. If they do, the field organization will be superficial and weak.

Remember that building strong sales leaders takes time, money, and effort. Invest in training them to become effective sales leaders, to build effective managers, and to recruit product retailers and recruiters.

Provide incentives for your top performing sales leaders. Avoid having the plan quickly max out or the top performers will wonder "What's next?" and you won't have an answer.

5. Retention

Retain people by helping them receive significant reward for their time. You compete for their time and attention with many other opportunities and distractions. Make it worth their while early on.

As a distributor works the business, they build an equity investment in their down-line organization. They will continue to work the business if their down-line continues to work the business. This is why a balanced emphasis on product retailing and recruiting is so important.

Distributors who build a down-line are far more likely to continue to be active than those who do not.

If your product is consumable, use an *autoship* program to build repeat business from both retail or preferred customers, as well as wholesale to distributors.

Promote contests and competitions that can be won by everyone. Avoid "top ten" contests where everybody loses except the top ten performers.

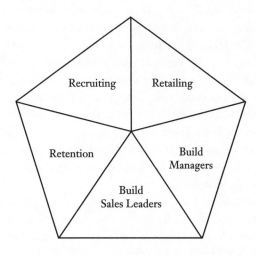

Figure 4.1 Five Objectives of a Successful Compensation Plan

Other Principles of a Successful Compensation Plan

Reasonable Compensation Percentages Most compensation plans today pay between 30 and 50 percent to field distributors. If a company promotes a plan paying only 25 percent or so, they will have a hard time recruiting and keeping distributors unless other factors offset this competitive weakness. These factors might include how well the public accepts the product (telephone service or other common consumables) or intangible incentives that motivate distributors. Real percentage pay-out should fall between 35 and 42 percent. Higher percentages are possible with high product margins. Theoretical pay-out (the percentage the plan would pay if *all* commissions were paid out in every case) should not be more than 8 percent above actual to avoid disappointing distributors who expect more.

Keep It Simple Unfortunately, many plans are designed by MLM professionals for MLM professionals. These plans often assume most people already understand terms and principles of MLM or can at least learn them quickly. This is most definitely not the case. While experience is essential when designing a compensation plan, you must never forget that *ordinary people are the ones who must be motivated by your plan.* If new recruits aren't motivated early, they quickly fall away. The more complex a plan becomes, the fewer people it will motivate. The plan needs to affect the heart of a distributor first, *before* it can affect his or her pocketbook.

Avoid Novelty or "Fad" Plans Changing a compensation plan is costly in terms of lost momentum and distributor commitment. When a distributor recruits another person, the compensation plan is often a significant part of the selling process. To change it later is, in essence, admitting that the original plan was not very good after all. Some people may perceive the change as a "bait and switch" tactic. By staying within more traditional plans, plans that have proven themselves over the years, a new MLM company can still be innovative but know that the plan has staying power. It's often joked that compensation plans are like men's ties: When one plan goes out of fashion, you can count on it coming back a few years later. Stick to more traditional plans that won't need to be changed as new fads come and go.

Don't Put Too Much Credence in the Impact of Your Compensation Plan Many entrepreneurs come to Jenkon convinced that they have the best possible compensation plan imaginable. When asked what product or service they will sell, they sometimes tell us that they're still looking for the right product. Obviously, these well-intentioned people have focused on only one aspect of starting their business, assuming that the compensation plan is the key to their future success. The facts, however, are different. Many companies have gained great success despite poorly designed compensation plans. Put simply, the plan is only one part of the puzzle; it isn't the only part.

Don't Change It Often Those who experiment with their compensation plan are asking for frustrated distributors to join other more stable opportunities. Even good change can be traumatic. Be very reluctant to change the plan.

Avoid Recruiting "Heavy-hitters" These successful MLM professionals can bring tremendous short-term success, but can also be a major cause of failure when they grow bored with your company and join another, often taking thousands from their down-line with them. Wise companies always build slowly for the first few years until they have the critical mass to handle changes in business volumes. Don't design your compensation plan to focus on attracting these heavy-hitters.

Compensation Plan Types
By Dan Jensen

Direct Selling Plans

Traditional Direct Selling

One-on-one, the distributor sells direct to the consumer and earns commission on those sales. Management is limited, often appointed, and sometimes employed. Sponsoring is not aggressively pursued except by those in sales management. Retail commissions are a large percentage of sales and are paid to the distributor/agent or retained in cash payment. Example: Rainbow Vacuum sales.

Party Plan

A one-to-many sales environment with the distributor arranging sales "parties" typically through a hostess. Distributors earn commissions on the inventory sold directly to retail customers at the party. Sales management is usually shallow. Distributors can often promote themselves to management through their recruiting and sales efforts, though higher levels of management are often appointed. The distributor recruits other agents and hosts or hostesses who hold parties and recruit retail customers. The host or hostess receives purchase credit for his or her efforts based upon party success. Generally, there are several levels of management commissions, but only a small percentage of total sales dollars is paid to management. High retail profits (35 to 50 percent) are common. Example: Tupperware.

Network Marketing/MLM Plans

Stair-Step/Breakaway

This type of plan is characterized by distributors who are responsible for personal *and* group sales volumes. Volume is created by recruiting and retailing products. Various discounts or rebates are paid to group leaders. A group leader can be any distributor with one or more down-line recruits. Once a distributor achieves personal and group volumes, that person becomes a manager and "breaks away" from his or her up-line manager. From that point, the new manager's group is no longer considered part of his or her up-line manager's group—hence, he or she is called a "breakaway." Managers receive commissions on the group sales of their down-line managers, which often become the majority of their earnings. These plans pay unlimited commission on limited down-line groups. This is the most common type of network marketing plan.

Unilevel

Often considered the most simple of compensation plans, unilevel pays commissions primarily based on the number of levels away a recipient is from the original distributor purchasing product. Commissions are not based on title or rank achieved. By qualifying with a minimum sales requirement, distributors earn unlimited commissions on a limited number of levels of down-line recruited distributors. Typically, there is no sales management position to achieve. Example: Kaire International, Inc.

Matrix

This is similar to the unilevel plan, except there is a limited number of distributors who can be placed on the first level. Recruits beyond the maximum number of first-level positions allowed are automatically placed in other down-line positions. Matrix plans often have maximum width *and* depth. When all positions in a distributor's down-line matrix are filled (maximum width and depth is reached for all participants in a matrix), an additional matrix is started. Like unilevel, distributors earn unlimited commissions on limited levels of volume with minimum sales quotas. Example: Melaleuca, Inc.

Australian, or 2-up, Plan

This plan is based on a large commission on unlimited depth of a small amount of a distributor's total group. Large-scale recruiting is necessary to drive the program. The distributor gives up the first two of his or her recruits to their qualifying up-line. This pass-up may move through an infinite number of levels. Typically, sales management positions are minimal. Volumes accumulate through unlimited depth but limited width. Earnings are unlimited.

Binary

The binary plan requires distributors to constantly assess their personal recruiting and sales management. Distributors activate *income centers* (also called *business centers*), then recruit distributors into each one. Income centers can be considered a distributorship entity or business. Volume in each income center accumulates on each of its two legs (only two legs are allowed per income center, a left and a right leg). Successful distributors in a binary plan must constantly watch their down-line to ensure that volume accumulates evenly. Compensation is made at fixed intervals of evenly accumulated volume up to a threshold where the maximum payment is made during a pay period. Volume accumulation starts again in the next period after maximum payment. Binary plans pay limited commission on unlimited levels of volume.

Compensation Plan Breakage: Why and How

By Dan Jensen

Breakage is defined as the commission left unpaid each month compared to the theoretical maximum of the plan. If a compensation plan pays a maximum of 45 percent but the actual pay-out is 35 percent each month, then the breakage would be 10 percent. On the surface, one might suggest that breakage is unfair, unethical, or at the very least, misleading, considering that a plan may represent itself as paying 45 percent but actually pay 35 percent. Upon further study, however, a plan that uses breakage wisely will reward the producers much more generously than one without breakage. It allows a company that can only afford 35 percent for commission expense to pay perhaps 45 percent or more to the distributors doing the greatest amount of work. Breakage can be a strong competitive advantage if it is used correctly and for the right reasons.

Objectives for Breakage in a Plan

Every piece of a good compensation plan has a specific purpose or desired result. With breakage, the goals are to:

o   Keep the total commission expense at or below a target maximum. If we can only afford to pay 30 percent, with breakage we can often afford a plan that can pay out 35 to 40 percent (or more) to the most productive distributors.

Chapter Four

o   Reward specific behaviors that are most desired by the
    company such as recruiting, retailing, building managers
    and leaders, and retention. (See *Principles of a Successful
    Compensation Plan* above.)

o   Reward those who exceed minimum levels of perfor-
    mance more than those who don't.

o   Avoid rewarding distributors who fail to perform
    consistently.

Benefits of Breakage

Breakage is applied by imposing reasonable rules to qualify
for commissions. If a distributor fails to perform at a desired
level, the company retains the commission that he or she
would otherwise receive. For example, if a distributor failed
to meet his or her $100 minimum personal volume require-
ment, the company might keep that person's commissions instead of paying them to another distributor. This allows the
company to pay more to other distributors who are meeting
or exceeding the desired level of production. In essence, the
company withholds commissions for lack of performance and
increases the compensation of those who perform well. The
advantages are obvious:

o   Distributors who meet or exceed expectations are re-
    warded more generously using commission dollars
    that would have been kept by distributors who are not
    performing as well.

o   The company can afford to pay more than it could oth-
    erwise afford to pay, expanding the capacity of the plan
    to provide incentives for desired behavior. The company
    gets more of what it wants (desired behavior) and the
    performing distributors get more of what they want—
    compensation and recognition. Breakage can be a win-
    win deal for both company and distributor.

There are many ways to implement breakage and methods
vary according to the type of plan used.

Example #1

Bob, a breakaway manager, fails to meet his minimum $100 personal purchase for the month. He would have otherwise received a 25 percent commission of $200 on his group volume. Rather than paying it to his up-line, the company retains Bob's $200. The company determines that about 1 percent of total pay-out is retained from unqualified managers like Bob each month. The company decides to put this 1 percent into a bonus pool paid to every distributor who sponsors at least three people in the month. For each new recruit, the participants in the bonus pool receive one share of the pool. The company happily discovers that redirecting the commissions into the pool has resulted in a 10 percent increase in recruiting and a 4 percent increase in sales volume for the fiscal year from those new recruits. Equally important, more than $100,000 has been paid to those distributors recruiting three or more people in a month, making a number of very happy and committed distributors.

Example #2

After a recent compensation plan change, the plan calls for a 4 percent first-generation bonus to managers who achieve $100 in personal volume and $1,000 in group volume. If a manager achieves $2,000 in group volume, the commission goes up to 7 percent. When the 4 percent is paid instead of the 7 percent, the company retains the difference as breakage. The company has determined that about 25 percent of its managers achieve the $2,000 GV level, so it pays out the 7 percent first-generation bonus about 25 percent of the time. The total first-generation bonus paid is about 5 percent. In its old plan, the company paid out a 5 percent first-generation bonus if the manager achieved $1,000 GV. In its new plan (4 to 7 percent), it pays out the same commission, but has achieved a 50 percent increase in managers achieving $2,000 GV each month. The company can afford to pay 7 percent to the higher producers out of the 1 percent obtained by lowering the original 5 percent to 4 percent.

Strategies for Using Breakage

○ Don't set performance thresholds (GV, PV, and so on) too low. Breakage is only available when there is a gap between poor performance and desired performance. If you need to set low levels of performance, then offer graduated compensation opportunities for those who are willing to work harder. Low performance requirements produce low performance.

○ Redirect the breakage into *new* incentives when possible. Increasing the fifth-generation bonus from 5 percent to 6 percent may make a few leaders happier, but they may not do anything different to obtain it—bigger checks for doing the same old things (no wonder they are happier!). Putting another 1 percent, however, into a new sixth-generation bonus (assuming the old plan paid only five generations) that is contingent on adding another three personally sponsored breakaway leaders will stimulate leaders to recruit and build more front-line breakaways than before.

○ If your plan uses titles or ranks like Stair-Step/ Breakaway plans do, then always use "paid as" titles. Let distributors keep the highest title they achieve, but always pay them as the title they actually qualify for each month. To continue paying them based on performance that occurred months ago is wasting incentive dollars that could be applied to the better producers. It also reduces breakage opportunities.

○ For group volume incentives (front-end stair-step), consider rewarding the breakaway manager based on his actual group volume instead of his title. For example, if a plan calls for a breakaway manager to receive a maximum of 25 percent on his or her group, consider requiring a minimum volume level to receive the full 25 percent. If the manager falls below the minimum, he or she would earn less, perhaps much less, than 25 percent. The difference between actual and maximum would be retained as breakage and added to other incentives in the plan.

o   Never roll up volume from an unqualified breakaway to his or her up-line. Rolling up commissions (called *compression*) is often desired, but avoid rolling up *volume*, which would add to the group volume of up-line managers. This results in phantom qualification volume for up-line managers not related to any real performance, and often rewards the poor performers, who receive nice checks and wonder what they did to earn it. The net effect is to eliminate breakage and waste your incentive dollar.

o   Distinguish between *active* and *qualified* when qualification levels are defined. *Active* usually refers to personal performance, often measured in personal volume (PV). *Qualified* often goes beyond active, adding group volume or sponsoring requirements. Breakage rules can be defined differently for active and qualified. For example, the company might keep as breakage some commissions for unqualified distributors who fail to meet their group volume requirements, but roll up commissions (no breakage) for those distributors who are not active.

o   A common technique when a company changes their compensation plan is to *grandfather* existing leaders and distributors into former (often lower) levels of performance requirements to "soften the blow" of the new plan. While this may be essential to winning their support for a much needed plan change, it is often unwise to offer these special arrangements for long periods of time. Wise companies often make grandfathering a temporary or transitional arrangement because the practice often reduces the breakage the company would otherwise receive due to poor performance. The net effect is that the good producers are compensated less while the poor producers are compensated more.

Other Sources of Breakage

Shallow Company Down-lines Companies that sponsor wide and new start-up operations find a "windfall" in the commissions left unpaid because there is no up-line to pay them to. Be careful, however, because as the down-line grows and matures, this short-term windfall diminishes.

High-end Titles and Ranks Many companies implement plans where the top-end ranks or titles are achieved so rarely that few, if any, collect the corresponding commission benefits. These unpaid commissions provide breakage until more and more leaders achieve these higher titles and collect the commission benefits.

Finding Breakage Opportunities

To determine where your breakage opportunities are, follow these steps:

1. Write down each type of commission your plan pays and what its maximum pay-out could be. For example, if your plan pays out five generations in the back end of 5 percent, then your maximum generation bonuses total 25 percent. Try to identify each individual type of commission such as first-generation, second-generation, group volume bonus, and so on.

2. Determine how much each type of commission actually pays out. Jenkon's Summit V Commissions Module provides standard reports each month that provide this valuable information.

3. Subtract the actual pay-out from the maximum for each commission type. The difference is your breakage.

Once you know where you already have breakage, you can also spot areas where you don't. Look at these areas and determine if you *want* more breakage and modify the plan accordingly.

Conclusion

Breakage can be a significant competitive advantage, if you use it wisely, and a terrific tool to reward the producing distributors more than you could otherwise afford. All plans have some breakage opportunities that can be tapped to make the plan an even more powerful motivator. As in most things, moderation is more prudent than extremes when applying the principles of breakage to your own plan.

Roll-up and Compression: to Do or Not to Do

By Dan Jensen

Compression. Of all the techniques used to fine-tune a compensation plan, compression is one that is most often used, but seldom understood. For many companies, compression is a source of massive waste in their compensation plan—dollars being spent with little return. For others, it is a source of focused and well-planned incentives on distributor performance that is otherwise difficult to obtain.

Roll-up and Compression: What Are They?

While they actually have different meanings, *compression* and *roll-up* are terms often used interchangeably in network marketing. Compression can be defined as: *The impact on a genealogy when a distributor is terminated. The down-line of the terminated distributor is linked to the sponsor of the terminated distributor, causing a "compression" effect on the down-line.*

63

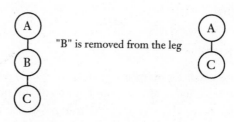

Figure 4.2 **Example of Compression**

Compression, therefore, relates to the effect of removing a distributor from a genealogy leg as shown in Figure 4.2. In this example, distributor B is removed from the genealogy, resulting in distributor C being relinked to A. When B is removed, his entire first level is linked to their new sponsor, A, and all other down-line distributors move up one level closer to A, compressing the down-line by the one level vacated by B.

Roll-up occurs when a commission payment cannot be paid to a distributor due to that distributor's being inactive, unqualified, or not eligible. The payment will then roll up to the next qualified, active, and eligible distributor. For example, a simple unilevel plan pays 10 percent to Level 1 and 10 percent to

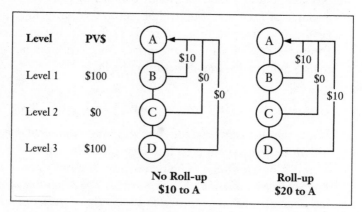

Figure 4.3 **Example of Roll-up**

Level 2, but only if the distributor purchases $100 in the month.

The example in Figure 4.3 shows the effect roll-up has on the commission of A. Without roll-up, A receives a Level 1 commission from B's $100 purchase, no Level 2 commission from C because C purchased nothing, and no commission from D because D is at Level 3, beyond the reach of A (the plan only pays two levels).

With roll-up, A receives $10 from B, nothing from C (no purchase volume), and for this month only (next month C may be active again), D is counted as second level to A, and A receives 10 percent on D's $100 purchase. Conceptually, A receives commissions on two active levels with roll-up and, therefore, reaches deeper, ignoring inactives when counting levels.

If C *had* purchased some product, but not enough to be active, then C would also be counted as second level to A. In this case, *both* C and D would be counted as second level to A, but only for the current month. Confused? Who said network marketing was simple?

Why Offer Roll-up?

A golden rule of compensation plan design is to apply the incentive dollars toward the desired behavior (see *Are You Wasting Your Hard-Earned Commission Dollars?* following). What behavior can roll-up buy?

Roll-up can help sales leaders work deeply in their downline. Sales leaders often find one or more distributors many levels below them who need their help and attention because they cannot get it from their immediate up-line. Sales leaders are forced to work around the inactive or uncooperative manager(s) directly with the needful distributors. Would sales leaders spend their valuable time with these needful distributors, however, if they felt there was little potential reward? The deeper a group is, the less the potential reward for the up-line sales leader because when the group catches fire it will build below itself even deeper and eventually move out of reach of the sales leader's commission check. Hence, sales leaders soon learn that without roll-up, it is in their best interest to ignore the deep distributors who may need help and focus on the closer ones. With roll-up, however, the inactive sponsors in between are ignored, so the sales leaders can expect to reap the benefits of their efforts on a long-term basis, since depth is determined only by those who are active. Roll-up, therefore, entices sales leaders to work deep because it offers them a return on their time.

Roll-up also entices sales leaders to move up the ranks by reaching deeper. The deeper people can reach for commissions, the larger their checks will be (assuming they have a large down-line). Sales leaders know that the largest earnings come from the volume at their deepest reach, because there are more producers there: The deeper you go, the more people there are in the down-line, level by level. Roll-up can be used as a significant enticement for ambitious sales leaders who want to earn from even deeper ranks of distributors in their organizations. For example, if a plan provides roll-up to only the top three ranks of sales leaders, then lesser sales leaders will strive aggressively to reach those top three positions because their commission checks will grow substantially as a result of the existing volume being generated. It would be like getting a huge raise!

Mistakes to Avoid

Mistake #1: Offering Roll-up to Most Distributors

Many plans I have seen offer roll-up to most distributors as if it would turn on a huge amount of additional performance across the board. This is not so. Roll-up works most effectively with sales leaders who have large organizations. It offers little incentive for distributors with shallow organizations because they already earn commissions from them.

Mistake #2: Everybody's Doing It

Don't fall into the trap of using roll-up just because it seems all your competitors are doing it. Do it because it's right for you. Roll-up costs your competitors a *lot* of money; depending on your situation, you could put that money into other parts of your plan and get higher returns.

Mistake #3: Giving Roll-up to Nonproducers

Once you understand what behavior you're buying with roll-up, it becomes apparent that it should focus on active, qualified, performing sales leaders. Giving roll-up to poorer performing distributors is a waste of precious incentive dollars.

Mistake #4: Not Budgeting for Roll-up

Roll-up is expensive because it almost always pays out to the maximum limit of the plan. Without roll-up, the company retains breakage to a much larger degree. Plans with roll-up should expect to pay out close to their theoretical maximum.

Conclusion

Roll-up can be a tremendous incentive for your active sales leaders who have large down-lines. If you are giving away roll-up commissions to nonproducers, to the less active, or to those with shallow down-lines, consider making some changes in your plan in the future.

Are You Wasting Your Hard-Earned Commission Dollars?

By Dan Jensen

As you look at the bottom line on a profit and loss statement, you quickly realize that the largest cost factor is for commissions. For many companies, this ranges between 30 and 50 percent of revenue. While executives search for ways to reduce expenses, "commissions" are seldom touched because they drive the motivation and loyalty of the distributors. Cut the commission check and distributors leave. Increase commissions, and distributors are more motivated (theoretically, at least), but the bottom line suffers dramatically.

The real question an executive should ask is not "How do we reduce our commission expense?" but rather "Are we wasting any incentive dollars?" If there was an accurate way to measure it, I believe many companies would find they are wasting between 10 and 50 percent of each commission dollar. In other words, incentive money is being spent without any resulting behavior or effect.

Identifying Wasted Commission Dollars

Step 1: Is your plan accomplishing the five basic objectives in a balanced manner?

In *Principles of a Successful Compensation Plan* I described five objectives or behaviors a compensation plan should include. They are:

1. Sell product to end consumers (retailing).
2. Build organizations (recruiting).
3. Build managers (people who train others to sell and recruit).
4. Build sales leaders (people who train others to manage).
5. Retain sales leaders (keep them active).

As you look at your compensation plan, determine how well it accomplishes these fundamental objectives. Figure out where it's weak and where it's strong. For example, suppose you look at your plan and realize that there are few incentives to retail product. Symptoms might include garages full of inventory or distributors who have to sell product to other distributors because they bought too much. Perhaps distributors focus on recruiting, but fail to train recruits how to sell the product. As you look at the plan, you realize that the retail profit is poor (maybe only

20 percent) and that the presentation of the plan doesn't emphasize retail profits as part of the overall compensation system.

Try making a chart like the one in Figure 4.4 to see how each commission type contributes to the desired behaviors (your types of commissions may be very different than in my example).

Behaviors	Retail Profit	GV Bonus	Break-away	Infinity	Recruiting Bonus	Total
Retailing	3	2	0	0	0	5
Recruiting	0	4	2	0	3	9
Build Managers	0	2	4	1	0	7
Build Leaders	0	0	4	5	0	9
Retention	0	1	3	4	0	8

Figure 4.4 **Chart Your Compensation Plan's Impact**

For this example, suppose your compensation plan has the five types of commissions. Now, assign a point value from 1 to 5 based on how well each type of commission (top row) produces the five desired behaviors (first column). I've filled in some sample numbers to illustrate the point. Total them up and see how balanced your plan is, where your weaknesses are, and where your strengths are. Is it accomplishing the five basic objectives?

Step 2: *Is each type of commission obtaining a desired behavior?*

Look at each component or type of compensation by itself and ask "What behavior does this type of commission create?" or "If this type of commission was removed, what behavior would stop occurring?" For example, if you took away the retail profit, what would happen? (Correct answer: Sales would stop.) If you eliminated your breakaway overrides, would leaders continue building other leaders and managers? Too many times, plans are designed to redistribute the sales dollar to others without any specific expectation. The result isn't as much a compensation plan as it is a form of "welfare" (no political message intended). Successful plans focus on behavior. Reward distributors for good behavior. Avoid rewarding them for undesirable behavior.

Step 3: Are there any duplicated or overlapping behaviors being paid for?

Compensation plans usually have at least four types of commission incentives. If two or more types of commissions are being paid for the same behavior, would it make sense to combine them or eliminate one? Sometimes it does.

Step 4: Are there disincentives in your plan?

As you look at each type of commission and how it interacts with the other types, you might find some conflicts or opposing forces at play. Eliminate them.

Step 5: Are you rewarding the nonproducers?

If a distributor fails to produce, what happens? Do they continue receiving compensation at the level of their performance? If not, you're rewarding nonperformance at the expense of the performers. *What one man receives without working, another man works for without receiving.*

Conclusion

Every plan has weaknesses that are opportunities to add to your bottom line. While you may not need to reduce your commission expense, I promise that you will increase sales and profits by redirecting some of the wasted commission dollars to strengthen the weaker areas of your plan. And who knows—spending a few hours on this may give you enough money to buy that shiny new Jenkon computer you always wanted.

MARKETING THE OPPORTUNITY

Objective

THE PURPOSE OF this chapter is to remind you that the Opportunity your network marketing company offers to people to start their own business is in and of itself a product that must be packaged and promoted. Just as McDonald's has to find customers for its hamburgers, it must also must package and promote the franchise opportunity in order to open enough stores to service customers.

One of the keys to success in network marketing, especially at start-up when a company needs to attract as many new distributors as possible, is to devote a lot of time and resources to packaging the Opportunity attractively and demonstrating how the process of presenting the Opportunity can be easily replicated. You will find that this need never goes away.

Your Second Product Line

In network marketing, a key to success and an integral part of the success system is recognizing that your Opportunity is indeed its own product; it needs attention and support in the same way the tangible product or service you are selling does. As such, significant resources and time should be spent putting together presentation pieces and supports that clearly identify your business opportunity. This term is not to be confused with the official term that is governed by business opportunity laws. However, as you plan the components of your business kit, be sure to take those laws into consideration (see Chapter 16, "A Legal Primer").

Just as you want to know the needs and desires of your primary product customers, likewise you need to know the makeup of the "customers" you are seeking to recruit for your business opportunity "product." Your target group will have specific tastes to which your opportunity image must appeal, as well as social or financial needs that must be considered. While the category of individuals (or couples) you want to attract is often fairly broad and diverse, you still need to know the hot buttons and key benefit phrases to use to get their attention. Remember, as the business owner, you will only present the business opportunity directly to prospective distributors at the beginning of business start-up. Thereafter, your distributors (most likely the newest ones) will most often be the presenters.

For that reason, it is important to keep your business opportunity presentation simple, visually attractive (so that it projects the right company image), and diverse enough to capture the attention of recipients with varying needs and interests. You should offer your presentation via different media (print, audio, video, CD-ROM, and so on) to allow your distributors to present it most effectively both for them and their target prospect. For one-on-one presentations, it can be a presentation book or desktop flip chart that outlines a script for the presenter and prospect to follow. Alternately, it can be a video for appropriate support of someone who has the opportunity to utilize a VCR, either in their own home to a group or in the prospect's home. This is often a comfortable way for someone starting out to cover the presentation, because they may be unfamiliar with all the key points about the company, or they may be uncomfortable trying to present the complex details of the compensation plan.

Other supports can include audiotapes and full-size flip charts. You also may want to encourage group opportunity meetings hosted by local area leadership so newer local distributors have somewhere to take their prospect to see a professional presentation. This is also a good chance for newer distributors to see the presentation role modeled, so eventually they will be adept enough to do their own.

Prospecting and Recruiting

Before I get into what these pieces should contain, let's first explore the various steps you should support to keep the prospecting and recruiting pipeline well oiled. By way of introduction, there are a couple of terms to define. A *prospect* is any individual who may be a candidate for the business. Distributors generally identify prospects from their sphere of influence, and prepare a contact list containing the names of all the people they want to contact to set up an initial meeting to discuss the business. The *prospecting phase* is simply the concept of making a connection with someone identified as a prospect, and the objective of the contact is to get a presentation meeting set up to begin the recruiting process. Prospecting can also encompass the activity of developing new leads for one's contact list through ads or other means.

Recruiting is the process that takes place during a business presentation where a distributor engages in the solicitation of a prospect to join in the business. It is where a distributor uses materials provided by the company to entice and recruit the individual observing the presentation. It is where they "ask for the order" and get the prospect to sign on the dotted line.

There are many places from which prospective distributors can come. They may come from the customer base of individuals who currently use the core product line. They may be members of a current distributor's family, a warm circle of friends, or anyone on the distributor's prospect list. They may respond to an ad in the paper or a lead box, or result from a cold contact that a current distributor has mustered up the courage to approach. The first contact can be made in person, by phone, or even by mail if it's an out-of-town contact. All of these possibilities must be considered; it is best to offer materials to support each person and approach. The company must support the process to the extent that it makes it as easy as possible for distributors to approach anyone they come in contact with. If you can accomplish this, you will have an important component of the Success Formula in the bag.

Support Materials

Some of the supports needed are:

○ Materials that allow distributors to make a contact list, and keep it updated.

○ A prospecting piece that functions as an attention-getter or thought-starter (not a fire hose full of information, but rather a sample to whet the appetite and get the prospect to agree to a presentation meeting).

○ Attractive lead-generation boxes or materials that can be picked up by individuals.

○ Appropriate, company-approved solicitation ad slicks.

○ Audiotapes that can lay the foundation for a follow-up call and meeting.

Additionally, you may want to encourage or sponsor weekly opportunity meetings in specific cities where local leadership exists; or, you can host a weekly opportunity contact from the home office. This can take the form of a live phone call or taped message to which prospects can connect to get some basic information and good feelings about the company. If this works as it should, the prospect should be sufficiently interested to allow the sponsoring distributor to at least schedule a presentation meeting to start the recruiting process.

Customers of Your Opportunity

In order to build some background on how to structure your approach and support pieces, it will be helpful to determine why people want to join direct selling or network marketing companies. In 1996, the Direct Selling Association commissioned a research study to determine who the "Customer of the Opportunity" is.[1] Individuals currently performing as distributors with direct selling or network marketing companies were asked to rank the following reasons to see how well they represented why these individuals joined their companies.

1. In 1996, the Direct Selling Association (DSA) commissioned Wirthlin Worldwide to conduct a study of public attitudes toward direct selling. Reports on the results of that study are available for purchase from the DSA, 1666 K St. NW, Suite 1010, Washington, D.C. 20006. (202) 293-5760

Some of the top reasons (in descending order, from 91 percent to 84 percent of those who agree with the reason) they shared were:

- It's a good way to meet and socialize with people.
- It is a business where the harder they work the more money they can make.
- It is a good way to supplement income and make a little extra money.
- It allows them to be independent and work when they want to.
- It is a way to develop a business of their own.
- It is a possible full-time career.
- It allows them to buy product at a discount.

While these findings will help you structure your communications piece to appeal to new prospects, it is also important to consider some other key findings about why people do *not* join. You need to be aware of these to help your distributors overcome objections they are sure to hear. Reasons given for not becoming a distributor when approached about an opportunity include:

- They dislike selling or feel they are not good at it.
- They perceive the time requirement to be a negative factor.

Your materials must overcome these objections by hitting head-on what selling is actually involved and how much time a person needs to have to do the job. It does not necessarily have to be "free" time, but one must be able to show a prospect how they can free up the necessary time or better utilize existing free time to achieve the benefits they seek.

It is also helpful to know that many distributors and customers of the Opportunity were customers of the product before becoming distributors. Six of ten were identified as such in the DSA-commissioned study. Even after leaving the ranks of distributors, more than half still purchase and use products from the companies they represented.

Another key finding was that seven in ten of the current representatives polled use one-on-one sales approaches exclusively, especially among traditional direct selling companies. If this is your company's approach, be sure to provide materials that support this method, such as a tabletop or brief annual report–style presentation book.

Current representatives also revealed the source of their recruiter. In other words, they answered the question "What was the relationship of the current distributor or representative to the person who recruited them?" Following are the findings:

Someone known only as a company representative	28 percent
A close friend	23 percent
An acquaintance	20 percent
A co-worker	9 percent
A relative	7 percent
An immediate family member	6 percent
A neighbor	1 percent

It is interesting to note that the most well-represented category is not friends or family of distributors, but rather someone who knew his or her sponsor only via the company they represent. Again, just some things to keep in mind as you develop support pieces and communications that present your Opportunity.

Investment in Recruiting

Because finding new distributors or customers for the Opportunity—I use the capital "O" because it should be thought of as the proper name for a product—is such an integral part of your start-up and ongoing business, an individual must be assigned full-time responsibility for marketing the Opportunity. It is your most profitable product over the long term, so why wouldn't you spend sufficient dollars here? This individual's role is a marketing function that operates in a similar manner to any other product line manager. In the same way product marketing encompasses the pricing, positioning, promotion, public relations, and so on of a personal care or other product you wish to move, marketing the Opportunity requires the same constant attention to keep recruits buying in.

Researching what the competition is doing to attract prospects and developing new and creative ways to generate leads is the responsibility of this Opportunity marketer. Additionally, constantly ensuring that the Opportunity gets attention in communications pieces and appropriate staging and time at all company gatherings is part of the role. This person would also be in charge of developing and maintaining an appropriate starter kit and recruiting support materials.

When promoting the Opportunity, you need to optimize what you have to sell and position who you are to the customers of the Opportunity. In the same way that your product should align with a mission and greater good as part of its appeal, so should the Opportunity be positioned. For the Opportunity, the cause may be financial freedom, extra income, the chance to have one's own business, meeting new social contacts, and so on. All the communications pieces developed to support the Opportunity need to project this appeal.

As an aside, prospecting and recruiting sales aids should be priced as reasonably as possible, and you should put several mediums into your starter kit. Since recruiting new distributors is the lifeblood of your business, you want as much help in the hands of your distributors as you can possibly afford.

The Success Formula

Because the Opportunity is an extremely important product, make sure you devote sufficient financial and human resources to this factor. Many companies fall short here. They simply forget that they need promotional dollars and a full-time person to focus on and be responsible for creating the ongoing support the sales group needs to have a truly contemporary and attractive Opportunity/Franchise product to market. Having a good performer in the position of brand manager for the Opportunity may mean the difference between success or failure, or slow growth and rapid growth. Part of the Opportunity brand manager's role is to create a *duplicatable* (the word used in network marketing to mean the ability to imitate over and over) recruiting process and recruiting strategy that measures up to the system outlined in the following section. The combination of a dynamic Opportunity brand manager and a duplicatable recruiting process is definitely a key ingredient in the Success Formula.

The Art of Duplication

There are many factors to consider in order to create a process and a successful recruiting strategy that can be duplicated. To help you analyze what you should be doing, Kirsten Park, principal of Mark Communications, outlines the key Success Factors required. Kirsten has seventeen years of experience in direct selling and network marketing. After having held several corporate positions with large companies, she established her own firm in Salt Lake City. Kirsten has worked with network marketing companies around the world, helping them create and implement the art of duplication through her system. Because recruiting is such an integral part of your company's future growth, pay particular attention to the principles she outlines here.

Creating a Process and Recruiting Strategy
By Kirsten Park

Duplication: Ideal or Reality?

Like all business, network marketing relies on a system; a verifiable, duplicatable, teachable system to ensure growth.

"What I do, I must teach you to do, and you must teach your new distributor to do."

In fact, we have only duplicated ourselves when we have developed a third level of distributors.

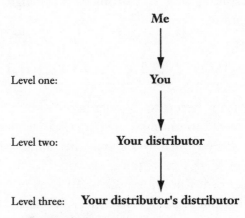

	Me
Level one:	**You**
Level two:	**Your distributor**
Level three:	**Your distributor's distributor**

Figure 5.1 The Duplication Process

You see, it is not enough for me to sponsor you; I haven't duplicated anything, I have just sponsored someone. And it is not enough for me to teach you to sponsor someone; I have just taught *you* to sponsor. I am still a critical part of the "system," which without me, would not exist.

But when I teach *you* to teach *someone else,* only then have I duplicated myself, or, in other words, taught someone to "do what I do."

Sound difficult? It could be, and it is, unless you recognize this undeniable fact: The key to a duplicatable system is to ensure that the method in which a distributor is sponsored into the system is the *same* method he or she is taught to use when sponsoring others into the system.

That means that the company is teaching what the sponsor does, and what the new distributor is experiencing. Period. Isn't this great? Your new distributors will be learning what to do before they have even joined your company!

If you have this, you have a duplicatable system; but if you don't, you have an approach that is dependent on personalities, circumstances, strong sponsors who never quit, tremendous teachers in the field, and a good dose of good luck. And another thing: You shoulder the liability that comes from not being able to present a legal, compliant sponsoring policy should you ever be confronted by regulators questioning your company's policies.

So, why do so few companies succeed in providing such a system? There is an undeniable paradox inherent in the industry of network marketing: The very skills that cause an individual to experience success in sponsoring are often the very skills that are by definition, nonduplicatable and cannot be taught.

Think about it: This is a personal, testimonial-driven business. The most visible leaders tend to be powerful presenters, either one-on-one or in a group. They are believable because the nature of their presentation is so honest and personal.

But on the other hand, the hue and cry from the field and from marketing departments is "systematize!" "Everyone needs to be on the same page!" "Standardize your presentation!"

Hmmm . . . the best presentations are personal, but everyone wants them to be standardized.

This is where a *truly* duplicatable sales system comes in. The desired system is duplicatable; in other words, it is taught to each distributor identically. But what is systematized also can be personalized, reflecting the honesty and believability that is so critical to a successful presentation. Think of a song that everyone knows the words and tune to, but is perhaps played on different instruments.

To do this, the company must know what it believes. In other words, you must have a philosophy that supports a strategy you are prepared to implement through appropriate training and tools.

Strategy: How Do We Sponsor?

What is your company's philosophy about sponsoring in a network marketing organization? While there are several strategies that work for the long term (party-plan, one-on-one presentations, or business opportunity meetings, to name a few), it is important to first decide *how* your company approaches the process. And it is important that your philosophy reflects what will serve your company in the long term.

For example, if your philosophy is that you will gain new distributors merely from approaching the pool of people who already use your products, you are automatically excluding people who don't use your products. "What's wrong with that?" you might ask. "We want our distributors to all use our products!" Well, that means that a cosmetics company will only sponsor women who use cosmetics; a company with a weight-loss product will only appeal to people who have a weight problem; and a cleaning product company will only appeal to people who identify with a particular cleaning problem.

With this approach you will exclude people who might be successful entrepreneurs, attracted to a business—albeit one sustained by a great product—but who personally don't take the time to meet with a distributor about a new product, or who don't perceive a need in their own lives for the product.

Did you know that virtually all successful cosmetics companies in the United States are led by men, who are not typically your average cosmetic company's consumer? Belief in your product is absolutely essential; a personal need, or personally using your product, is not.

If you asked ten people on the street, "If you had to choose, which would you be more interested in, a *product* that offered benefits (of better skin, more energy, etc.) or an *opportunity* that offered the benefits of financial success, freedom, a chance to travel, etc.?"—don't you think most individuals would select the benefits of an opportunity over the benefits of a product?

This doesn't mean we don't present both options to prospects, but doesn't it make sense to offer what people are more inclined to want, first? Some folks who use your products will then become active in building a business, but 100 percent of the people who are seriously active in business building will use and sell your products. And you can always present product to an individual who has rejected pursuing the Opportunity, but you can rarely present the Opportunity to an individual who has rejected the product.

If this becomes your company's philosophy, you needn't worry about losing your focus on product sales: You will get all you can handle (in fact more, if you consider that a prospect who is negative about "getting sponsored" will be much more open to looking at product when he or she has already rejected the Opportunity).

You will also find your distributors doing a better job of not just attracting customers, but attracting people who are more capable than themselves, able to develop a large organization, and highly likely to sponsor individuals in this manner.

So, what does this strategy look like in action?

The System: The Cycle of Sponsoring and Retailing

Regardless of your product, your service, your compensation plan, or your sales channel, the *system* of sponsoring, and of retailing for that matter, is the same. There are three critical components in a duplicatable sales system. While any two successful companies may appear to be completely different, upon close examination, you'll see that a successful sales system is identifiable within each. It is interesting that while many companies have a firmly established sales system for the retailing of product, they may not have one for the sponsoring of new distributors. Figure 5.2 shows what a duplicatable sales system looks like.

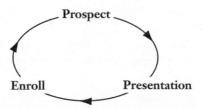

Figure 5.2   A Duplicatable Sales System/Opportunity

The first element is one that *prospects,* or identifies and opens the minds of, individuals to whom you will *present* your company story, which is the second element. If your company story is compelling enough, you will then be successful in *enrolling* your prospect as a distributor, which is the third element of the process.

A duplicatable system guarantees that the exact process you engaged to identify and open the mind of your prospect will then be used by that prospect in identifying and opening the mind of his or her prospect. And so the cycle is duplicated.

If your prospect is not interested in the Opportunity, the presentation focuses on product, and the enrollment element becomes a purchase (see Figure 5.3). And, while a customer can most certainly recommend other customers, the cycle for your customer purchasing more product begins again when you discuss new products with him or her, make a presentation on those products, and again he or she purchases.

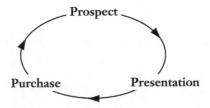

Figure 5.3 A Duplicatable Sales System/Product

Any time your retail customer is open to exploring the Opportunity (which often happens with satisfied product users), your system for then presenting the opportunity is no different than it was the first time you presented the opportunity: He or she must first be open to exploring the Opportunity, then must be presented with the company (from a business perspective this time, rather than that of just a customer), and then given the opportunity to enroll and receive a company Starter Kit.

The same steps occur at every stage, because each prospect, for product or business, has the same issues to address on his or her way to making a decision. By identifying these issues, you have identified the critical elements of your duplicatable sales system.

But identifying these elements is only the first part of your responsibility; the second part is to create the tools that support this strategy. Your success in developing a duplicatable system will lie in developing consistent, affordable tools that support your strategy and clearly communicate how they are to be used.

Tools

Now that you have established your company's strategy, your next responsibility is to create tools that serve that strategy. Each tool has a specific purpose, just as each step in the system has a specific purpose. Let's go through each element of a duplicatable sales system and identify its purpose and the contents of the tools associated with that element.

Step One: Prospecting Tools

Purpose: To open the prospect's mind to the concept of network marketing. The goal at this stage of the cycle is not to communicate everything about your company, but to get the prospect to the point of asking, "If I were to explore network marketing, which company would I look at as my vehicle?" Wouldn't it be great if your prospects were asking themselves this question?

Every successful network marketer understands and believes in the network marketing industry. Sure, some may have signed up in their company without that belief, or perhaps joined based on their faith in the products alone, but at some point before they committed to building a successful organization they developed faith in the industry. (For some, this may have taken place years after they signed up as a distributor!)

The purpose of your prospecting tools is to objectively communicate the power and credibility of network marketing. Many companies omit this step, thinking that the strength of their company story or their product make it unnecessary. Do not make this mistake! While a prospect may certainly join your company to buy product, as a favor to a friend, or even to retail a very small amount of product to others, he or she will definitely *not* build a business until faith in the industry has been established.

Contents: To convey the power of network marketing, include information that supports the industry, such as statistics from the Direct Selling Association or articles from mainstream news discussing the viability of network marketing. Other compelling information includes studies and case histories that demonstrate a trend toward self-employment, working at home, and the instability of a once-stable workforce.

You can also include testimonials from successful distributors attesting to the viability of their business: what they gained, both personally and materially, as a result of their business.

Once your prospects have agreed that the industry is a viable option for them, their minds are now open to exploring your company through a great presentation. (If their minds are not open yet, they need more information about the industry of network marketing, but they are not yet a candidate to hear about your Opportunity. You may choose at this time, if they are not open to the possibilities of network marketing, to present product instead.)

Step Two: Presentation Tools

Purpose: To communicate the information you would want to know if you were contemplating making the considerable investment (of time, if nothing else) in starting a business associated with your company. Whereas a product consumer may only be interested in the quality of a product and perhaps the product guarantee, someone investigating the opportunity will want to know many more details about the company.

At the end of your presentation, your prospect should be convinced that your company has all the critical components for a successful business, and he or she should complete a distributor agreement with you.

Contents: The presentation is really the heart of sponsoring, and the most personal part of the prospecting cycle. Through literature and training, distributors should be taught the critical components of a powerful presentation: one that is best presented personally, with their story, and that is supported in the corporate presentation literature.

A powerful presentation should include:

o   Network marketing: Provide a reaffirmation of the industry.

o   Company: Discuss the history, location, facilities, and top management.

- Products: Discuss the product industry, the different product lines, the technologies used to create them, the research that supports their use, and testimonials of use.

- Compensation plan: Provide an overview of the compensation plan based on both retail sales and business building.

- Support: Identify what meetings and training sessions are available, and some of the corporate tools available for business building, such as brochures, kits, and samples.

- Testimonials: Share your success, or if you are new, share your sponsor's success, and the success of others.

- Call to action: Challenge the prospect to make a decision about his or her future in the industry.

At the beginning of this article, I discussed the ultimate paradox of a duplicatable system: "systematized, yet personal." How do you accomplish that? The presentation is the one portion of a duplicatable sales system where a distributor's personal story is critically important.

It is duplicatable, because the content outlined above is the same from presentation to presentation. But it is also personal, because it reflects each distributor's experience and stories.

Consider advocating the use of presentation books. First discussed in John Kalench's book *Being the Best You Can Be in MLM*, presentation books are binders personally prepared by each distributor. Using the company-created brochures and materials to effectively present the company, presentation books also incorporate personal pictures, anecdotes, local news articles, and anything else that lends itself to the sponsoring distributor's experience. Binders or photo albums with blank pages to which personalized pages can be added work very well.

What is so significant about presentation books is that they are personal but also duplicatable. New distributors immediately recognize the need to develop their own "story," since that is what was presented to them in the presentation process.

What does a new distributor present? The great thing about a duplicatable sales system is that the key points of a great presentation are easily duplicated and communicated through a corporate brochure and/or corporate audio. New distributors also have the experience of their sponsors to draw from. But in each and every case, the type of information communicated is the same.

Step Three: Enrollment Tools

Purpose: The purpose of the enrollment process, including the delivery of the Starter Kit, is, contrary to many companies' belief, not to provide all the information necessary to succeed with that company! While providing basic information in the Starter Kit and in the enrollment process is beneficial, providing too much can be overwhelming and discouraging to a distributor who has little confidence or whose belief may be shaken by less-than-supportive family and friends.

The most important thing that a Starter Kit provides (especially if it is delivered days after enrollment) is the assurance that the new distributor has made a good decision. When a new distributor is confident and excited about taking the next step with your company, nothing will keep him or her from seeking all the information necessary to succeed. But if the new distributor is uncertain or unenthusiastic, too much information will merely appear daunting and will confirm the doubt he or she feels.

Content: This means the Starter Kit your company initially provides does not have to be costly or large. In fact, in many parts of the United States and in Canada, you are wise to offer a minimal Starter Kit that can be purchased for less than $50. But what your Kit must be is stunning, appealing, and simple, both in content and in look.

A Starter Kit should minimally include:

o   Some kind of "welcome piece" that clearly outlines what comes next, the new distributor's recommended "first steps," and how to take them.

o   The company's product catalog.

o   The company's compensation plan.

o   The company's policies and procedures.

o   A selection of the necessary forms and miscellaneous literature new distributors need to order product, enroll other distributors, and get necessary supplies for their business.

I also recommended that you assemble your Starter Kit in an attractive, substantial package that communicates prosperity and a commitment from the company to the distributors' success. Many companies assume that special packaging is much more costly than simple boxes, but that is not the case. While the development cost can be higher, the actual production is not; the value derived by encouraging a new distributor far surpasses the nominal design and development charges you incur. A first impression, here as everywhere in business, is critical for long-term success.

Please note that a minimal but impactful Starter Kit does not preclude offering enhanced Starter Kits at enrollment, or initial product packages that provide new distributors with an assortment of products to retail and to sample. These are simply offered as an additional optional product kit at the time of enrollment. Do not underestimate, however, the impact of the Starter Kit upon its arrival: Does your kit make your new distributors want to jump in and get started? And does it clearly provide them the information they need to get started? If it doesn't, you are losing distributors before you ever have the chance to introduce them to the benefits of building an organization in your company.

Prospect, Present, Enroll. Prospect, Present, Enroll. Prospect, Present, Enroll.

When your company effectively communicates a duplicatable sales system, and has the tools to support it, your distributors will find that they have already experienced the steps that they, in turn, will be sharing with their prospects. The strength of their sponsors, though always important, becomes less critical. Their personality and people skills, though helpful, become less critical. The circumstances surrounding their enrollment, though these always have an affect, become less critical.

What remains the most important is that new distributors can approach prospects and train new distributors with confidence, having seen the same system duplicated in company literature and materials that they experienced themselves.

STRUCTURING THE SALES ORGANIZATION

Objective

I N A L L S U C C E S S F U L network marketing companies, there is a person similar to Tom Sawyer who gets everyone to think that "painting the fence" is fun and rewarding. This person is often referred to as the *stage* or *sales personality*, or even the *rainmaker*. This chapter offers a description of that person, along with an observation of his or her importance to the field organization.

Some companies may want to align with a celebrity or create an expert panel, and the pros and cons of these options are explored.

Also included at the end of the chapter is a perspective from Al Wakefield, a partner in Wakefield Talabisco International, an executive recruiting firm that places many top-level *sales personalities* as employees with various network marketing and direct selling companies. For your benefit, he has also provided a sample job description developed for this senior-level sales position.

The Sales Personality

Before I describe the various sales organization structures that are working for MLM companies (some more successfully than others), let me share with you my view of the sales personality, or the person who becomes the rainmaker. This person is the one out in the field raising storms and bringing in the distributors. He or she is an invaluable resource in the recruiting process.

According to my observations, there are generally two types of human operating systems that direct people's actions—the brain or the heart. People whose first mode of reaction is the brain are the planners, the COOs, the CFOs, the strategic long-term thinkers—people who give structure to a business. People who operate instinctively from the heart are the fun-loving, free-wheeling souls who make good rainmakers, but who are not particularly attentive to detail. Both these types are important to an MLM organization, and they make a great combination of ingredients in the Success Formula. In order to get a quick start and build the sales force to support the business, the sales personality/rainmaker is needed to create sales momentum; the planners go ahead of and come behind to plan for, and clean up, the chaos or "flood" of business created by the sales personality.

Obviously, it's the free wheeler who operates instinctively from the heart, puts people first, spins the tale, the sales personality/rainmaker or the cheerleader and stage personality that the field sales force identifies with most. Every successful MLM company I know has a person so driven at the helm of their sales organization who is an inspiring leader. These people have wonderful personalities, a fun stage presence, a down-to-earthiness unencumbered by structure and planning, plenty of jokes, and generally a warmth and approachability that makes everyone with whom they come in contact very comfortable, and a way about them that makes you feel better about yourself just by being close to them.

This sales personality has a Tom Sawyer-like effect on an audience that makes everyone want to help paint the fence. These individuals are the best recruiters in the world and can incite the momentum needed in a company to launch and sustain the growth of a huge network marketing sales organization.

In many successful MLM companies the sales personality comes first to launch the business, or shortly thereafter to create momentum, and the back-end support systems come later. Even a mediocre product can create quite a stir if it's promoted by a super sales personality, even though, if that is the case, the company may not last in the long run. Those companies who have done all the right planning, have excellent products, and have made all decisions from the financial rather than the people aspects can be very slow to launch. Some of these companies are in business for two to three years, with all the back-end systems in place, but they never develop the front-end sales organization to take advantage of their plans. The question of why they haven't grown comes to mind. The answer is that they don't have the magic ingredient of a great rainmaker, who is needed to build a large field sales organization and create the strong binding relationships that attract and maintain a crowd.

On the other hand, companies who jump-start and don't seem to stop have one, two, or even more rainmakers who build the sales organization regardless of the company's ability to handle the growth. They worry about the details later . . . if at all. Generally, if the relationships are truly strong, the field is very understanding of the little inconveniences of doing big business before the company is prepared. They forgive product shortages, or long waits on the phone, because the sales personality can smooth ruffled feathers and even make the field feel good about the experience and better about themselves in the process. In general, companies that combine a great rainmaker with a great product and great service are the real long-term winners.

The Field Sales Organization

Ironically, the sales personality has an entrepreneurial nature, and therefore you would think he or she should be a distributor, not an employee. In my experience, companies have been successful both ways—by having the sales personality in the field or as part of the company.

The most common situation where the recruiting superstar is part of the company is when he or she is actually part of the company's founding team. He or she may be a part owner, or the person who approached a product formulator or patent holder to start the business. That person's role is to take the product to market by recruiting distributors to sell the product, who in turn recruit others to do the same.

A second type of company employee is one who has been recruited by the owners to be part of the management team to perform the sales function. This person could be recruited from another MLM program that has gone bad, or from another company with a good track record. Often an entrepreneur who has been stung by a company that defaulted will come in as an employee to protect losses and regain financial stability. In the long run, this relationship may end because it is the nature of the sales personality to need the freedom to operate independently without the constraints of being someone else's employee.

Other structures merely rely on recruiting independent people into the sales organization early on who later become "super distributors" with front-line positions directly to the company. They virtually own much of the field sales organization because they are everyone's up-line. Consequently, the field often thinks of these individuals as the company.

Another typical arrangement is a hybrid of the two, where companies engage top distributors as quasi-employees to work on programs and do training or opportunity meetings on behalf of the company. For their role at the corporate level they can be compensated either through special bonuses in the compensation plan, a fee-for-services arrangement, or an ongoing consulting fee. These arrangements can have shortcomings for two reasons.

First, I am concerned about how the IRS would view this arrangement, because the distributor wants to claim independent status. But by virtue of the special arrangement, the independent status could come into question, especially if the distributor now has a corporate or executive title such as National Trainer or National Vice President of Field Support.

Second, it is hard to determine if the suggestions made by one individual, whose personal organization stands to benefit, could truly be objective enough to make recommendations with the best interests of other distributors and the company in mind. While that could be the case, it's hard to conceive of them as not being at least somewhat self-serving, even if it's not intentional. It could work if the individual comes from the right perspective. However, the sales personality can't always think strategically, and may be most interested in solutions that require additional funding from the company coffers, even if he or she cannot fully ensure payback.

Also, with this arrangement, if the field leader doesn't agree on direction, you risk the organization following that person elsewhere to another MLM, or creating another company. Lately, more and more distributors have begun to create their own companies, either in the wake of their former company's failure, or in the desire to make a company that's truly their own, and to control the destiny of their followers.

Many companies get needed input from the field by creating prestigious committees of distributors. The company gets the benefit of various perspectives (rather than just one top leader/employee), and distributors get payback simply by the growth or impact on their organizations when the well-conceived plans they recommend are implemented. If your company creates such a group, it is wise to have a balanced representation of both established, large distributors along with a mixture of new, high-growth businesses.

The most successful companies I have observed have a true sales personality and inspiring leader as part of the company team and, along the way, recruit other leaders to help them in their quest. This is what causes the explosive growth that other companies envy.

Another Approach

An approach generally used by more traditional direct selling companies (such as Avon) that pay commissions to the sales force as opposed to a multilevel override program, is to employ a group of sales management individuals and trainees responsible for sales growth in specific geographic areas. They may be called *district, division,* or *regional sales managers.*

A few network marketing companies have adopted this structure. Some start off with the rainmaker, who develops the field, and then later add individuals to support or replace these efforts as the company grows. Individuals are hired to fill the role of regional sales managers, and it is their responsibility to train and lead distributors in various geographic areas assigned. Eventually a national sales manager emerges or is hired to direct the efforts of the regional managers.

These individuals work in tandem with the independent distributors to generate sales growth and boost recruiting efforts. It is also their responsibility to pass on the company culture.

One potential drawback to this approach of hiring a number of people at the corporate level is the tremendous price tag it creates in terms of fixed overhead. In addition to salaries and bonuses, the potential for significant travel expenses must also be taken into account. Also, the fixed costs will remain constant even if your business has a period when it doesn't grow.

On the other hand, an advantage to this structure is it does allow for a closely monitored effort, and if your company wants to tightly control and monitor the message—what and how it is said, and by whom—it is an approach to consider. If properly directed, it certainly can help to keep things straight from a regulatory point of view, so this insurance alone may be worth the cost.

My recommendation is to hire only a very small number—perhaps only one, or maybe two, high-level people—to lead the field charge. Support them with an excellent trainer, and other sales support staff whose main job is to "listen" to the field so that distributors feel they have someone to turn to when they need help. They also serve as a listening ear on behalf of the company. As a caution, remember that this only works in combination with the sales personality and great recruiters in the distributor ranks. Absent that, you will take on lots of fixed overhead, without getting the desired results.

Using Celebrities

Celebrities come in all sizes, shapes, and colors, and they may enjoy celebrity at the local, regional, national, or international level. Your choice of one will be driven by how you hope he or she will impact your business. You need to consider the target audience and what it is that your audience needs in the way of additional enticement for your product or company that a celebrity could bring to the table. Sometimes the need is to create credibility, other times it can be to enhance the recruiting effort, or to promote a specific product, such as sports nutrition or a weight loss line. Whatever the need is, it is good to remember that paid endorsers can sometimes be seen as such, and if they are not an integral part of the company, or do not have an exclusive arrangement with you, chances are they will not be the convincing endorsement you hope for.

There are *current* celebrities and *retired* celebrities. There are *general* celebrities such as actors, actresses, authors, or musicians. There are also *specific* celebrities such as sports figures, fitness gurus, nutritionists, alternative medicine spokespeople, do-gooders for specific causes such as environmental movements, and noted authorities on certain topics. There are product formulators or inventors whom you can develop into a company celebrity. This person could be a scientist or a doctor (Ph.D. or physician) whose background and story is compelling, even though it hasn't been told to the masses. You can build on this, and thus create their celebrity.

Let's explore the pros and cons of using a celebrity to endorse your product line or help in your recruiting efforts. We all know that companies use celebrities to give credibility to a product or service in hopes of making sales grow. It is often a highly compensated testimonial, and these endorsements have been used in mainstream advertising with mixed results. In the case of Michael Jordan, the success story continues, and he tends to stay with lines that are complementary to his field of expertise. In other cases, results have varied, especially when the talent is risky, or if they are used outside the scope of what they represent to the public. Celebrities create a risk because they are in the press and the limelight. If some skeleton comes out of the closet that reflects on them unfavorably, and raises the public's suspicion about the celebrity's character, then that person becomes a liability rather than an asset. Also, in many cases, if a celebrity is overused, and it is evident that it is just a paid political announcement, those who see it will find limited value in the endorsement. In either case, it becomes a bad investment.

To avoid this, it will help to first determine if a celebrity is needed or not. If you have the right combination of product, opportunity, and a creative rainmaker, you should be able to start the business with reasonable success. However, if your product is not that unique, is not patented, or you do not have a qualified rainmaker who can jump-start your recruiting process, you may want to consider the celebrity option.

Whether or not you want or need to use a celebrity is a decision you must weigh. If you bring someone in to partner at start-up, he or she may be willing to work for part ownership in the company, or as the head spot in the compensation plan. If they are not going to be a partner, you need to weigh the cost against the incremental revenue you expect to generate to see if it is a good business decision.

Expert Panels

Other forms of celebrity endorsements manifest themselves as expert panels or athletic sponsorship arrangements. Sometimes they are funded by donations from the company to sponsor athletic events that can then be promoted in the company communication vehicles. The athletes usually give testimonials about the perceived benefits of the products on their athletic performance.

Expert panels are sometimes a group of physicians, Ph.D.s or nutritional experts who, by virtue of their association, appear to endorse a company's products. They can be paid a retainer for input, speaking engagements, writing articles, and other occasional duties, or they can be bona fide distributors who recognize the benefits of the products and personally believe in them. In this case, they may just volunteer their credentials to endorse the products. It is becoming customary to assemble this type of panel and promote it in company literature to give credibility to types of alternative medicine or wellness products.

Because the use of celebrities and athlete endorsements is becoming so commonplace, depending on your product line and available resources, creating an expert panel is worth considering. If you offer nutritional supplements, weight loss or athletic performance products, not having such a panel may put you at a competitive disadvantage.

Initial Recruiting Strategies

When you first open your doors, you need to begin by actively recruiting people to buy and sell your product. What then is the first step to spreading the word about the company, its products, and the reason that individuals should join the cause? Well, publicity and word of mouth are the name of the game. (Also see Chapter 5, "Marketing the Opportunity.") Everyone associated with your company needs to put together a contact list. You can also strategically place lead-generating ads. This process is one you must learn, then teach, and then replicate throughout the life span of the company.

You need to start by having all company members create a *warm list* that includes their friends, family, and other familiar business or social contacts. Then move to the *cool list*, or expanded circle of influence, and then to the *cold prospects*, which come from the ads that you've run. Next there's the *three-foot rule* (approach anyone who comes within three feet of an individual—or whose path they cross). Additionally, if you have targeted audiences or cities you would like to open, it may help to place ads and spread information about the Opportunity meetings you plan to have there.

As you move into this arena, you must know who your target recruit is so that you can spend your advertising dollars wisely in the right publications. Sections of a local or regional paper or another publication that your target recruits are likely to read are good choices. If you have done your research, you will know where they are most likely located so you can choose the right cities to target. Also, by knowing the key benefits your recruit is likely to respond to—such as financial freedom, flexible hours, environmentally safe products, the ability to start their own business, or the social aspects you offer—then you can formulate your pitch. Once you have gone through your initial recruiting process and established your first wave of leadership, then you can get the duplication process started. This process is merely an imitation or duplication by each of your distributors and sales leaders who repeat the process that you initially created.

The Success Formula

As highlighted herein, the importance of having a rainmaker cannot be underestimated. In order to jump-start, gain momentum, and sustain the growth of your MLM sales organization—which in turn translates to business growth—a key ingredient of the Success Formula is the sales personality/rainmaker.

Searching for the Rainmaker

To assist you in your efforts to recruit the right sales leader for your corporate staff, Al Wakefield, a partner in the firm of Wakefield Talabisco International, provides some helpful advice. The firm, which was selected for inclusion in *The Career Makers: America's Top 150 Recruiters* and *The New Career Makers*, services numerous clients in the network marketing/direct selling industry to find the right match for each company's needs and culture. Al has more than thirty years of experience, both with Fortune 500 companies and three international search firms, in the evaluation and recruitment of senior-level management. This combination gives him in-depth insight into what it takes to make a good match of candidate and company. After Al's discussion on what he tags the "unspoken spec," he also provides a sample position description for a senior-level sales personality/rainmaker.

The "Unspoken Spec"
By Al Wakefield

As executive recruiters for senior management in the direct selling industry, we hold deep and serious conversations with our client companies at the start of a search, creating and going over and over the so-called "spec." This spec is the paper, generally one to two pages long, which defines the responsibilities of the job to be done and the specific characteristics for the person to do the job.

The spec typically is divided into categories such as the purpose of the position, reporting relationships, responsibilities, the skills, education and experience required, and "other." This other category can be anything from relocation requirements, certificates required, and so on.

Each direct selling company is very different. Whether the position to be filled is called vice president of sales, vice president of field operations, vice president of network sales, director of field development—or just chief sales developer—or whether this client is a $6 billion global, well-established, blue ribbon, "been there, done that" company or a newly established, small—"What is network marketing?"—entrepreneurial company, the description of the job and the specs for the individual typically sound very much alike. Give a little bit here on the specs, shave a little bit there.

If it is a requirement that the person must come from another direct selling company, we executive recruiters go to the same well for talent over and over again. We talk to the same known sources, and network through the same organizations. As new companies are created, we source these as well.

Fortunately, each time we do, because the direct selling industry is so dynamic and changing, we always discover new talent—that one jewel who is exactly right to undertake the challenging responsibilities for our client.

So then, if one candidate who is called a vice president of sales or vice president of field development is the same as the other, what makes one individual right for one company and so wrong for another? The answer is in the "unspoken spec."

This unspoken spec is essentially why companies frequently select a third party, that is, a direct selling executive recruiting specialist, to target specific companies, source a number of organizations, network through a variety of contacts, interview relevant candidates in-depth, and bring only those two or three outstanding candidates to them.

These are typically candidates who are not necessarily looking to make a job change, but those whose uniqueness separates them from all other prospective candidates. They look, feel, and act like they are right for the client company. This unspoken spec is sometimes called "fit," and often it is related to the culture and personality of the client company.

The fit is what makes the difference. The ability of the search firm to locate and develop interested prospects encompasses such aspects as style, potential, flexibility, leadership capability, tolerance, ability to manage change, charisma, capacity to endure pain, effectiveness with men and/or women, and the ability to influence. Performing this evaluation is just one way in which the search firm really earns—and deserves—its fee.

Other attributes such as integrity, honesty, and ethnic background (targeted searches for females, Latinos, African Americans, and so on are permitted) sought by companies are important for the client company to state and the search firm to know. The ability of the search firm to effectively assess these sometimes unspoken specs is what makes for a successful search versus just another hire who will eventually fail. These are frequently the make-or-break issues over the long run.

Some issues such as sex, age, and ethnic background (yes, depending on how these are used, they can border on being illegal) are left unspoken much of the time, and these preferences are often not discussed (or discovered by the search firm) until several candidates are rejected. So, while the specs, which are crucial to the success of the search, are either ignored or intentionally left unspoken, precious time, money, and resources are expended.

The savvy recruiter takes the time and is diligent in asking the tough questions—and the smart client is careful and smart to speak the unspoken. This honest, up-front communication between the two parties will result in the client getting what it so desperately needs—the selection of the best possible candidate for the right job in the right company—and the executive recruiter really earning his fee.

Senior Level Sales Position Description– Direct Sales[*]

POSITION OBJECTIVE:
To work with management and the field to plan, design, and lead programs necessary to motivate the field organization to increase sales and continually improve profitability.

REPORTS TO: President/Chief Operating Officer

STAFF REPORTS:
Regional Sales Managers
Director of Training
Director of Motivation and Retention
Director of Customer Service

KEY RESPONSIBILITIES:

○ Work with management to plan, develop, and implement long-term sales strategies.

○ Provide sales leadership to the company field sales organization.

○ Assist in the development and implementation of recruitment, training, motivation, and retention programs.

○ Work with marketing to insure inbound/outbound flow of communication regarding products, programs, communications, etc.

○ Conduct sales training and motivational meetings.

○ Plan and manage annual budget and profit plan.

○ Counsel staff on a regular basis. Evaluate staff and conduct formal performance appraisals.

EXPERIENCE:
Required:

○ Ten to fifteen years of direct selling experience

○ Success working in the field as well as in a corporate environment

○ Responsibility for sales development through recruitment, training, and retention of field sales personnel

○ Experience in planning and development of seminars and conventions

Desired:

○ Developed programs for training field sales representatives

○ Worked in both a large established direct selling organization as well as a small more entrepreneurial one

109

○ Worked in fast-growing network marketing environment

KEY SKILLS:

○ Proven ability to recruit, train, and motivate

○ Knowledge of how to develop sales plans

○ Good at stand-up presentations

○ Ability to lead and motivate field sales people at all levels

PERSONAL CHARACTERISTICS:

○ Articulate, well spoken, an excellent presenter

○ Charismatic

○ Image of a leader

○ Honest, trustworthy

○ Credible to people at all levels

○ High integrity

○ Outgoing, easy-to-be-with style

○ Pep in the step/high energy/vitality

○ Entrepreneurial style

○ Organization- and team-minded

OTHER:

○ Bilingual English/Spanish language preferred

EDUCATION:

○ Minimum of a bachelor's degree required

○ Specialized developmental courses, seminars, etc., in leadership, organization, human resources, compensation, and sales techniques highly desired

* Provided by Al Wakefield of Wakefield Talabisco International.

FIELD SUPPORT

Objective

THIS CHAPTER PROVIDES an overview of the role of the field support department. The field support group has to be proactive and operate as a watchdog to ensure that interaction with the distributors or representatives in the field is "high touch," combined with the right mix of high-tech support.

Further, I'll recap the minimal supports needed for success in the field. Technology plays a big role in making your field salespeople feel they are with a company that is sophisticated and has their needs in mind. Because your competition will offer high-tech support, it is important that you be prepared to do the same.

Supporting Distributors in the Field

Field support has taken on an expanded meaning with the advent of technology that is complementary to the network marketing industry. When distributors want help, it is usually in the form of collateral materials and support technology to help them do their job, both in the area of product sales and recruiting. The home office must provide them with the tools and support that make their business easy to run and duplicate.

In addition, distributors need to know that a group exists in the home office who is looking out for their best interests. This home office staff group is known as the field support department. The individuals in this department have the dual role of being advocates in the home office on behalf of the field and being vigilant and knowledgeable on new and creative ways to provide high-tech solutions to support the distributors' efforts. This group extends white glove treatment to the field leaders and trainers, and, in general, offers high touch support. In contrast to distributor services staff, who react to events and problems in the field, this group is proactive in providing services that help people in the field succeed and feel good about their accomplishments.

Field Support's Role

Generally, in a network marketing company, it is one group's responsibility to provide support to the field. In addition to making sure the field has what it needs in the way of technology and proper sales aids, this group is most likely the main point of interaction between the home office and the field in a variety of situations. Often, they are responsible for administering travel schedules for corporate personnel going into the field, as well as processing field information that needs to be tracked in the home office for publications.

Such information includes the dates of meetings to be held by distributors in the field that are open to the public or that qualify for publication in the company magazine. Field support provides the information that can be put into other vehicles of communication, such as a voice-response system that provides meeting locations or other important information needed by the field.

Additionally, this group often manages the recognition program. Generally, reports are generated monthly by the compensation plan system that show promotions through the ranks of distributor levels. When this report is received, the field support group performs a number of functions. Sometimes letters of congratulations are sent out, award pins are mailed to qualifiers, and at certain levels, other forms of recognition are managed.

For instance, if your company wants to show promotion listings in its monthly publication or newsletter, this list is managed by field support personnel. If at certain levels a distributor qualifies to have his or her picture in the field publication, field support personnel request a photo (matching predetermined requirements outlined by graphics personnel) from each distributor, and they are responsible for tracking and filing upper-level distributors' photos for current and future publications.

When contests and incentives are run for the field, most likely the field support group will monitor and manage information on the qualifiers and winners. In order to keep interest in longer running programs, often the field support group will provide the publications group with monthly standings for potential winners. And when the contest is over, winners need to be notified and duly recognized at an upcoming event or through the monthly publication.

Often, there is a council of individuals made up of field leadership that provides input to the home office. Field support schedules regular meetings and collects information from the field to put together an agenda of items for top management to use as a basis for the discussions. The field support group arranges itineraries for the leadership group, schedules social activities for evenings during their stay, and even arranges to be at the airport for their arrival.

Because of their key role in communications, field support staff are highly valued by the field, and are often are available throughout meetings to handle miscellaneous duties that come up such as registration, arranging bus transportation and hosting functions, or getting merchandise from the home office for attendees. They can also arrange tours of the home office or manufacturing facilities for distributors coming to the town where the home office is located.

Individuals and management for this department need an in-depth knowledge of all areas of the business, and most importantly, they need to have great people and communications skills because of their ambassador-type role. Administrative support in this area is generally recruited from the order entry/customer service personnel within the organization.

Other Supports

Order Entry and Customer Service

At the minimum, distributors expect to have a toll-free (800 or 888) number to call to place orders and submit enrollment applications. There is also an expectation that the company will have live distributor services personnel to contact at hours convenient to distributors, regardless of the time zone in which they live. While distributors prefer toll-free customer service numbers, requiring them to call at their expense is not uncommon. Additionally, as you grow larger, and before you go to a twenty-four-hour-a-day operation, you may want to consider a voice-response, automated-order option that will allow you to offer expanded service without additional human resources.

Communications and Publications

Other supports your distributors will expect are a monthly newsletter or magazine and other ongoing pieces from the home office that inform and motivate them about their products and business. Remember, communication is not a one-time event, so plan to keep the field informed on a regular basis.

It is also wise to seek the free publicity available through public relations efforts. Stay vigilant for opportunities to provide "filler" for television or radio talk shows and news magazines. It is best to research local markets where your company is headquartered or where distributors live. Distributor and product stories could provide valuable material for local newspaper coverage, too. Magazines related to network marketing are sometimes looking for interesting distributor stories. Examples of some that could be interested in your story are *Working at Home*, *Upline*, and even *Success* magazine. All of these publications feature articles from the industry.

Other Supports

Order entry, customer service, and communications pieces are only the very minimum supports that are required. Above this minimum service expectation, your distributors can measure the true support and value a company places on them by reviewing the following sections.

Voice Mail Voice mail, if designed properly, can be an efficient tool used by the corporate office through its broadcast message function. It can be used to keep the field updated, recognize accomplishments by field performers, promote product information, and to publicize meeting locations, dates, and times. Services can be offered to distributors (for a fee) to participate and utilize it as a business tool to communicate with the company, their down-line, and each other. It works best when the company finds a vendor that can interface organizational information with the voice mail system. Then, because it interfaces with a distributor's down-line organization and the company, users can stay informed on corporate information and can easily communicate with their field sales organization. Distributors can also utilize the system's broadcast capabilities to interact with their entire down-line organization at once.

Organizational Information Electronic assistance is an interactive automated system that allows distributors to get volume and other important genealogy information about their organizations, either by phone or computer, directly from information established in a database. The information would not come directly from your mainframe, however, because you would not want to risk someone breaking into that, but rather from a file that is downloaded for access.

At start-up, this information is often provided through distributor services via a phone call from distributors in the field. As you grow, remember that this can be an overwhelming task for distributor services because these calls generally come at month's end or near your qualification cutoff date. This is already a very busy time because everyone is getting in last-minute orders or resolving other issues to ensure that their checks are correct. As you search for the data processing system provider for your business, you should check to see if an automated phone- or dial-in option or interface with a VRU is available. If it is, and if you can afford it, buy it. It will pay off in the long run.

One word of caution: Be sure you only include information in the down-line report available in hard copy or on disk that you feel comfortable releasing. Don't forget that this is your customer list, the most valuable asset you have. If you allow access to it, and someone at the top of the organization can get a complete report with all names, addresses, and phone numbers, they have captured your most valuable property. If for some reason they become disenchanted with you later, it can make a great recruiting list for them to take elsewhere. While it is good to give distributors as much information as they need to effectively manage their businesses, do so without risking your most valuable business asset. It is wise to include a phrase such as "Confidential Information" on any list sent out, and state as part of your Policies and Procedures that this list is only for use in conjunction with your business.

Fax The fax machine can be used to provide various supports to your field organization. It can be used as an alternative vehicle for the field to submit orders, enrollment applications, or contracts, or to otherwise communicate with the home office at a convenient time. The fax machine is accessible twenty-four hours at day, which makes it attractive. It is important to establish rules for receipt of faxes, especially at month's end, because timely receipt and processing of documents can play a role in compensation and distributor status.

Another way the fax machine can be used is to offer a fax-on-demand feature. This allows your field sales organization to access information via fax. Set up specific documents you want in your "library"—anything from product or company information to third-party literature, or other pertinent documents. The documents can then be disseminated both to current distributors and prospective customers or distributors via fax-on-demand. A phone number is given to the field to access the service, along with a code number for each available document that they might want to order. A great advantage to the company is that legitimate product information can be controlled, and important articles can be distributed easily. You need to assign someone to select which literature to include and maintain the library of articles with appropriate updates and document numbers.

Conference Calls A conference call can tie the field together. It can occur weekly, monthly, or at any given interval to provide a presentation by a noted distributor or product authority to all conference call listeners. You can also provide for question-and-answer time, if it is a two-way setup. Otherwise, if it is listen only, information can only be shared one way, outbound from the broadcast point. This media is also used to connect to leadership councils or other input groups when in-person meetings are not feasible.

Recruiting/Opportunity Calls Often, a home office executive will conduct a recruiting call or provide a prerecorded call for individuals in the field to tap into. The live or recorded call should include sections on the company, its products, its earning opportunity, and it should showcase leaders. This can be a great starting place for a new distributor to direct their prospects to get firsthand information on the company. The listener gets a feel for the top-level people while observing a duplicatable process with which they can introduce their new prospects to the company.

It is a nonthreatening way to make a top-notch Opportunity presentation available to the field. You can control your message, ensure that it is completely legal, and still get across the enthusiasm and confidence that established distributors can bring to the party. With prerecording, the message can be made available to individuals across the country at a time convenient for them. If you are doing it live with a listen-only feature available to call-ins, it is necessary to repeat the message at different times of day (preferably evenings), to accommodate the various time zones. The message can be made available via a toll-free or toll call, whichever you can afford.

Training and Meetings Information on all corporate-sponsored meetings or meetings attended by corporate personnel should be widely publicized. This information can be disbursed via any publication that goes into the field. Or, it can be inserted with checks when they are mailed, or dropped into orders when they are shipped. Another option is to set up an interactive voice-response system that all distributors can access. They can use their city, Zip code, or area code to access information about meetings near them or their down-line.

While the corporate office cannot personally run or sponsor all training sessions in the field, it is in everyone's best interest to disseminate information about distributor-sponsored meetings so individuals can attend one led by leaders in a location near them. You must establish a process to collect and broadcast information about these functions—your distributors will expect nothing less. You can set up the rules by which meetings are published when you grow larger, but at start-up it will be helpful to publish information about as many as possible, to build the momentum. These gatherings can be opportunity meetings or other forums sponsored by distributors for the purpose of teaching more about your company's products, the Opportunity, or how to recruit.

The Internet It's a good idea to provide a Web site that distributors or prospects can visit to learn more about your company, your products, your compensation plan, and your mission. An interactive technology, the Internet can be used for presentations, offer the capability of "what if?" interaction, and include chat rooms that will allow interchange among distributors about specific topics. Be creative! You could even have company VIPs host chat rooms at preplanned, publicized times.

Be sure to establish rules for distributors' Web sites in order to protect yourself from misrepresentation by them. It is difficult to contain distributors when it comes to product and opportunity claims, or the use of your name, so it is important that your advertising policies and procedures cover the Internet. It comes under the same section where you restrict printed pieces created by anyone other than those authorized by the home office.

A safe way to allow your distributors to create sites is to support the process. You can sell a service and develop a template outlining information they can include, and have them submit the completed form to you or your site vendor to post online. Then you can orchestrate a way for their individual site to link to your home page, where you can control product and opportunity information, not to mention the image you want associated with your company. Since attorneys general have indicated that they surf the Net looking for offenders, it is wise to get this process under your control right from the get-go.

Another way the Internet can service your distributors is through the ordering and enrollment processes. Programs can be developed to facilitate the ordering process over the Internet with the use of credit cards, or by having a preauthorized credit or debit card or authorization for a fund transfer from a checking account on file. In addition to being a support for the field, such a service could have a cost-savings benefit to the company because it eliminates both the toll charge and wages for order processing personnel. It also facilitates the ability to offer "24 × 7" (twenty-four hours a day, seven days a week) accessibility.

Enrollments can be facilitated on the Internet, too. Sponsors can fill out applications on the Net to speed up first-time order processing. However, in order to pay commissions, it is best to be sure you have an original signed contract on file indicating agreement to adhere to your policies, and authorizing credit card or checking account use.

Audio/Video/CD-ROM Support Audio, video, and CD-ROM materials are created by the home office to present various aspects of the business such as the product line, company information, the business presentation, or an explanation of the compensation plan. These materials should be provided at a nominal charge for use by distributors to support recruiting efforts, and to disseminate product and motivational information. Many include the stories of others who have had great product results or financial success.

Choose the best vehicle for your company based on what equipment your audience has and uses. You can be reasonably sure that most people have audio cassette players in their cars. This is a great place to listen to a teaser or a motivational/educational tape because people generally are alone while driving and the tape fills up otherwise void space. Companies often have their top distributors tape their stories of success. These are great motivators for new distributors already in your organization, or they can be used to pitch the Opportunity to someone who starts from a similar place.

While videos are widely utilized in this industry, and virtually everyone has access to a VCR, I am not sure how many people take the time to watch those provided by many network marketing companies. If a video is really well-done and concise it can be a great way to present a new concept to a large audience, or even an entertaining way to teach concepts in a small or large group meeting. Particularly intriguing business information videos can support long-distance recruiting efforts because they are easily mailed to a contact to introduce the company in your absence. However, my advice is to keep the length under eight minutes and the information succinct enough to be interesting. Follow this advice and a lot more people will watch your video.

Because videos are so expensive to produce—especially truly creative ones that capture the appropriate message, excitement, and image—use caution as you consider this idea. Be sure you select the most important things to communicate this way, and ask yourself, "Will my distributors really find this the best way to support what my company is trying to communicate?"

CD-ROM is a relatively new medium for recruiting presentations and training of new distributors. Because it is so new, it is wise to determine how many individuals have equipment at their disposal to truly make this a venture with adequate payback.

TV Broadcasts Several MLM companies produce TV shows and training elements to broadcast over satellite TV to their audience. Others use satellite up- and down-links to broadcast large meetings or training sessions to be viewed by individuals in remote cities. Since this is something to consider only when you have a large enough viewing audience to benefit from it, I do not recommend it for start-up.

The Success Formula

While basic field support, such as toll-free ordering and company publications, is essential, companies that take advantage of the plethora of other high-tech and high touch vehicles to support their field definitely have an edge. Advanced supports that effectively and positively impact recruiting efforts are the ones that are most important to the Success Formula.

RECOGNITION AND INCENTIVES

Objective

THIS CHAPTER HIGHLIGHTS the importance that recognition and incentives play in a network marketing company. Acknowledgment and rewards for achievement are cornerstones of human emotional satisfaction. Recognition can be the factor that cements distributors to a company. This universal principle is widely practiced in network marketing, but it is a useful concept to put in place regardless of the company's structure. You will find in this chapter one very distinct advantage of network marketing's appeal: Everyone has the opportunity to get promoted without threat to up-lines, down-lines, and peers, and there truly is a feeling here that everyone can join hands and cross the finish line in victory together!

Our Need for Recognition

I once read that all human beings long for only one thing: acknowledgment of their existence. Never has this been more understood than through public reaction to two recent highly publicized events: the deaths of Princess Diana of Wales and Mother Teresa of Calcutta. Both were very different in stature, dress, and in their roles in life, but each had a wonderful mission and relationship to other human beings. Over and over, the message resounded that both of these enormously popular and giving individuals bestowed a sense of self-worth and dignity to those they touched. They seemed to recognize and acknowledge the commonality of human existence through a spirituality that affirmed the internal oneness of being. They showed us that feelings and compassion supersede material status among people of all ages, races, economic levels, and illnesses.

People felt uplifted from whatever they were suffering with a mere glance or touch from these women. Even individuals who did not come in personal contact with them considered them friends or heroes. People seemed to sense that by meeting either Diana or Mother Theresa their human existence would be acknowledged as meaningful. What a powerful message to witness.

This is such a simple key to unlocking many of the mysteries of life. It's also the key to helping us understand one very crucial ingredient in the Success Formula. It explains the attraction of people to network marketing; and it's a key component of the success of network marketing companies. That key is *recognition*. If you think about it, recognition can be used interchangeably with *acknowledgment*. For instance, if you recognize someone, you can use his or her name, and thereby acknowledge to that person that you know who he or she is and likewise acknowledge her or his existence. Perhaps this is why we all like to hear our names, because it acknowledges that we exist as separate individuals from all others. This reinforces in us that we have meaning to others. It is basic, but extremely important. As we discuss recognition programs, keep in mind that they are just enhanced forms of the human courtesy of acknowledging the self-worth of individuals.

Universal Application of Recognition

In my opinion, recognition can be more universally applied to achieve success even outside network marketing. If Corporate America embraced the concepts contained in this chapter it would enhance the attractiveness of that career option. Instead, because such a lack of acknowledgment of human existence, effort, and appreciation exists, many corporate evacuees turn to network marketing to fill the void.

As a matter of fact, at their corporate offices, some network marketing companies don't even have a good recognition program. The principles that draw people to the status of independent distributor are often overlooked right in those companies' own backyards. In my experience, the people at the home office who service the field are very loyal and dedicated individuals. This includes behind-the-scene staff as well as the customer service people who have numerous contacts with the sales force. They too are drawn to the principles of financial freedom, setting your own hours, and being treated with respect. However, they are sometimes overlooked in the scheme of recognition programs. That's why some of them are lured away and recruited by great field people who treat them well and acknowledge their existence and importance.

So let's just say here that everyone who is employed or self-employed, and even those who are independently wealthy, needs recognition. The concepts discussed in this chapter can be universally applied. Companies that have top distributors know that even with all their financial success, the input, status, and existence of those top people must be continually acknowledged and recognized, or trouble will appear on the horizon. Regardless of who the person is, the basic need for acknowledgment exists.

The Missing Link

I have always felt in some ways that it is sad to need recognition from your network marketing company because it reflects how little people feel acknowledged in other areas of their lives. They often do not feel appreciated for their contributions on their "regular" job. Often they are not even acknowledged or sufficiently appreciated by their own family or spouse. People take loved ones and employees for granted or get so wrapped up in their own needs and agendas that they forget this basic need for respect as an individual, which we call acknowledgment.

On the other hand, I feel elated to be part of an industry that so aptly fills this wide, wide gap. The nice part of network marketing as opposed to regular corporations and jobs is that it is very much a you-do, you-get environment. What I mean by this is that the rules for success as they relate to levels, promotions, status pins, and contests are all spelled out; and when you accomplish what is laid out, you are rewarded.

Rules of the Game

As we all know, it is often difficult to determine what the rules of Corporate America are; and when you go by what you think they are, rewards are often elusive. How can anyone win when this is the case? Even when you have a set of objectives to reach, when you "deliver," are you always guaranteed that you will get the percentage raise you deserve? Or, will you hear that raises have been capped by a corporate salary survey, or that management dictates a maximum of 5 percent, when you deserve 10 percent or more? Bonus plans may sound good initially, but over time have you seen them decline in amount, or has the bar been raised so high to achieve them that you don't even attempt to jump?

Have you ever been overlooked for a promotion and didn't even know why? Have you seen people you thought undeserving get promoted even though they made no apparent contribution? Because of this, you are left to wonder, was it political; did the boss have a personal favorite unrelated to ability; if you are a woman, was it above the glass ceiling? All these reasons make people feel that they are not acknowledged, which creates a feeling of helplessness and lack of control. Often these situations create feelings of self-doubt and lowered self-esteem. How sad, especially when we all need positive feedback. It just shows that corporations, much like some families, can be very dysfunctional.

Luckily, you can make your network marketing company a place people can turn where their individual efforts can be both acknowledged and rewarded, regardless of who does or does not like them. Network marketing is the greatest leveler of people there is. Your background, sex, ethnicity, age, education level, or personality doesn't matter: The rules for promotion, pay scale, raises, and recognition status level are the same. And regardless of who you are, once you achieve them, you get the rewards. Sometimes it is the quiet reward of an increase in your paycheck because you have two more customers consuming the product. Other times it can be very public recognition when you walk onstage in front of five thousand people at an event to receive your pin or ring for achieving a designated level. What sweet revenge to be at a higher level in your network marketing company and earning more money than your nonproducing boss who was holding you back at your previous corporate job.

Room for Everyone

The beauty of success in network marketing is that there is room for everyone to achieve higher status, and it is not at the expense of someone else. In the corporate world, there is generally a predefined number of slots at the manager, director, and vice president levels. It's called the organization chart. If one slot comes open, everyone below that level has to fight each other to get it, and only one person "wins" while all the others "lose." What a demoralizing concept.

On the other hand, in network marketing, the higher-level positions are unlimited. Your organization chart is often called your *genealogy*, *down-line*, or simply your *organization*. Everyone at the same level can be promoted at the same time and no one is left out. Instead of threatening your peers to go for one open position, everyone can get a raise (the percentage is predefined) and be promoted together. Individuals know that if they perform the required work, they control their own destiny and promote themselves to the next higher position.

As a matter of fact, instead of feeling threatened by you, it is in the best interest of people who are your superiors to get you promoted. Your promotion can mean they get promoted too, or at the very least, it often has a positive impact on their bonus check. What a different environment this creates when everyone is motivated to help everyone else succeed. Now this is a great program!

Good Recognition Programs

Given all this background, let's explore how you can develop a good recognition program. Here we will be covering what the company should offer. It is helpful to remember that recognition programs create distributor loyalty, and as such are an important part of your investment dollar. In addition to the home office–sponsored recognition programs, you should expect and endorse the efforts of independent distributors to create their own special way of recognizing their organization at local meetings. Often, they will even create their own incentives to motivate and acknowledge individuals in their group. Encourage it, as this too creates a loyalty connection to your Opportunity.

My friend Char Knox, a very successful corporate sales executive, told me that one of her mentors gave her this advice, "Never pass up an opportunity to recognize someone." This was and still is great advice. As I review the various types of programs, please remember that recognition is not just a program, but an ongoing process. It should have a prominent place in every meeting and gathering in the field, in your communication pieces, and whenever the opportunity presents itself. It should always be done tastefully and in a dignified manner.

At large field events, the act of just standing up or walking across the stage can be as important as the award that is given. Not often do ordinary people get to take a bow in front of five to ten thousand of their peers. When selecting recognition pins, plaques, and certificates, be sure that they are tasteful and that they project the classy image you want for your company. It is better to give tons of praise and a handshake and forgo giving anything tangible if you can only afford something junky. Instead recognize people by public acknowledgment and publications until you can afford something nice. There are many sources for inexpensive but tasteful pins and rewards; just be sure you deal with a reputable company so that they not only look good but also wear well over time. Remember, recognition programs are desirable because they acknowledge individuals; if they achieve that they will be motivational, regardless of what you spend. Banks learned this by handing out titles rather than large salaries to employees.

There are a number of ways to implement recognition programs. They include: position promotions and stair-step advancement levels in the compensation plan; achievement of various pay-related bonuses and earning lapel pins for specific performances; certificates for completing training programs; or other tangible pieces that acknowledge outwardly to others the accomplishments that have been achieved. Other short-term programs can be used to move key indicators, such as recruiting goals or sales of a specific new product. Some easy ways to create status for distributors are to develop field councils for corporate input, assign area leadership designations, create training positions, and assign titles for various levels of achievement.

A key question to ask yourself when designing a program is, "What behavior am I trying to influence?" As in your compensation plan, you need to be sure that you push the right buttons to deliver the outcome you want. Just like your compensation plan, to get the best payback on your investment develop a program that helps you achieve your overall corporate goals.

As a matter of clarification, let me briefly explain the subtle difference between incentive and recognition programs. Incentive programs are pull programs to motivate your sales organization to move sales or recruiting at an accelerated level for a specific period of time. They are generally announced, then implemented, then have an ending date at which time winners are announced and the reward is granted. Incentive rewards can include trips, prizes, special seating or event privileges, and more.

Recognition programs are generally well-promoted, ongoing programs and processes that anyone entering your organization can strive for and achieve. Once certain criteria are met, the recognition is bestowed.

When putting together your initial and annual budget and business plan, be sure to allow dollars to cover these important programs. In actuality, incentive programs should be funded out of the incremental impact they have on sales, but you still need to show an expense line in your budget to cover the up-front costs. As I mentioned in Chapter 4 on compensation plans, be sure to build into your plan a series of levels that serve as platforms for recognition and rewards. But hold back enough money from the pay-out to support specific and necessary short-term incentive programs to positively impact growth.

The Success Formula

Recognition is a vital ingredient in the Success Formula. The more sophisticated and efficient you can be in executing your recognition programs, the more powerful this factor will be in your success. Everyone loves to be recognized, and the effort expended and resources you allocate to allow people to participate will pay off with huge rewards. Recognition and incentive trips cement relationships with your company. Effective recognition is what gives network marketing companies a competitive advantage in drawing people in from the corporate world and from lives that often lack appreciation.

SPECIAL EVENTS

Objective

UNTIL YOU ACTUALLY attend a well-orchestrated event sponsored by a network marketing company, you cannot have a perspective on the magic. These events are where the field sales force and home office connect in a special way and each recognizes in awe the role of the other. In this chapter, you will get a sense of what types of events are held in the industry, the purpose of each, and what it takes to make them special. To be truly successful each event requires a "show business" feeling.

Events vs. Meetings

Corporate-sponsored special events need to be special in every sense of the word. These events should capture the essence or soul of the MLM company sponsoring them. This forum gives the distributors and their prospects a showcase to introduce others, and to reinforce in themselves, the mission and culture of their supplier company. These events expose the larger-than-life aspects of this touchy-feely industry.

When a company sponsors a special field event, the purpose should be to link together their chain of many independent distributors—some of whom are geographically isolated and don't often get a picture of how large the company is. The objective is to make everyone feel part of something bigger than his own down- and up-line. When special events aren't taken seriously, or not enough time and energy are devoted to the big picture, such as the purpose and desired outcome, then they end up just being meetings. And, I might add, meetings just as boring as mandated meetings in a corporate environment.

The reason many people join MLMs is to experience something different. When a special event sponsored by the home office of a network marketing company is well planned and executed, *magic* happens. It's this magic that keeps distributors motivated and sends them home to recruit, recruit, and recruit some more. This is a good thing; it is the lifeblood of your company's growth.

The Agenda

First, let me cover some of the generic processes, or agenda items that are always part of good special events (notice I don't say meetings, because meetings are easy to put on and bore people with). Later, I will recap some of the reasons companies should have special events, and when they are the most effective.

The components of good special events are as follows:

o   Recognition: Always use these group forums to recognize success.

o   Motivation: Have someone inspire the troops.

o   Education: Give distributors at least one or two simple things that they can take away and put into practice to move their businesses ahead.

o   Announcements: This is the perfect place to introduce new products, services, and/or personnel that impact the field.

o   Focus a spotlight on your two offerings: product and Opportunity. Always highlight recruiting tips and urgency.

o   Storytelling: Have successful distributors share how the income opportunity has changed their lives—always spoken from the heart.

o   Testimonials: Have individuals share how the products have worked to improve their lifestyle.

o   Call to action: Ask for the order. Tell them what you want them to do and when you want it to be done.

That's what you need to cover at your events. Another important element is how you produce your message.

The Production

In this world of instant gratification via TV, videotapes, the Internet, and interactive multimedia, plain old "talking heads" just won't cut it. To keep meetings interesting, a multimedia combination of live, videotaped, musical, and slide presentations keep things rolling. Everything from the selection of music to be played at the walk-in and walk-out periods, to the projection of the speakers so that people in the back feel included, to the decoration of the room and the staging—it is all important to the creation of a mood.

A whole book could be written just about the elements that need to come together to take a meeting into the special events category; but, suffice it to say, this is a whole area of expertise. It's well worth having someone experienced to consult with to make yours a success. I have created events for as small as thirty couples to more than six thousand convention attendees, and each event is similar to producing a live Broadway show. The staging, music, and the little touches, whether they be a room gift or reserved seating for the most successful distributors, are long remembered after the words have disappeared.

In my experience, companies that approach corporate-sponsored events in terms of pushing out information—as opposed to creating an emotional production—fall short of getting the best return for their buck. The small incremental amount you spend to make your meeting an "event" will have huge payback in solidifying your field sales force to you with an emotional bond. The credibility of the company is at stake, and it is vitally important to combine substance with the warmth to complete the process.

Event Planning

There seem to be several logical events in the course of a company's development. Obviously, events will start out with small attendance and as the company grows—and depending on the perception of how much value is received at company events—your audience will expand. First, let's cover what you should do to prepare for an event. I'll follow with when these events generally happen.

Preparation and considerations prior to announcing an event:

- ○ What is the purpose of the meeting?

- ○ Who is the audience? Prospects, distributors, customers, or sales leadership?

- ○ Where will you have the event? Geography of intended audience is important to site selection. Remember, your image will be inferred from where your meeting is held.

- ○ Who are the speakers? Identify a combination of both corporate and field people, and don't forget an emcee. After all, someone has to say, ". . . and here's Johnny!"

- ○ When will each person speak? An agenda is a must!

- ○ What types of media will you use? Video will need to be preproduced. Is satellite broadcast a consideration to expand your reach? The answer to this question will also help you plan your onsite audio-visual needs.

- ○ Who will pay (the company or attendee), and how much will you charge attendees, or how much of the event will your company subsidize?

- ○ What handouts will be given? A manual or new product information flier, or a program, for instance. All of these require advance preparation and a plan for distribution during the function.

- ○ Will product be sold onsite? This can be your worst nightmare or a dream-come-true, depending on the planning process. (Don't forget sales tax collection and nexus considerations.)

- ○ How will you promote the event? Will advance reservations be taken, or will you accept onsite walk-ins?

- ○ Can you utilize local distributors as "greeters" or hosts to help decorate, do sign-in duties, handle sales or registration?

- ○ What type of atmosphere do you want to create? This will dictate the decorations, staging, and music.

- ○ How will you memorialize the event? Will you take photos to share with nonattendees via your company newsletter? Will you record part or all of the event to sell in the form of video- or audiotapes later? What about a candids video or slide show to close the event? Can a photographer be available to take official pictures of distributors with the president or other VIPs?

When to Host Events

Another issue you face is when to stage an event. Following is an overview of events companies have effectively used to propel their business growth. I also include a brief explanation of each. Some more expensive events, such as a national convention, are best held after you have achieved a critical mass; others are needed earlier so that you can create a widespread population of distributors.

Types of Events

Initial Launch Once you have decided to start your company and all the plans are in place for product, mission, key personnel, operational systems, and so on, it's time to let the world know that you exist. It's now time to share information about your mission, vision, products, and compensation plan with potential distributors. Your initial launch can be localized in a small geographic area, or it can be a road show to cover several geographically desirable areas. Prepromotion through word of mouth, advertising, and mailings are necessary to get people there.

Regional Events Regional events cover various regions of the country where your population centers are concentrated. They can be used for training, promotions, or recruiting. They can be a combined effort on the part of local leadership and VIPs from the home office.

Opportunity Meetings Generally these meetings are held by distributors in the field to recruit new prospects. They can be hosted by one person or by a group of individuals who present various parts of the agenda. These are often referred to as business presentations because they expose people to the business opportunity. I have seen the home office support these meetings in various ways. Home office sponsorship of these meetings at start-up is essential because field leadership does not exist to support this function. Some companies supply an outline or script for these meetings, as well as appropriate audio-visual supports for the presentation. Room setup diagrams should be provided to help guide the moderator with some suggestions for a good meeting.

A typical opportunity meeting includes presentations on the following:

o   The company: its history and ownership.

o   The products: what makes them unique, the demand for this type of product, the size of the market for the products, and testimonials to their effectiveness.

o   The compensation plan: an overview of how money is paid to distributors for their role in selling, training, and recruiting.

o   The people: distributors who tell their stories of successes they've achieved and how their lives have changed.

○ Motivation and call to action: a section where someone highlights the benefits of signing up and explains
how to become part of the action.

Leadership Training Once your distributors start being
promoted into leadership positions, it is in the best interest
of the company to offer training for these leaders directly
from the home office. Its purpose is to educate them on their
position as role models and to ensure that they fully understand and are solidly behind the corporate ideals and management. Training can be offered as a benefit at a certain level
where it is earned and paid for by the company, it can be training that is paid for solely by each attendee, or some combination of the two. The purpose of these leadership gatherings is
to pass along the culture and to teach leaders to duplicate the
home office message.

Seasonal Product or Motivational Launches Many
companies have field meetings twice a year to kick-start or
reenergize the business after a lagging period. The month of
December is often slow due to family events, and January
launches are used to kick-start each new year. Again in the late
spring, launches are held to reenergize the business before the
slower summer season. A team from the home office supported by local leadership hits the road to stage rallies or product launches in various locations to accomplish this objective.
Sometimes incentive contests are announced or special provisions are temporarily enriched in the compensation plan to activate a push on a necessary business indicator.

As your business grows larger, you may want to consider
satellite broadcasting to reach larger audiences without the toll
of travel to numerous cities. In my opinion, there is no substitute
for live performances, but sometimes practicality has to enter the
equation. Even with the broadcast option, it is good to have
someone from the home office or local leadership onsite to host it.

Annual Convention This is the biggest production the home office sponsors each year. It is held at one location and everyone from throughout the country convenes at the selected site for a few days. It should be a positively electric event that sends your distributors out on a cloud. The production and message should be of such a scale that many of the other meetings pale in comparison to this event. An awards night similar to an academy awards event is a standard element.

The national—or international as the case may be—convention is usually undertaken once you can attract at least one thousand or more paid attendees. Up until that time, launch or rally meetings are more appropriate. But to pay for the production required, a crowd of one thousand is the minimum. Usually you need to hire a production company to help with the staging and creative parts of the event and an audio-visual group to handle onsite production. You need to create multimedia presentations to elevate the meeting to status of special event/convention.

At this event, much of the experience goes on outside of the meeting room. Distributors are exposed to other distributors from all over the country, and they can interface with each other to get ideas and help on how to run their businesses. This happens informally during free time and is also orchestrated by incorporating distributors as speakers and presenters from the stage.

While the agenda includes the components outlined earlier, they are presented here on a much grander scale. Include yearly recognition of your highest performers in select categories. They can be called onstage and presented with special trophies or awards. New products can be launched with a great deal of conviction, and you can allow distributors to buy them onsite right after they are announced. It can almost be like a feeding frenzy if you properly introduce your product.

Companies have different names for this event. While most simply call it the National (or International) Convention, others use more creative names. For example, Excel calls its annual convention Excelebration, while Mary Kay, Inc., refers to its annual event as Seminar. You can name yours creatively to communicate the desired effect.

Excel hosts more than ten thousand attendees, and Mary Kay, Inc., has five consecutive back-to-back Seminars hosting close to fifty thousand attendees over a two-week period. The production is so large that Mary Kay, Inc., keeps Reunion Arena in Dallas set up for production for weeks to accommodate its needs.

While you won't start this big, it is important to recognize that at some point you will be ready to host your first national event. Look forward to it, and learn from your smaller meetings what works well for your audience. Be sure to incorporate all those special touches, looks, and processes that best fill the bill for your distributor base.

Convention Follow-up Events Because the national event cannot be attended by everyone, but you want the message to get out to your entire sales force, it is wise to schedule follow-up meetings in the field. These can be hosted by local distributors who set up and fund the meetings, but who are supplied with information from you at the home office. This way, the message continues to flow to the masses, and the roll-out will have impact for weeks to follow. You can utilize the theme, agenda, scripts, and videos made for the central meeting to do your own road show or you can share this information with your field leaders to carry it forward. Your money is best spent when you can get the message out to the masses. And don't forget, communication is not a one-time event. The more you reinforce it, the better off you will be.

Executive Leadership Events Meeting with your top producers—especially the advisory board and executive leadership council—provides a great forum to discuss upcoming plans and to get feedback from the field on what is and is not working. Because these meetings generally involve field VIPs, it is important to make them feel special for attending. So often the leading distributors give of themselves to make others in their down-line feel special, and these leaders are forgotten. The home office mistakenly thinks the big check is all the leadership needs, but in fact they need their giving cup refilled, too. Take advantage of this meeting experience to reinforce how important the leadership is to the company.

Most companies pick up travel and accommodations expenses for this small elite group, and add an element of fun by incorporating an exciting evening at a local attraction. No payment is made to the members of the council for their time, but their ability to speak and participate is usually enough satisfaction for them.

Other Events and Meetings There are a myriad of other times and reasons for the home office to have meetings or events for the field. They are so varied that it would be futile to try to cover them all here. The main thing to remember is that each time a group meets in your name, the event should reflect the image and culture of the company, and attendees should go away feeling better for having attended. The spark they take away with them fuels the flames of their businesses and in turn keeps your business growing and exploding into a huge success!

The Success Formula

As you can see, events play a big part in the Success Formula. If they're done well, they give a company instant credibility and they help distributors get the big picture and vision of greatness. Events also serve as a bonding experience that will pay back big dividends in the area of distributor retention. Once you get a distributor to attend a well-orchestrated major company event, he or she will generally stay with you for years to come.

CUSTOMER SERVICE: DELIVERING ON THE PROMISE

Objective

IN THIS CHAPTER, you will learn about the importance of delivering on the promise of customer service in the network marketing industry. Distributors have high expectations of the home office in the area of customer service because their reputations with their customers are on the line. Also, if orders are not properly filled and shipped, serious consequences can reverberate through the compensation plan, since qualifications for commissions and bonuses are contingent upon the movement of product and the activity of customers.

I will also provide many useful examples of how to get a read on the service of all operational areas at any given time. I will outline tips for planning and resource allocation to ensure that you will be able to successfully follow a fast growth curve, or deal with peaks and valleys in the workflow.

A Philosophy—Not a Department

We have all heard the saying "Customer service is a philosophy, not a department." Read this at least *three* times because this chapter will be devoted to your overall service philosophy, not just the customer service department. The department only answers to your customers when initial service is lacking somewhere else in the company.

Critical areas of customer service are numerous and readily apparent to your customer. Your performance will be measured against the best, so be prepared to do it right the first time. Be sensitive to the fact that your customers and distributors have alternative places to shop. If properly managed, the dollars you spend on excellent customer service will be rewarded with the retention and loyalty of your sales force.

In this increasingly demanding society, where instant gratification, overnight delivery, and everything-on-demand are expected, customers' expectations are high. You need to deliver accordingly. Following are some of the key areas to consider when developing your standards.

Accessibility

There is a standard to strive for when planning your call center hours for order taking and customer service support. The premier companies offer 24 × 7 service (twenty-four hours a day, seven days a week) with live operators available via a toll-free number. At first, you will most likely be unable, nor would it be wise, to accommodate this. Following are some alternatives that let you "be open" longer to service your customers at a more reasonable cost.

Alternatives to 24 × 7 Service

o   Automatic, around-the-clock touch-tone ordering by phone o   Fax ordering

o   Voice mail with appropriate callback procedures

o   Internet ordering capabilities

Toll vs. Toll-Free Calling As I mentioned earlier, the best direct marketing companies offer toll-free numbers for both ordering and customer service, but at minimum you should offer toll-free calls for ordering. Hybrids and combinations of toll-free and toll service depending on a distributor's level can help offset some complaints. Offering unlimited toll-free service requires careful analysis to ensure that you do not become a lonely hearts toll-free advice line. However, if you offer excellent service on the front end, the number of customer service calls on the back end will be minimal.

Interdepartmental Communication

In my experience, the worst communication is the internal communication between field operations, marketing, shipping and maufacturing operations, and a company's customer service department. Often, the first time internal departments learn of new products and programs, product shorts, or problems in shipping is from customers over the phone. You can imagine how inconvenient this is.

Some of the best organizations I've seen have a daily update meeting at a predetermined time. Present are representatives from Operations (product availability and shipping schedules); Sales; Marketing (new programs, plans, upcoming events, and contests); and Customer Service management (feedback on issues reported by the field, wait times on the phone). They exchange information on the status of the various areas.

These daily meetings should be quick, stand-up, maximum of fifteen-minute exchanges. Their purpose is to keep each department informed and to minimize, or more preferably, ward

147

off, any problems early on. It's a surprisingly simple exercise. But because many companies do not adhere to the daily meeting, problems have escalated to the crisis level at the weekly or monthly management meeting.

If you learn nothing else from this book, this one tip will save you thousands of dollars—and you and your customers numerous headaches over the life of your business. At the end of this chapter (see Figure 10.1), you will find a form that may be of help in determining what types of information you can capture and exchange during this meeting.

Service Standards and Turnaround Times

First you need to consider the level of service or standard that you want to deliver. Then you can set up procedures and checkpoints to determine if your service levels are being attained. These standards can cover many areas in the operation, and are the key measurements of your service goals. By monitoring them, you can determine your success rate. Following are the key areas that can be reported on a daily basis.

Product Availability Your minimum standard needs to be no product shortages or back orders. It's very frustrating to a customer to place an order and receive a notice instead of the products. "Sorry, item X was unavailable; we will ship it when it comes in," is small comfort to an empty-handed consumer. Now, you may be a new company, and it can be hard to forecast accurate product sales and growth patterns. Or, you may be an established company that offers a hot new product that skyrockets beyond your wildest imagination. Both of these are tricky situations. Getting merchandise availability in the right balance is a true art, but one that has tremendous ramifications for your business. Obviously, overstocking and excess inventory can be costly, so the more skilled you are at the estimating game, the more successful your "just in time" process will work.

One industry we can all learn from is that of energy production, or the delivery of electricity. In speaking with an authority in the field, I learned that power generation is tricky because companies never really know their exact demand until their customer flips a switch. But they are ever vigilant and ready to produce to meet their customers' needs. Talk about a "just in time" philosophy. Since virtually every home is wired and anticipates regular delivery of electricity, when excess demand occurs, or a storm causes a breakdown in the system, everyone experiences a "blackout." We all notice those, and your customers will notice too when they experience a blackout—or a shortage due to product unavailability.

Response Time Every customer request that comes into your office should be handled according to a standard for turn-around time or completion. Whether it is a call, an order, a fax request, a letter requesting information, or a request to management that needs resolution, your company must establish and monitor appropriate and timely turnaround standards. I cannot tell you what your internal rules should be; but put yourself in the customer's place when determining your plan. What would you expect? Following are some thoughts to guide you, but let your customers, your service philosophy, and your competitors be the final judge.

Phone Calls Try sitting quietly for just thirty seconds, and see if it doesn't seem like an eternity. When your customers are on hold, that is what they experience. Or, even worse, they're stuck listening to a repeating tape that goes on and on trying to entertain them. Experts say that companies should target hold times of no more than fifteen to twenty seconds.

Response to Written Inquiries Out of respect to your distributors, customers, and potentials, an established reply time is appropriate. Forty-eight hours should allow you plenty of time for research and to create a response.

Order Processing and Shipping In this day of overnight everything, delivery time of more than five days is too long. Three to five days is acceptable; two to three days is a competitive advantage. The delivery speed of an order starts right in your order department. Once an order is taken and credit is verified, it should be processed and go directly from data processing to your shipping floor with shipping labels attached. It should be picked and packed that day (at least for orders taken up until 3 or 4 P.M. local time) and put onto a truck.

What happens next will determine how soon the customer gets the order. In the United States, if you are located on one coast or close to it and you develop a customer base in a remote geographic area, ground service can be very slow. But you can overcome this obstacle in one of two ways.

When the volume warrants it, you can set up an additional strategically located distribution facility so that delivery will be made by common carrier, such as UPS or the U.S. Postal Service, in two to three days. This is an expensive alternative and one that will require a critical mass to get the payback you need. Until you grow large enough, you can look at a third-party warehousing and shipping service near your remote populations to drop ship items for you.

A second alternative is to ship second-day air to the remote locations. Often, carriers will negotiate special rates for this service for large-volume customers. Economically, this may make more sense for a while. Do a cost/benefit analysis to help you determine your best approach.

One last thing to consider is the size of your products. As you expand your product line, you need to involve your shipping/distribution department. The last thing you want to do is to catch your staff off guard by introducing a large product that won't fit into existing shipping boxes. If the first time the shipping staff finds out about the size of a new product is when the oversized product arrives in the warehouse, they may not have time to order the right size boxes before you want to launch. This puts your new product launch on hold. Believe it or not, I have seen this happen!

Another reason to keep distribution involved in new product development is so that they can advise you how, as you change the product mix, your shipping and handling charges are affected. If the weight of the new mix shifts toward heavier products, you may have to consider raising shipping and handling charges. Your distribution experts can evaluate this equation and advise you appropriately so you will not get caught on the short end.

Payment Methods A former associate and prince of a guy, Gil Fuller, who served as CFO in a company I worked for, always reminded me that "cash is good!" Any time cash is an option (onsite sales, will-call, company stores, and so on), I suggest you accept it. However, since so much of network marketing business is done via phone, fax, mail, or Internet, cash is often not an option.

This leaves you with the choice of accepting credit or debit cards, or electronic fund transfers from checking accounts. With orders by mail, you can accept checks, but mail is not the most attractive option for speedy turnaround.

Even with credit cards and electronic checking options, you incur additional expense. First there is the discount rate charged to merchants for every transaction processed. This varies by volume and type of credit/debit card (American Express generally runs more than Visa and MasterCard). Unfortunately, the cost varies even by industry. In the mail order/phone solicitation or order-taking arena that MLM is usually lumped into, fraud and abuse have been widespread, and the industry is paying a premium price. Until you establish your own history, or unless you can show that you attract an unusual customer who could help exempt you from high charges, you will most likely be at the higher end of the discount rate, so plan accordingly.

In order to even take a credit card, you must establish a merchant account with a bank. There can be application fees, and sometimes a deposit against future write-offs is required for new clients. Your prior relationship with your bank and good credit/cash flow history will work in your favor. Any disputes in credit card charges often result in "charge-backs," which reduce your overall collection rate. Also, the volume of charge-backs has an impact on your future percent discount charge.

Co-branded Credit Cards Many wise companies have chosen to affiliate with an issuing bank to offer a co-branded credit card. This card shows the company logo and is called an affinity or co-branded card. This card serves several purposes. First, it can be easier for your distributors to get a card, because the bank can develop credit guideline criteria that meet the often yo-yo-like earnings patterns of network marketers. Second, your distributors may get a better interest rate on their balances than they are currently paying on other cards. Also, since your card should sport an impactful color scheme and great graphic version of your company logo, it may start prospecting conversations with others when it is used to pay for meals or merchandise. This in turn can lead to more distributors for the company.

Even better, these affinity credit cards can be a source of revenue both for you and your distributors. The way the system works is that the bank shares the revenues with you—generally a percent of charges made on the card. You can then split out a couple of bonus points to assign for purchases made by a distributor's down-line that then get added to that distributor's bonus points for the month. These are then added to other bonus points generated from product movement, and the payout is included in the regular monthly bonus check. Usually, the bonus reports include a line showing the points earned from credit card purchases. If you have a large enough distributor population, it can be a great marketing tool for the bank to gain new customers, for you to make money, and for your distributor to share in the profits, too. A true win, win, win situation.

Electronic Funds Transfer Electronic funds transfer is a direct deduction from someone's checking account that is credited to the merchant from whom they make a purchase. Generally speaking, electronic funds transfer is cheaper per transaction than credit cards. However, the public is more apprehensive about this process and does not choose the option as often. With the current surge toward debit cards, which in effect accomplish the same thing, electronic fund transfers may become a thing of the past.

Distributors Accepting Credit Cards Before I leave this topic, another area to mention is helping your distributors to become "merchants" so that they too can make it convenient and easy for their customers to purchase from them by credit card. If your distributors have high-ticket retail sales (and who wouldn't want to encourage this?), it is a must.

There are companies who target MLM distributors to fill this need. Two that I know of are Voxcom in Dallas, Texas, and Cardservice International in Agoura Hills, California. Both can partner with MLM companies and work directly with their distributors to set them up. This concept is a great support for your distributors if you have made it an easy step to take. It really seems to make distributors feel that they are truly in the retail business once they become a "merchant" and can take credit cards from their customers for purchases. Customers love it too, because they are accustomed to making purchases this way. Your retail tickets may go up too, because impulse purchases can be easily accommodated.

The Check Is in the Mail It is impossible to stress enough how important it is to pay your sales organization *on time every time*. Nothing, *nothing* else you can do will jeopardize your reputation and integrity as much as not paying what is due when it is due. If you lose credibility on this front, you lose momentum, and your business could come to an abrupt halt.

The field sales organization–corporate office relationship is fragile, and if disrupted causes bad news to travel fast. The only thing faster than the speed of light is the "bamboo wireless" informal communications chain that carries rumors through your field organization. So if news is going to travel that fast, be sure your news is good.

I once had a client company who had a problem with their check run. The date was entered incorrectly, so calculations were one cycle off, causing shortages on the checks. The error was discovered during the audit process and the check run was done over. On the rerun, another error was discovered. The second run calculated two pay cycles, added them together, and made the checks close to twice the amounts actually due. Unfortunately, the processing cycle to calculate and run checks took anywhere from one to two days, so, after the second run, timing was down to the wire and getting checks out on time was in jeopardy.

It was agreed in advance that a third run would be made, but, if the checks were still incorrect and the error not found, that the checks for double the amount would be sent out. Accompanying them would be a note explaining the situation, telling the field sales force that the company was keeping their best interests at heart. So, the note and larger check would go, instead of no check or a late check (which would be very inconvenient for the distributor). This larger check would be sent to allow distributors their current amount due, plus an advance on their next check. The explanation would go on to say that any overpayment would be deducted from the next check.

Extreme decision? You bet! But what a better message this sent out (healthy cash flow/good financial underpinnings, etc.)

than the one of an envelope with no check, but an apology letter saying the computer messed up so the distributors would have to pay the price and wait a few extra days for their check.

The story ended happily: The third run came out correctly and in time, but the thinking shows how important customer service is with regard to mailing checks on time. Imagine how it would affect employees if on payday they got an apology letter rather than a check! Scary, huh? Don't let it happen to you. Do what it takes to deliver commission checks on time. As you choose your MIS vendor, be sure that the turnaround time for check production is minimal and that other systems can continue to work while it operates. In the case cited, because of an outdated software program, even order entry could not take place until the checks were sent out. Also, in your promises to the field for check delivery, leave yourself some time to run checks, audit them, and if necessary rerun them if operator errors occur.

Usually, mailing checks on the fifteenth following the month's close is the industry standard. Any way you can improve on that will give you and the field an advantage that will result in higher sales. Direct deposit is a great advantage to the field, but may negatively impact your cash flow. Another option may be to allow upper-level distributors the ability to pay for their checks to be delivered overnight. This helps them receive their checks quickly and makes them feel special.

Month End Normally *month end* in network marketing is like the Christmas season in retail. Everyone rushes in at the last minute to get his or her qualifying order placed. Some companies have chosen a weekly pay plan. This is fun because it makes everyone stay on their toes weekly and you have four "mini month ends" instead of just one big one per month.

In a monthly cycle, the workload is usually heavy at the first of the month to clean up the prior month, and for those who want to be the first at everything. Then it slows down in weeks two and three, and then in week four—watch out! Chaos breaks loose. In a weekly qualification plan, this cycle has a similar pattern. Monday is like week one, Tuesday, Wednesday, and Thursday like weeks two and three, and Friday becomes a "mini month end."

The last day of the month, or month end, can be humongous. One of my clients has even caused an entire regional phone circuit to be busied out due to the large number of distributors and customers calling the company's order department on the last day of the month or quarter.

The challenges here are 1) how to manage and schedule your workforce to efficiently handle this peak period in operations, 2) still maintain excellent customer service, and 3) to avoid being overstaffed the rest of the month. The phones in order entry, customer service, credit checking, and shipping are all taxed at this time.

I've seen these challenges met in numerous ways. Generally there is a core full-time staff that works all month. This group is then supplemented by part-time or temporary workers at peak periods. Also, other companies cross-train workers from staff areas and pull from those departments to staff the phones and shipping lines during month end. For instance, some people from product manufacturing may move to shipping, and someone who generally operates as a secretary may switch off to take order calls at month end.

Staffing Decisions History, coupled with a future vision of your growth plan, is your best indicator of how to staff order entry, customer service, and distribution. Once you have captured historical information on the length of each call and the number of calls received daily by order entry, and you know the approximate wrap time and time allowed for breaks and lunch, you can determine how many calls per day each staff member can handle. This in turn will lead you to the number the entire group can handle.

For example, if your average call time is four minutes, and you expect individuals to be available to take calls 80 percent of every hour (allowing for wrap-up, breaks, and so on), then:

80% × 60 minutes = 48 minutes available per person to take calls

48 minutes ÷ 4 minutes per call = 12 calls per hour per person

Twelve, then, is the average number of calls per hour a person can take. Therefore, in an eight-hour work day, they can generally take ninety-six calls. If, according to your trends and historical data, you expect to receive 960 calls per eight-hour shift, then you need ten people to take the calls. This assumes your calls come in evenly over this eight-hour period, however, which rarely happens.

This example does not take into account shifts longer than eight hours, flexible work times, part-time workers, or extended hours over eight hours per day. Further, in addition to peaks and valleys over the period of a month, each day your call volume will fluctuate by the hour, you will have employees absent, and so on. All of this complicates my simple example, which was used just to give you an idea of how it works. Luckily, there are many software programs that can do the calculations for you. Your job then becomes to feed accurate data and projections into the formula so it will give you the correct answer to your staffing needs.

I won't bore you with a more complex formula, but you do need to have a basic understanding of how it works in order to maximize your resources. Suffice it to say, real analytical expertise in this area of staff planning, coupled with useful software programs to run the numbers, will pay back huge dividends in efficient resource allocation. Remember, in addition to the people, you will need adequate workspace, phones, and computer terminals for everyone to use at your peak period. While this can be a tricky balance of investments, if it is properly managed, you will realize payoff from satisfied customers who don't get put on hold or into a queue for an eternity while you rack up toll charges and ill will.

A similar formula and process can be used for staffing your shipping line, too. Numbers of orders to be shipped will follow the curve you develop for phone order taking, if estimates were accurate. Many companies have developed a process to smooth out the month end logjam.

One such program is known as "early bird specials." The theory here is that by giving an incentive for ordering early in the month, you can entice customers to change their ordering patterns. Depending on the nature of the offering, I have seen this work very well on the company's behalf.

An example is to offer a special price on a particular item if you place your order by the twentieth of the month. After that, the special is no longer available. If this is an attractive discount, distributors will be moved to change their ordering patterns, and will place their order prior to month end. Then they can take advantage of your special and you will be able to help smooth out the peaks and valleys in your order curve. Another option is to offer a "buy one, get one free" or "half-price" special, but only if the customer purchases within the designated time frame. "Free" always sells, so this can do the trick.

What you need to do is determine the financial advantage you achieve by keeping your staff at a more even level throughout the month, which allows you to better utilize your equipment and overhead on a regular basis as opposed to paying overtime and having underutilized resources throughout the month. Once you have this number, you will know exactly how much you can afford to give away on your monthly special to break even in costs. Any special offer that costs less than that number will be realized on your bottom line.

Autoship and Backup Orders Another concept that until recently was only used by a few companies, but which now has widespread usage, is that of an automatic shipment. It can be called autoship, or a backup shipment program (also referred to by some companies as an insured or preferred customer program). This concept promotes a predefined or custom-selected order that a distributor or customer can sign up for, and it authorizes regular automatic shipment—kind of a modern-day book-of-the-month club. When it ships only if a distributor has not placed a qualifying order in any given month, it is considered a backup order. When this preauthorized order ships regardless of what else is ordered, it is an autoship program.

These programs have several advantages, both to the company and to the distributors. The company virtually assures an order count for the month because anyone on the program who doesn't meet their requirements automatically gets product anyway. This creates a great reorder rate, which is an attractive feature that helps distributors sell the program to other potential distributors. Also, idle time in your shipping area during the mid-month slump can be used to build or pack the inventory of these orders whose contents are predetermined. Backup orders are generally shipped after the month end has closed and the rush is over, because a month end computer run must determine who gets one. Autoship orders can be sent at any time the company designates in its program guidelines, so if you choose mid-month, you may help to smooth out your distribution curve.

For predetermined packages (not custom orders) a computer run can produce labels by category and the only thing shipping needs to do is apply the label to the preassembled package, cutting a lot of paperwork and hassles. Once a customer or distributor has signed up and given you authority to charge his or her credit card or debit a checking account on a monthly basis, the amount stays the same each month because the order contains items of a similar value. This package can be identical each month or it can be rotated on a quarterly or any other predetermined schedule.

This again points out the need for a consumable product. For this type of program to work, the items must need to be replenished. A great example may be a vitamin/mineral supplement that comes in a thirty-day supply. This not only becomes an easy choice for that reason, but it is also a very small package that can be easily and inexpensively shipped. You couldn't do this program with nonconsumables because the reorder need doesn't exist. You might be able to do a hybrid if you have a nonconsumable that has replacement parts or components, or an ongoing service or maintenance need. An example might be a bottled water dispensing system that needs the bottled water replaced on a regular basis.

The advantage to the distributor and/or customer varies. At the very least, distributors have a convenient way of getting product and they are protected for commissions even if they fail to place a phone order because the backup order satisfies the purchase qualification requirement. Another way the distributor benefits, if he or she has sold the program and has most of his or her down-line on it, is that activity in the group is high because everyone on the program gets an order. This product movement generates bonus volume toward the up-line commission and bonus check.

Often, in exchange for the commitment to the purchase requirement, a lower price for the predetermined package may be given to those on the program. Another option is to lower or completely eliminate shipping charges on these packages. In either case, the distributor benefits by getting a better value.

A caveat on these programs: While they have tremendous upside potential, there can be a downside. This downside occurs if your distributors are not properly explaining the program to new recruits. When this happens, new customers don't understand why products keep showing up that they didn't order; and, even worse, charges appear on their credit card statements that they were not expecting. In the worst-case scenario, a person who didn't realize what he was signing up for, and who used the debit to a checking account as method of payment, could end up with bounced checks for his or her mortgage payment or other necessities because he or she had counted on the balance in the checkbook without realizing the direct debit from your company would conflict.

The best approach to this program is education, education, and more education. This way it can work to both the company's and the distributors' benefit, not to the detriment of your business and reputation.

Amazing Customer Service

The last word on overall customer service is this: The best road to satisfying customers is to treat them as you would like to be treated—and noticeably better than your competition treats them. I have gotten so accustomed to being put on hold and into a queue, or having to provide push-button responses to what seem like a million trivial questions, in order to get through a voice-response maze, that recently I was *shocked and amazed* when I called my dental insurance carrier because a live person answered on the first ring! I won't forget this for a long time. This translated into what I call amazing service. This is how you want your customers to feel about you, so plan to offer it. To paraphrase the Lexus philosophy, when it comes to customer service, keep on the "relentless pursuit of perfection" and your customers will remember you by being loyal and continuing to be part of your organization for years to come.

The Success Formula

Customer service is an integral part of the Success Formula, and specifically important when it comes to retention of distributors and customers. The two most critical elements of customer service in the Success Formula are 1) *always* make sure your distributors' checks go out on time, and 2) avoid merchandise shortages. In addition, one of the secrets to enjoying a competitive advantage is to set the amazing service standard, and establish a daily meeting with an accompanying system to monitor your performance.

Customer Service Daily Meeting:
Potential Topics for Review

CALL CENTER UPDATE

Total number of calls received _____

Average queue time _____

Number of abandoned calls _____

Average length of call _____

Number and percent of calls monitored
_____ / _____%

Average rating of calls monitored
(scale of 1–10, poor to excellent) _____

Quantity per associate _____

Accuracy of responses _____

Attitude rating of associate _____

CORRESPONDENCE RECEIVED

Number of pieces _____

Oldest date unanswered _____

Number answered _____

Figure 10.1 Daily Update Meeting Topics

162

MANAGEMENT PHONE MESSAGES

Number of voice mail messages taken _____
Voice mail:
Answered _____ Unanswered _____
Oldest date of unanswered _____
Number of live messages taken _____
Live messages:
Answered _____ Unanswered _____
Oldest date of unanswered _____

TOTAL NUMBER OF ORDERS RECEIVED

Total _____
How received:
Fax _____
Phone _____
Mail _____
Internet _____
Voice response _____
Oldest date unfilled _____
Date currently shipping _____
Average delivery time _____
Number in tracing/delivery status _____

PRODUCT AVAILABILITY

Items shorted or on back order _____
Reason(s) _____
_____
Resolution date _____
Items off sale _____
Reason(s) _____
Resolution date_____

Figure 10.1 *(continues)*

Bonus/Commission Check Status

Due date _____

Plan run _____

Audit date _____

Mailing date _____

Problems _____

_____

New Product Introductions

Number scheduled _____

Product name(s) _____

_____

Date due in inventory _____

Date on sale _____ On target? Yes _____ No _____

Resolution for No's _____

_____

Other Issues

Manufacturing _____

Shipping _____

MIS/computer _____

Operations _____

Sales _____

Finance _____

Customer service _____

Hottest item reported on phones _____

Resolution of issues assigned to _____

THE HOME OFFICE TEAM

Objective

THE OBJECTIVE OF this chapter is to lay out an organizational structure for use as a guideline when creating your home office staff. Even though this section covers an up and running organization, all functions will most likely need attention from the beginning. For this reason, you may have to select individuals who can perform multiple functions on a small scale at first, then later move to a staff with more specific functional expertise.

The Organization

Functionally, your organization will include these roles and responsibilities:

President and CEO Visionary—overall responsibility for all company functions and interfaces with the owners, shareholders, investors, etc.

Sales Overall responsibility for recruiting, developing, training, and recognizing the field sales force of independent distributors. Another key responsibility is to provide field support and appropriate motivation and promotions to enhance recruiting efforts. This chief sales executive is the owner of the Opportunity and compensation plan, and has the responsibility of developing and promoting the Opportunity as a product, including designing and updating the materials in the starter kit. The sales personality is the major communicator with the field, and should provide information from the field to marketing for inclusion in the monthly publication and other communications.

While some of my clients include order entry and customer service personnel with operations, I would consider putting internal sales and customer service personnel either in sales or marketing. I see this function as an extension of the sales support function. Order entry and customer service personnel on the phones directly impact sales (up-selling and providing product information to distributors and customers), recruiting (what better testimonial than great response from customer service agents or TLC callers?), and customer retention by appropriately solving problems. Also, by reporting to sales or marketing, there is a better chance that new offerings and programs will be properly communicated to the field on a timely basis.

Marketing Overall responsibility for selection and maintenance of an appropriate product line for the sales organization to sell. Pricing, promotions, public relations, positioning and marketing communications, and profitability responsibilities lie here. Marketing is also responsible for new product launches, the company image, and the positioning of the company and its product line. Brand management includes the management of concept promotion, pricing, and ensuring each product and category is achieving desired productivity and profitability throughout the product life cycle. This group must manage the size of the product line and eliminate or upgrade SKUs as needed. The marketing group is responsible for the success of each product's introduction, and it must support sell-through to the consumer. Also, market research, competitive analysis, and segmentation of the sales force and customers are performed by the marketing group.

Special events are a joint function of sales and marketing, each bringing focus and creative thoughts to the process. Often, sales brings in the recruiting and training parts of the agenda and requests locations that work best for the sales force. Marketing focuses on product and creative ways to deliver the company's message at the event.

Operations This group is responsible for support functions such as manufacturing, purchasing, third-party sourcing, distribution, shipping, and inventory control.

Finance and Administrative Support Includes functions of management information services (MIS), human resources, legal (including compliance), financial planning, and accounting.

Product Development This should be a joint function (in the form of a Product Development Committee) including representatives from sales, marketing, operations, a scientific/R&D team, and finance. New product development should be driven by market need, deliver an incremental contribution to average order or recruiting efforts, and it must fit into the overall marketing strategy or umbrella product categories already established.

Customer Retention This function is jointly owned by all corporate management staff. Many thousands of dollars are spent to gain new customers as you create and implement your initial recruiting strategies to grow the business. An additional (often overlooked) large expense is incurred if customers and distributors join your plan and, because of a bad experience, drop out or cancel shortly thereafter. As you develop your investment strategy for MIS, operational programs, customer supports, inventory policies, your general commitment to customer service, and your internal quality culture, don't be cheap up front because you will pay for it on the back end. Be sure to factor turnover into your investment equation; the short-term cost savings—if they are at the customer's expense—will actually add to the overall expense in the long run.

You can determine the opportunity cost attributed to turnover by calculating the average cost to recruit a replacement distributor for each one lost, and then adding the value of the average distributor—found by taking your average order ($100, for example) multiplied by the average number of months a distributor stays. The combination of these factors is the opportunity cost of turnover; as you can imagine, these "hidden" costs can be substantial.

As mentioned in the last chapter, product availability, mailing checks to distributors on time, and the overall quality and attitude of customer service greatly impact company credibility. If you don't deliver on the promise, your turnover will increase and profits will suffer. And once credibility and trust are lost, so is momentum. Optimal trust in and the credibility of a company are what separate great companies from others in the pack. With these elements intact, the field can be very forgiving for many other mistakes.

At start-up, many functions will fall under a small number of individuals with more general management skills; or, more likely they will fall to the owners or start-up team, regardless of their skill level. Later (assuming the start-up hump is crossed), as the company grows, experts in specific areas can be brought in to carry things forward. In some ways, this is a little backwards because experts could be very helpful in making the organization grow and flourish early on. However, there are often not enough funds to underwrite all the employees you would ideally like to hire.

The effectiveness of using one or a limited number of people (especially the lone entrepreneur who developed the product or concept) to wear many hats with multiple responsibilities depends on their breadth of knowledge, desire, experience, and exposure to the issues that lie ahead. Unfortunately, sometimes not all the issues are known, and therein lies a big risk. You can be blind-sided by a truly fatal business-stopping error, or a mistake that negatively impacts potential growth. However, in my experience, it's not what my clients have known and considered that has created problems, but rather *what they didn't know they didn't know.*

Utilizing a Consultant

An alternative for help at start-up or at "stuck" (a term I use for companies who have reached a certain sales level and plateaued), is to hire a reputable consultant who has expertise in one or more of the areas where a skill gap exists, or where time and objectivity is of the essence. Often everyone on staff is duly overloaded—or too close to the trees to see the forest. While this may seem like an expensive alternative, think of it as an investment that may actually save you money. In the long run, costly major obstacles can be avoided with a qualified consultant, and you just may avoid the million-dollar mistake. A caution here: Be sure you check out who you work with because not all self-acclaimed consultants have what you need. Legitimate consultants have a good track record and reputation in the industry. They can provide references. Be sure you get references, and take the time to check them out.

While consultants may seem expensive at a time when little cash flow exists, if you choose your resource carefully, hiring one will be a great investment with residual (you know that term!) payback throughout the life of your organization. It can also be insurance that there will be a future life for your business.

As a consultant and partner to my clients, I view my role as being similar to a tour guide in a foreign country where my clients may not know either the geography or the language. In either case, eventually they can find their way and learn to communicate, but not without considerable time and money being wasted. But when I step in at the strategy development stage, I can help clients avoid big detours on a road they would have chosen, simply because they did not know a roadblock existed. Because I have been down the road before, I can advise them to take a more direct and appropriate route around the roadblock, one that will more easily and quickly lead to success.

My recommendation is that you consider investing whatever you can afford (and perhaps even a little more) at this stage. It can mean the difference between your trying to do some wrong things right, instead of being advised to do the right things.

The Success Formula

Having the right team or talent pool at the home office is definitely a component in the Success Formula. If competent resources exist, regardless of the size of the team, they will have a positive impact on success. Even at first, when you cannot employ separate expert individuals to perform each function required, someone with appropriate cross-functional skills must be available and assigned responsibility for each function. If you cannot afford even this level of full-time staffing, utilize a consultant who brings the skills you need to bridge the gap. It may feel like you can't afford one, but if you choose a consultant wisely the money you spend will save you thousands of dollars in mistakes you may make without proper guidance.

CAPITALIZING ON THE CHANNEL

Objective

IN THIS CHAPTER, I will explore the various ways that
network marketing companies can capitalize on their
most valuable asset—their base of distributors and channel of distribution. Once your sales organization is established,
there are various approaches you can take to make use of beneficial products or services that support your core business.
These distributor benefits items can also help your distributors
in the execution of their businesses or provide them with additional merchandise to share with their customer base.

The decision to add third-party merchandise or services is
strategic, and it can be a win-win proposition if approached
correctly. We will explore the value of these options along with
a discussion of whether to consider the ultimate consumer for
these items as your distributors, or, as an alternative, their customers. Timing is critical as you consider this option. New and

emerging companies should focus on the core business, whereas midsize and maturing companies can find extremely lucrative alternatives through this option.

Also, as a closing thought, maintaining your channel—known as retention—is an important consideration. Once you have recruited someone, it is in your best interest to keep them in your organization; spending some resources to ensure a high level of retention can be key to continued growth and success. Ways to do this are explored here.

The Basics

During my tenure at Avon, an important but basic lesson I learned was that there are two proverbial ways to increase sales: Get more representatives (read: stores) or get each representative to move more merchandise through her current store (read: boost average order). This logic is so basic that we often forget it.

As you start up your network marketing company, the approach is to open many new stores—meaning find new distributors. This focus is important at start-up and will always be the number one way to move your business forward. Generally you have a volume requirement that each distributor commits to for purposes of qualification for compensation, and this relationship can be the basis for establishing the value of each new distributor. Coupled with your turnover rate, you can determine the value of each new distributor brought on board. Your core product is what supports this requirement; its effectiveness, value, attractiveness, and the level of service you offer will determine whether or not it is reordered, extending the life cycle of new distributors. Of course, the training, support, and understanding given to new distributors at start-up also impacts your distributor turnover and retention rate.

Assuming that you offer a great core product line and that the other Success Formula ingredients in your system are working, your distributor base will expand rapidly with the right sales leadership. Over the years, your distributor base will become large and, thus, your most important asset. As your distributors mature through the compensation plan, and they help sufficient numbers in their organizations likewise to succeed, they will be looking to you for new and exciting challenges. They will likely express a desire to have more to offer than just the core products. Requests will come from your top distributors, first to make the compensation plan richer, and second, for additional ways to add volume to their BV or GV requirements. Often, it can also come as a request for additional "employee-type" benefits such as health care alternatives, or other benefits the company can offer to help sustain their own motivation and retain their organizations, in which they have invested significant time to build.

The Avon Example

To illustrate the value of a distributor/representative base, let me give you some examples of what I have seen to demonstrate the incredible value of your channel as a vehicle to move merchandise. At Avon, it quickly became apparent how valuable the representative force (approaching one million in number) was in the 1980s. When a fragrance was launched during the fourth quarter, more sales dollars and units of fragrance passed through this channel in the matter of a month (two campaigns) than department stores could move in a year.

Often, Avon would offer premiums or purchase-with-purchase promotions of items not germane to the core product line. These could be anything from a dated trinket to a music tape. It finally occurred to me what an impact Avon had on making these premiums successful in their own right, when gold and platinum record awards began to appear in the hallways. For example, when the premium item was a tape of Christmas music, that tape would often become a gold, or even platinum, recording, demonstrating the immense impact on the success of a product when delivered by the direct sales channel. No wonder vendors were persistent in trying to get their items added to Avon's product line.

On the downside, if wrong items were chosen, the warehouse could be filled with overstocked or obsolete merchandise. This lesson must be applied to the types of items you choose to put into your product line for distribution through your channel.

Sideline Products and Distributor Benefits

In addition to expanding your core product line to take advantage of your distributor channel, as you become larger you will be approached by other companies with the options of putting their products and services into your distributors' hands. Many will be sales supports positioned to drive your distributors' businesses (voice mail, Web pages); services that support specific needs distributors have during the course of conducting their businesses (credit cards, long distance phone service, or travel services); or benefits that can lure them away from a traditional job (medical insurance). Others will be products or services for distributors to sell (some of the same supports you've made available for them).

Strategic Objectives

Before jumping into the "distributor benefits," or "world of services" options, there are questions to ask to determine their strategic fit with your overall plan. In most cases, when you add the appropriate products or services that benefit your distributors, there is a matching benefit to the company. But different options have varying degrees of payoff, and some even have hidden costs.

The first bridge to cross is to determine if your objective is to develop products and services to support your distributors in the execution of their duties; that is, for their own personal use, or if your goal is to add sideline (non-core) products or services for them to sell. Either way, there are options and philosophies to consider before you enter this arena.

Some companies decide that they want to make a sideline product for resale with margins equal to their core product profit margin. Others merely pass along attractive cost-saving supports to the field sales organization with only minor margins built in. These supports are intended to make distributors' jobs easier, and to save them money on business expenses. The philosophy here is that cost-saving supports will allow distributors to sell more core product, or sell it more profitably, both of which are good for the company and the retention of distributors.

Exciting and appropriate distributor benefits can also serve to make your Opportunity more attractive and competitive to potential recruits, thus allowing your distributors to more easily recruit additional distributors. In all cases, services are offered to support growth, with a byproduct being the creation of more dollars through the increased sales of your core product or interest in your business opportunity.

Timing

Timing is also an important consideration. When your company is relatively young, it is best to focus on your core product. Introducing new products or services for your sales force to sell (especially if you have a small, specialized line) that are off strategy and do not fit with your mission statement can be detrimental. If you take focus away from your core line, and your sales force has to spend time learning about a product or service to sell that is different from what attracted them to the company, it can be confusing, time-consuming, and paralyzing to the business. The time spent on this diversion is taken away from the core, which can cause sales of your leading products to suffer. Additionally, depending on how complementary or diverse the additions are, focus on your best margin product can be lost.

As a start-up or for a relatively new company with only a small number of distributors, it is best to focus on building the down-line and opening new "stores." It is the simplest and most focused strategy for success. However, after you become a medium-size organization, your asset of the field sales force has enough meaning to start exploring optional supports. At that point, the group has the critical mass needed to be an attractive catch for a credit card issuer or long-distance provider to approach you with a partnership deal.

At this point, which is when you have fifteen to twenty thousand active distributors, the channel is big enough to add enhanced services to support your distributors, perhaps services you couldn't afford at start-up. At this point, the group is also large enough to be an attractive audience for a partner service provider, and large enough for you to negotiate a win-win contract for you. The winners are you, the vendor, and the distributors who share a portion of the profits.

In the ideal case, everyone participates in the profit and the cost savings large groups can command. This means you can pass along significant savings on a service or even have room to grant a percentage bonus value (BV) toward the compensation plan on which you can afford a small pay-out to the sales organization. Generally, this is simply an increase in volume for calculation of pay-out only, not for qualification or achievement of new levels.

Unless your strategy is to offer a wide variety of product categories—as with Amway, and to a lesser degree Avon—it is my opinion that you are better off targeting your distributors and their down-lines as the ultimate consumer of these benefits rather than utilizing your sales force to resell these services to their customers. There are exceptions to this thinking (especially when the core product is already a service) and my opinion may change over time. But for now, it seems to me that if you create a company to sell and focus on product X and then change the focus to selling a third party product or service Y, it is a confusing message to those attracted to product X and its mission.

On the other hand, if you create a company to be X, and later expand with a logical category of X-related items that stick to your overall concept umbrella, you are most likely to succeed. If you add Y, an unrelated item, you may attract additional people who want to sell Y, but it will be so off strategy and mission, that the sales force may become confused as to what the company stands for. It may feel to them that they are trying to serve two masters. And instead of focusing your resources where your expertise and reason for being lies, you end up watering down and clouding the company mission.

Compatible Options

To clarify this point further, here are a couple of examples of where a product line extension makes sense. If you are a beauty and skin care company, a logical extension may be nutritional supplements, because they support the concept of beauty at a deeper level, and sales to consumers of both can be compatible. Likewise, if your core product is long-distance services, a logical extension of the product line may be selling local phone service or electricity to ultimate consumers, because both are services that come under the utilities umbrella, which makes sense to the ultimate consumer.

However, it would not make sense for the beauty products company to resell electricity to its ultimate consumers, or for the long-distance service sellers to add nutritional supplements, because the product lines are not compatible with a single focused mission. But it may make perfect sense to offer a value-priced long-distance service, or even electricity services, to a distributor sales force regardless of what they sell, because, as a business owner, distributors have a need for attractive alternatives that support their businesses by lowering expenses.

Likewise, for any company, a credit card that has the company logo, or a travel club with special advantages for its members, makes perfect sense as a business support to offer to distributors. Because all companies have distributors who use these services in the execution of their businesses, they are reasonable to consider. But to have distributors resell these services seems off-strategy, and perhaps it would be confusing for their customers who fail to see the connection. It would be easier to make the leap if your core product is services and the new offering is just an expansion of them than if your core product is a tangible, unrelated product with a finely positioned story.

Other services that make sense to offer to the sales force for their purchase, but not for them to learn to resell, would be voice mail; Internet support such as Web page production; on-line, real-time organizational information; logo merchandise; and customized checks, direct deposit, or other banking services. One of my client companies even went so far as to apply for a charter to open its own bank, which would allow it to offer direct deposit, credit cards, loans, and investment opportunities to its distributors. It is for their distributor's use as a business support though, not a product they will initially sell.

Another attractive benefit for distributors is in the area of life, health, and umbrella liability insurance, as well as discount cards that allow savings benefits for related items not covered by insurance (eyeglasses, prescriptions, dental care, hearing aids, and more). Insurance is a tricky area, because in order to get the best rates for your distributors, they should be categorized as a defined group for experience ratings and they must be diverse enough to create an attractive insurable group. However, because they are independent contractors and not your employees (and you do not want to give the appearance of employee status), the best you can do is shop for competitive rates among insurance companies that have experience pricing individual health policies.

A downside to offering health insurance is that you will be hard-pressed to find a company that offers coverage in all states. Further, getting attractive rates significantly better than what the distributor could already obtain on their own is tricky. Sometimes the rates are better, and sometimes they are not; and this puts you in a sensitive position if you have offered the product.

A new arrival on the health insurance scene in 1997 that is valuable to independent contractors because it has tax-advantages is the Medical Savings Account. It combines a high-deductible health insurance policy with a tax-favored savings account. It is somewhat like a medical IRA in that you get to save pretax dollars to cover your deductible, and you can earn tax-free interest on the balance. It also offers the privilege of carrying unused funds forward until retirement. Its intricacies are too vast to explain here, but it is an option worth educating your sales force about. It may even be worth setting up strategic partnerships with appropriate insurance carriers and a bank to handle your distributors' needs. This becomes especially important as members of your sales force desire to transition from part-time to full-time, and need some alternative for health insurance as they leave a traditional corporate job.

Logo Merchandise

An easy first step into the third-party non-core merchandise arena is logo merchandise. Your sales force is already favorably disposed to you and your company name, and you can capitalize on this by offering quality merchandise for your distributors to wear or use that advertises their business. It is important that you choose items that reflect the tastes of your sales force, and of the quality that speaks to your core image.

Cheap T-shirts will sell, but they will not properly reflect your image. On the other hand, expensive, tasteful, understated merchandise will go a long way in promoting the correct image both to your field and to others who observe it. Get the best merchandise and your distributors will buy it and wear or use it proudly. After all, it may be a deductible business expense for them, and they appreciate really nice things. And, if properly selected and executed with the right vendor, it can be a great profit center for the company while still maintaining a real cost–benefit value for your distributors.

Some easy items to start with are short- or long-sleeve, tasteful, 100 percent cotton T-shirts, golf shirts, portfolios, pens, collared sweatshirts, etc. The best ways to sell them are onsite at an event or through a small catalog or four-color sheet that is dropped in orders going to your distributors. Additionally, if you have a monthly communications piece, promote them there. Companies often put information about logo merchandise in starter kits, but I feel this is premature. This merchandise sells best to your longer-term people who have belief in the company, not to new recruits who are just testing the waters.

Another great way to promote logo items is to have company management and top field leaders wear or carry and use the merchandise. Logo merchandise makes a great gift to give to your upper-level leadership when they attend company-sponsored events or training sessions at your home office, or for participants in your leadership council. Remember, if you get the right vendor, you can offer quality and value to the field while making a nice profit. Again, approach this carefully and tastefully with timing considerations (near an event to launch the items) because it will be an investment in inventory.

Retention Aids: TLC Calls

One relatively easy thing to do to solidify a distributor to the company right from the get-go is to make what I call tender loving care or TLC calls. Most of your turnover will occur among the ranks of new distributors. These are the ones who don't know exactly what hit them. All they know is that someone presented this business opportunity to them, and they signed up. It sounded like fun, and made sense then, but they really didn't understand everything, and surely they don't want to look foolish by asking dumb questions. They can even be stricken by buyer's remorse.

At this moment, this person needs to be rescued and given the chance to get comfortable with what they have gotten into. A great way to help them over this desperate period is to have a cheery person from the home office call to welcome them to the company, and invite them to ask questions. Since the new recruit doesn't know the person on the phone from the company, and aren't likely to see him or her any time soon, the recruit can ask all the "dumb" questions in the world and find a friendly answer for them. Even better, the TLC caller can be equipped with a script that includes the most commonly asked questions and most often under-explained aspects of the business presentation. This type of TLC call may make the difference between another cancellation and a long-term distributor. If and when you can afford to do this, please do so. At first, when the order entry clerks have open times between calls, they can even make a few calls a day, without any added personnel expense.

The Success Formula

The area of distributor benefits is not of significant importance as an ingredient in the Success Formula at start-up. However, as your company grows and more of the competition offers services, you need to be aware that they will become important both as an additional source of income and as retention support. Since retention is a vital success factor and important at all times, the best thing to start with early on is the TLC call. The next step would be to offer a limited logo merchandise line. Later, significant supports and benefits that help distributors in the efficient execution of their duties are the best choice.

VIEWS FROM THE TOPSIDE

Objective

To BROADEN YOUR perspective, I felt it would be good to share with you ideas from individuals who have been in the industry and have learned important concepts through their experience. I chose a variety of executives from both direct selling and network marketing companies, whose sales range from the low millions to more than a billion dollars in sales. Some of their comments reflect the most important aspects to consider at start-up, while others encompass ongoing considerations.

Bill Spears, president of Tupperware, shares his views on how being a good listener is not only important but critical in a direct selling company. Dallin Larsen, vice president of sales for USANA, captures the "magic" needed to grow a large sales organization. Kenny Troutt, CEO of Excel Communications, shares with you why network marketing works in the communications industry and the importance of relationship selling. And last, Craig Keeland, CEO of Youngevity, Inc., and Keith Harding, CEO of Sportron International, both answer the question, "What are the most important factors to consider at start-up?"

Being a Good Listener

By Bill Spears

President, Tupperware North America, Orlando, Florida

Keeping an open line of communication is important in any organization, but it is critical in a direct sales company. You cannot dictate to a direct seller. You can influence behavior, you can motivate. And motivating a sales force of independent contractors is a complex process based on many factors. Not the least of those factors is a sense of relatedness and the loyalty and desire to please that flow from it. Therefore, how you communicate is often as important as what you are communicating.

The sales force, particularly sales leaders, want to know that their concerns are heard and their ideas are considered. Dr. Stephen Covey expresses it well when he writes in his book, *The Seven Habits of Highly Effective People* (New York: Simon & Schuster, 1989):

> Next to physical survival, the greatest need of a human being is psychological survival—to be understood, to be affirmed, to be validated, to be appreciated . . . and after that vital need is met, you can then focus on influencing and problem solving.

To many people, being a good listener means you did what they asked you to do. With a sales force that may number in the tens of thousands, that's impossible. And sometimes, it is not even what the speaker really wanted. So just being a good listener and hearing what is said is not enough.

True listening is a process of connecting with the motives and feelings of the other person so that the issue and their relationship to it are understood. It is empathetic. And when you listen empathetically and acknowledge where the other person is coming from, it builds a very different kind of relationship.

In any organization, sharing the rationale behind a decision is helpful in selling it. In a direct selling organization, it is vital. Acknowledging everyone's point of view may help build credibility by inferring that they were considered in the decision-making process. And it can be even more powerful to acknowledge the feelings behind those points of view. That shows you not only heard but heard empathetically what was being said to you. That you truly listen at a deep level and understand others' perspectives is motivating to those with whom you work and speak.

Developing a reputation as an empathetic listener won't always guarantee success in selling an idea, but it can't hurt. And it will help to grow trust and strengthen the relationship between you and the listener.

The "Magic" Ingredients of Growing a Network Marketing Field Sales Organization

As told to me by Dallin Larsen

Vice President of Sales, USANA, Inc., Salt Lake City, Utah

Dallin Larsen is the individual who helped convince Dr. Myron Wentz, the CEO and founder of USANA, that utilizing the network marketing channel would be the best way to build the business into the successful multimillion-dollar publicly traded company it is today. Dallin's role, which typifies a great rainmaker, has been to build the field sales force to more than eighty-two thousand distributors in just five years. He continues in this role in the United States, while beginning to create a worldwide sales force as USANA goes international.

Dallin indicates that the major Success Factor to grow your business is recruiting. In order to do this well, a company must have a *compelling story*, and be able to crystallize the story so that it can be told thousands of times by thousands of people over, and over, and over again. A successful company never misses an opportunity to tell its story because it reminds everyone of the reason for the company's existence.

Dallin further advises that companies must never forget that the distributor is their customer, not their employee. He recommends that you always keep this in mind in your dealings with them, and in making decisions that impact them.

Last, Dallin indicates that at start-up, management and ownership has to exercise patience, patience, and more patience, because it takes longer to build the business than they think.

Why Network Marketing Works in the Communications Industry

By Kenny A. Troutt

Chairman and CEO, Excel Communications, Inc., Dallas, Texas

From the moment I founded Excel Communications as a reseller of long-distance and telecommunications services, I believed that it would work because every home and business needs and understands these services. I also knew that relationship selling was a natural vehicle because everyone has his or her own network of customers that increases over time.

It took years of hard work and development to get Excel where it is today. The opportunity was made possible by the breakup of AT&T in 1984, and the emergence of competition in the long distance market beginning with other providers like Sprint and MCI. It wasn't long before a number of long distance resellers entered the market as well.

I viewed reselling as a way to enter the market and build a subscriber base without having to incur all the debt that comes with building a network. By negotiating with the facilities-based carriers for large blocks of time, I could then resell the services at a discounted rate.

At the time, most network time was used by businesses during the day, leaving access capacity on weeknights and weekends. I felt I had found my niche and targeted the primarily evening residential market through a nationwide network of Excel independent representatives.

Excel is not limited to long-distance products and services. We have already added paging products and services, and are currently evaluating the possibility of entering other communications markets such as digital broadcast satellite, local service resell, Internet services, wireless services, and eventually expanding to international markets. We already have the customer base. Our goal is to offer our customers the most cost-effective products and services by bundling them into a single bill.

With Excel, our independent representatives have the opportunity to build a business of their own. Although many representatives choose to work on a part-time basis for supplemental income, there are a number of individuals who have used Excel as a way to find financial freedom and leave the ranks of the corporate ladder. The opportunity attracts individuals from all walks of life ranging from business professionals to stay-at-home housewives and moms.

The Excel opportunity is designed for entrepreneurs on all levels. We know that relationship selling works. Our job is to continue implementing the types of products and services that consumers want and need, which leaves only one factor in completing the transaction, *the relationship.*

Cash Is King: Answer to the Question, "What Are the Most Important Factors to Consider at Start Up?"

By Craig Keeland

CEO, Youngevity, Inc., Dallas, Texas

The most important aspect of starting a network marketing business, or any business for that matter, is capital, capital, and more capital. When one or more people come up with a vision to form their own company, then lay it out step-by-step in a business plan, part of the business plan will be pro forma income and expenses. Almost without exception, in every new business, expenses will be higher than what was projected, and income for the first thirty-six months will be lower than what was projected. To guard against this happening, plenty of cash reserves are necessary to sustain your new business venture. You can overcome almost any obstacle in a new business except running out of cash. When you run out of cash, the party is over and everyone goes home!

Pro forma expenses should be fairly easy, at least in theory. However, the reality is another matter. You will find, for example, when new telephone lines are installed, they are much more expensive than what was budgeted on a monthly basis. Then you find out that you need your own phone system. Do you lease a unit, buy a new system, or buy a used system? The same holds true with copiers, postage machines, and so on. You spend a lot of time you hadn't counted on setting up the services, so instead of working on your business, you spend a lot of time just trying to get your business up and running, getting telephone lines and systems installed, and other tasks. Then you find that one vendor will blame another vendor as to why what you want can't happen.

For example, one telephone company runs the lines to your building. Another installer will take those lines from the building to the outlets, and then another vendor will hook up the instruments and/or computer modem, fax lines, etc. What happens when they don't work? Everybody blames everyone else and you spend all your management time trying to get up and running.

The next thing that occurs is that everyone wants credit references, and you don't have any. Again, a massive amount of time is spent on items that seem unproductive, but yet must be done in order to get your business going. As you can clearly see, there is one item after another that takes up much more cash and/or time that wasn't planned for in advance.

In reality, to get up and going (or as we would say in Texas, "to come out of the chute") takes a tremendous amount of time and capital. Other expenses you may not have allowed for are the printing of literature for the second and third time because you counted on the amount of money that you allocated for the literature to be right the first time. You'll find that as soon as it is printed, you will find a mistake or multiple mistakes, or you will change things and have to reprint the literature. If it's a black-and-white copy, no problem. But if it's in color, it's a big problem because of the large press runs required, and that eats up capital, especially when you have things printed for the second and third time. Even if it does get printed right the first time, you may find out thirty, sixty, or ninety days after you've been in business that there is a modification needed for the products, compensation plan, or policies and procedures, and guess what? Here we go back to the printer after throwing away 95 percent of what was originally printed.

Income projections on a monthly basis for the first twelve months, and usually the next twenty-four to thirty-six months, often don't live up to expectations. There are many reasons for this, but one of the most important is that you don't get up and operating as soon as you expect. What looks really good on paper doesn't always happen in actuality because, as I mentioned above, a tremendous amount of time and money is spent "coming out of the chute." Once your business is up and running, you will be making modifications that take time and money to implement, and all these factors reduce the projected income that you had planned.

Every time you make a change, it has to go through your sales organization, and while change is a daily part of business, it is something no one likes. When change happens, your sales force will slow down to try to understand the change, and while they're slowing down, they don't recruit as many new distributors and/or sell as many products as they did before the change. Therefore, you have a slight dip before the takeoff begins again.

In 1991, I founded Youngevity, and after two years of research and development, started selling product in late 1993. While I had extensive experience in previous start-ups, as well as acquisitions of other businesses, I prepared a very thorough business plan. Although people who reviewed this business plan were very impressed, I knew that once I got the company rolling, the pro forma numbers wouldn't be anything like the real ones, due to the items mentioned earlier.

Sure enough, we came out with the latest and greatest compensation plan, only to find that new distributors we were slowly bringing in weren't as enthused about it as we were. Needless to say, the six-color brochures went into the dumpster, and $10,000 later we had designed a new compensation plan, new brochures, and had to do another printing. Not only were expenses higher than expected, income was lower because it took longer than I had planned to attract distributors.

The moral of this story is that in any new business venture, once you have budgeted your pro forma capital, *increase it* because you will find that expenses will be higher than you had planned and income will be lower. The only way to survive is with more capital. You will learn very quickly in the business world that cash is king!

Product Is King

By Keith Harding

CEO, Sportron International, Dallas, Texas

If you are going to be successful for the long term, product must be king. There is always a company who can give more, and unless you have a product that distributors are bonded to—you will come and go. It is of utmost importance that the products do what you say they will do, and that they work. If you say the products help people lose weight, then they must help people do that. If you say consumers will have more energy, then the product must deliver on that claim.

You must have a business plan before you start the company operations. After you do your business plan, expect half of the revenues you project, and double the expenses you planned for the first two years.

The Success Formula

In reviewing important aspects of the Success Formula as discussed by those who have been there, they say: Listen to the sales force; remember that your distributors are your customers; develop a compelling and crystallized story and tell it often; build on relationships to grow the business; have lots of capital; and make product king. While all of these things have been mentioned in other chapters, it's best to hear them straight from someone at the top.

AN EDUCATOR'S PERSPECTIVE

I N THIS CHAPTER I would like for you to see how an educator perceives the industry. Because this particular educator serves as a member of the Board of Directors of the Direct Selling Education Foundation, he has great insights into direct selling and network marketing. He shares his observations on how the industry provides ongoing education to professors, students, and consumers.

Raymond W. "Buddy" LaForge is the Brown-Forman Professor of Marketing at the University of Louisville. He is the founding editor of the *Marketing Education Review;* he has coauthored *Marketing: Principles & Perspectives; Sales Management: Analysis and Decision Making; Marketing Interactive: Building Skills for Your Career* (in press); and *The Professional Selling Skills Workbook;* and he coedited *Emerging Trends in Sales Thought and Practice* (in press). His research is published

195

in many journals, including the *Journal of Marketing*, *Journal of Marketing Research*, *Journal of the Academy of Marketing Science*, and *Journal of Personal Selling and Sales Management*.

Buddy currently serves on the Direct Selling Education Foundation Board of Directors, DuPont Corporate Marketing Faculty Advisory Team for the Sales Enhancement Process, Family Business Center Advisory Board, Board of Trustees of the Sales and Marketing Executives International Accreditation Institute, and the Strategic Planning Committee for the National Conference in Sales Management, as vice president of marketing for the American Marketing Association Academic Council, and as associate editor for the Sales Education and Training section of the *Journal of Personal Selling and Sales Management*. He is coauthoring *Professional Selling: Text and Workbook*, and he is establishing The Sales Professional Network to link sales faculty, students, and executives to improve sales careers, education, research, and practice.

As you can see, Buddy LaForge has an impressive résumé, and I can tell you he is a joy to know. He is always willing to share with others, and I know you will learn from his perspective on the industry.

The Direct Selling Industry: An Educator's Perspective

by Buddy LaForge

I attended an Academic Seminar held by the Direct Selling Education Foundation in 1983. The two-day seminar brought marketing professors and direct selling executives together to discuss the direct selling industry. This was my first exposure to direct selling and the beginning of a long-term relationship. Since 1983 I have been involved in a variety of DSEF activities and currently serve on the DSEF Board of Directors.

During this period, I have worked and developed friendships with many direct selling executives that include Dick Bartlett of Mary Kay; Dick DeVos of Amway; John Fleming from Avon Products; Stan Fredrick of Colesce Coutures; John Frere from World Book; Erick Laine of CUTCO/Vector; Alan Luce from DK Family Learning; Charlie Orr of Shaklee; Neil Offen, president of the Direct Selling Association in the United States; and Bob King, who was instrumental in founding and served as past chairman of the World Federation of Direct Selling Associations. These experiences have given me an insight into the direct selling industry in general and the practices of specific companies.

The purpose of this article is to share this insight with you. I'll begin by discussing what DSEF is and what it does. Then I'll examine the development and implementation of a Code of Ethics by the direct selling industry via the DSA. The article concludes with several personal observations and recommendations for those establishing or involved in direct selling companies.

The Direct Selling Education Foundation

The Direct Selling Education Foundation was established twenty-five years ago. Its current mission statement is:

> To serve the public interest with education, information, and research, thereby enhancing acceptance and public awareness of direct selling in the global marketplace.

DSEF achieves this mission through consumer and academic programs. Because my personal experiences are with the academic programs, I will only provide a general overview of the consumer programs. I will, however, discuss the academic programs in detail.

Consumer Programs

The DSEF's consumer programs are designed to assist consumer advocates and their organizations in mounting and operating programs in the consumer's interest. They deal with important current consumer issues. DSEF helps consumer groups, such as state consumer affairs departments, to achieve their goals by increasing public awareness of consumer issues and promoting consumer protection measures. Current important consumer issues include the safety of food and drugs, security and privacy issues on the Internet, credit card usage, the environmental impact of products, and telemarketing fraud. Some examples of DSEF consumer programs are:

o An interactive satellite conference on telemarketing fraud cosponsored by the South Carolina Department of Consumer Affairs; the Howard County, Maryland, Office of Consumer Affairs; and the DSEF. Broadcast over public and university television systems, the program reached thousands of senior citizens, university students, and government officials.

o The DSEF organized the third Transnational Consumer Protection in North America conference. This conference was held in Mexico City and examined consumer rights under regional and national trade agreements such as NAFTA.

o The DSEF brought government and private consumer advocates to the University of Utah campus. They taught six hundred students in fifteen classes about the key consumer issues facing the nation today.

This glimpse of consumer programs highlights some of the DSEF's important work. The success of these programs is evident from the remarks of Alan Kennedy, past chairman of the Direct Selling Association and DSEF:

"Our industry is now regarded by consumer advocates as a partner, not a problem. . . . Because of our efforts to keep consumer advocates informed, we are able to prosper and grow both domestically and internationally."

Academic Programs

The basic objective of DSEF academic programs is to educate marketing professors about the direct selling industry. These marketing professors, in turn, educate students and other professors about direct selling through classes, textbooks, cases, and journal publications. Marlene Futterman, DSEF executive director, has developed close relationships with marketing professors around the world. Because of these relationships, leading marketing professors such as Jerry Albaum (University of Oregon), Larry Chonko (Baylor University), Morris Mayer (University of Alabama), Bob Peterson (University of Texas), and Tom Wotruba (San Diego State University) have worked with the DSEF for many years. The major academic initiatives are academic seminars, academic symposia, classroom materials, and the Direct Selling Days on Campus program.

Academic Seminars Academic seminars are held on a regular basis. These seminars bring marketing professors and direct selling executives together to discuss the direct selling industry. The seminars are of two basic types. One is an introductory seminar designed to establish relationships with marketing professors. Similar to the one I attended in 1983, these seminars introduce marketing professors to the direct selling industry. Direct selling executives typically present general industry information and specific company practices over a two-day period. Professors from more than 125 universities have attended these introductory marketing seminars.

The second type is an advanced academic seminar. These seminars are intended to expand relationships with marketing professors who have previously attended an introductory seminar. Although different formats have been used, the typical approach is to have the attending professors and executives discuss a case about a direct selling company. Typically, an executive presents a case study about a direct selling company with accompanying materials. Breakout groups of professors and executives discuss the case and present their recommendations to the entire group.

A new type of advanced seminar was introduced in 1996. This CEO/Professor Seminar included direct selling CEOs and marketing professors who had attended the introductory and advanced seminars. The seminar topic was "How to Preserve Relationship Marketing in an Era of High Tech Global Communications." A mixture of general and breakout sessions was used to discuss the key issues of relevance to direct selling companies. This type of seminar was very successful and is likely to be continued in the future.

Academic Symposia Academic symposia differ from academic seminars in several ways. The symposia are held on an irregular basis, usually span three or more days, and have a larger group of participants. Each symposium focuses on a specific topic and generates a publication summarizing its results. I have attended three of these symposia.

"Retailing in the Year 2000" was held in 1990 at the University of Texas in Austin. Distinguished professors and retailing executives made presentations on basic retailing topics including direct selling. The attending professors and executives then met in small groups to formulate recommendations and predictions concerning the retail marketplace in 2000. Presentations from the symposium were published in a book titled *The Future of U.S. Retailing: An Agenda for the 21st Century,* edited by Bob Peterson (University of Texas). Dick Bartlett of Mary Kay and Bob Peterson wrote "A Retailing Agenda for the Year 2000" as a conclusion to the book. A brochure, "How to Achieve Retailing Leadership by the Year 2000," was also published.

The symposium "Non-Store Retailing" was held in Berlin in 1993. Marketing professors and direct selling executives from the United States and Europe attended this symposium. Presentations and discussions focused on the growth of non-store retailing with special attention to challenges and opportunities for direct sellers. Symposium presentations were published in a proceedings titled *Non-Store Retailing: An International Perspective on Issues and Opportunities in an Evolving Industry*, edited by Bart Weitz (University of Florida) and Jerry Albaum (University of Oregon).

The most unique academic symposium was held in the Czech Republic in 1995. Direct selling executives and marketing professors from the United States and Central and Eastern Europe met in Prague and at the Czech Management Center in Celakovice to examine direct selling issues. A major focus of the symposium was for the U.S. professors to share their direct selling knowledge and teaching approaches with European colleagues. The symposium presentations were published in a proceedings titled *Direct Selling in Central and Eastern Europe*, edited by Tom Wotruba (San Diego State University).

These symposia are beneficial to both academic and direct selling participants. Marketing professors learn more about direct selling, while direct sellers are exposed to the latest marketing thinking on specific topics. Both groups learn from each other and develop closer relationships based on mutual benefit.

Classroom Materials Although the publications cited above are often used by marketing professors, the DSEF also promotes the development of specific classroom materials. One approach is to support the writing of cases on direct selling companies. The DSEF typically provides a modest grant for expenses and often helps to link the case writer with a direct selling company. The completed cases are usually published in various marketing textbooks. More than fifty direct selling cases have been published in marketing textbooks to date.

Another effort is the development of videotapes about direct selling for use in marketing classrooms. The videos are produced by the DSEF and distributed directly to selected professors and indirectly as supplements to marketing textbooks. The first tape, "The Personal Touch," was an introduction to direct selling funded by sixteen direct selling companies. Marv Jolson (University of Maryland) wrote teaching notes to suggest how the video could be used in different marketing classes.

The second video, "Direct Selling in the Global Marketplace," emphasized the global nature of direct selling and examined issues involved in international marketing. A specific case study of the international experiences of CUTCO was also included. Amway Corporation provided funding and Larry Chonko (Baylor University) prepared teaching suggestions for professors.

A third video is in development. This video will address issues within the direct selling industry. Since many ethical issues involve areas outside of marketing, this video is expected to be used in marketing and other business courses. It should be completed in 1998.

Direct Selling Days on Campus Direct Selling Days on Campus is a program where direct selling executives visit a campus to talk with professors and teach various classes over a two-day period. The program has been held at many universities, including the University of Texas, Baylor University, San Diego State University, University of California at Los Angeles and at Fullerton, University of Missouri at Columbia, Northern Michigan University, University of Alabama, University of Florida, University of Dayton, and University of Central Florida. My school, the University of Louisville, participated in the program in November 1996. The results were outstanding, with both students and professors learning a great deal about the direct selling industry.

One of the reasons for the success of Direct Selling Days on Campus is the participation and preparation of direct selling executives. Each executive normally teaches four to five classes during the two-day period. These classes are usually part of different courses, which requires personal contact and planning with several professors prior to coming to campus. Some of the most recognized executives who have taught these classes are Jim Preston, CEO and chairman of the board of Avon Products, Inc.; Dick Bartlett, vice chairman of Mary

Kay, Inc.; John Frere, president of World Book International; Rick Goings, chairman and CEO of Tupperware; Jerry Heffel, CEO of The Southwestern Company; Chris Pair, EVP and COO of Herbalife; and Erick Laine, president and chairman of the board of CUTCO. In addition, countless other individuals from DSA member companies have given their time to make this program a success.

The DSEF is clearly valuable to the direct selling industry and direct selling companies. Many marketing professors have minimal knowledge about direct selling and often have negative perceptions. DSEF programs provide direct selling knowledge, and change perceptions. Marketing professors now talk favorably about direct selling in their classes. Examples of and cases about direct selling companies are now routinely included in many marketing textbooks. Direct selling executives now speak at marketing professor conferences and are quoted in marketing textbooks. The DSEF leverages its resources by teaching marketing professors, who then teach students about direct selling.

The DSA Code of Ethics

"Good ethics is good business" is the guiding principle for leading direct selling companies. Realizing this, the Direct Selling Association developed an industry Code of Ethics in 1970 and has amended it on a regular basis. Initial and continuing membership in DSA requires direct selling companies to agree to abide by this code. An interesting historical discussion of the development of this Code of Ethics is available in *Moral Suasion: Development of the U.S. Direct Selling Association Industry Code of Ethics* written by Tom Wotruba (San Diego State University) and published by the DSEF.

The purpose of the Code of Ethics is eloquently stated in its preamble:

> The Direct Selling Association, recognizing that companies engaged in direct selling assume certain responsibilities toward consumers arising out of the personal-contact

203

method of distribution of their products and services, hereby sets forth the basic fair and ethical practices to which member companies of the association will continue to adhere in the conduct of their business.

The code specifically outlines ethical practices related to communicating with consumers, recruiting salespeople, terms of sales, warranties and guarantees, seller identification and buyer privacy, inventory purchases, and earnings representations. Procedures for administering the code are also presented in detail. A code administrator, who has the power and independence to enforce code violations, implements these procedures. The DSA Code of Ethics has "teeth," and provides direct selling companies with ethical guidelines for conducting their business.

Since the direct selling industry has experienced and continues to experience tremendous international growth, the need to expand to and maintain ethical standards in international markets became evident. With this in mind, the World Federation of Direct Selling Associations was founded in 1978. The World Federation currently consists of fifty National Direct Selling Associations around the world that exchange information and promote principles similar to the U.S. DSA. The WFDSA embarked on the difficult task of developing ethical guidelines for direct selling and network marketing around the world. The result of this effort was the establishment of World Codes of Conduct for Direct Selling. This code consists of two parts. One is the World Direct Selling Code of Conduct Toward Consumers; the other is the World Direct Selling Code of Conduct Toward Direct Sellers, Between Direct Sellers, and Between Companies.

These codes establish ethical practices for different direct selling constituency groups and have been approved by Direct Selling Associations around the world. It is a requirement that each national association that participates in the World Federation appoint and maintain a code administrator. Additionally, because the U.S. code contains extra territorial provisions (which means it covers business operations in countries without an in-country DSA organization), members of the U.S. DSA agree to be bound by the U.S. Code of Ethics in those extended countries, too.

The establishment and enforcement of ethical codes for direct selling around the world is an important accomplishment. Successful direct selling companies are built on strong relationships with their distributors and customers. Ethical behavior is the foundation for these relationships. Since a few bad apples can ruin the barrel for everyone, the DSA and WFDSA codes are important to worldwide direct selling, and the preservation of ethical direct selling and network marketing companies everywhere.

Observations and Recommendations

My experiences with direct selling during the past fourteen years have been enjoyable and rewarding. I have met many wonderful people and learned a great deal about a very unique industry. The direct selling industry has a proud heritage and a promising future. For those of you starting or building a direct selling or network marketing company, I offer several recommendations.

First, learn about the historical development of the direct selling industry. A good way to do this is by reading *Direct Selling in the United States: A Commentary and Oral History* written by Morris Mayer (University of Alabama) and published by the DSEF. The author conducted thirty in-depth interviews with industry leaders, many of whom are founders of long-term successful direct selling companies. The information obtained from these interviews is synthesized into a discussion of the nature of the direct seller, the characteristics of the direct selling industry, the importance of corporate culture in the industry, and the future of direct selling. I can think of no better way to develop an understanding of where direct selling has been, is, and is likely to be in the future than by reading this monograph.

Second, join the Direct Selling Association and participate in its activities. This is the association for direct sellers and network marketers in the United States. DSA membership offers your company credibility, and it is an important factor in the eyes of potential distributors and consumers because of the rigorous membership screening process and the strict enforcement of its Code of Ethics. Many checklists prepared for potential distributors to review before signing on with a company include this qualification because membership in the DSA enhances the company's reputation. Led by President Neil Offen, the association provides members with useful industry statistics, effective lobbying efforts, and various educational opportunities. Participation in association activities will make it possible for you to meet and network with executives from leading direct selling companies. You can learn more about the DSA by visiting its Web site at www.dsa.org.

Third, support the DSEF. Your support can come in two forms. The DSEF's operating budget comes largely from contributions made by DSA member firms. Although these financial contributions are important, DSEF programs also require the participation of executives from direct selling companies. The many successful DSEF programs discussed earlier owe much of their success to the active role played by direct selling executives. Many direct selling executives take time from very busy schedules to participate in DSEF activities. They do this because they know that the DSEF makes an important difference for the direct selling industry and their companies. They also benefit from the programs through the interaction with marketing professors and executives from other direct selling companies.

Finally, never stop learning. The business environment is extremely complex and turbulent. New technologies are constantly being developed and improved. What is successful today may not be successful tomorrow. Although the personal contact between a customer and direct seller will remain at the core of this business, new technologies and new approaches are being integrated with these direct selling efforts in various ways. The use of the Internet and intranets is just beginning, but will undoubtedly increase in the future. Learning must be ongoing for continuous success in the global and dynamic direct selling industry. The DSA and DSEF provide many learning opportunities for direct sellers.

The Success Formula

As we have seen, education is significant to the Success Formula. Because there are so many entities and individuals who may have misconceptions about the industry, it is important that everyone involved helps to educate others to ensure a better understanding of what we have to offer. Also, joining the Direct Selling Association and contributing to the Direct Selling Education Foundation, as well as participating in their educational seminars, serves as a way to keep yourself updated on industry-wide issues. Because executives of member companies are open to sharing ideas with one another, and new members are assigned an executive mentor from an established company, you can also pick up inside tips to apply to your business and help accelerate its success.

THE TEN MOST COMMON MISTAKES

Objective

I N THIS CHAPTER you will learn some of the common mistakes to avoid as you begin to build your business. Dan Jensen, CEO of Jenkon International, shares these words to the wise to help you avoid pitfalls he has observed over a long span of time. Adhering to these warnings can save you time, money, and even your business's future.

The Ten Most Common Mistakes in MLM

By Dan Jensen

Multilevel/network marketing is the essence of free enterprise. Thousands of MLM companies have sprouted during the last few decades. Sadly, many are no longer in business. Having been entrenched in the MLM industry for over a decade, seeing hundreds of companies come and go, I have observed a pattern that might be of help to an entrepreneur wanting to build a successful MLM organization in today's competitive marketplace.

This pattern includes at least ten common mistakes that weaken these start-up ventures, often to the point of tragic failure. While there are many reasons for failure, it is my hope that by understanding some of the more common mistakes, an aspiring MLM business owner might have a better chance at success than those who failed to see the picture clearly. These common mistakes are:

1. Inadequate funding
2. No business plan
3. Poor management and leadership
4. Poor staff training
5. Computer systems that don't work
6. Poor compensation plan
7. Failing to have the plan reviewed legally
8. Poor customer service
9. No corporate marketing personality on the road
10. Growing too fast

While these mistakes are not in any particular order, they carry with them differing levels of severity. For example, while a poor compensation plan can become a major obstacle to the success of the organization, it isn't too difficult to correct the problem by changing the plan to make it a good one. Lack of funding, however, can quickly force a company out of business, sometimes within a few weeks. Both problems can be fatal, but one is easier to correct than the other. Let's review these mistakes in more detail.

Mistake 1: Inadequate Funding

Let's suppose you want to build a house and have borrowed $150,000 to complete the project. You have $50,000 of your own money to add to the mortgage and expect the house to cost no more than $200,000. During the construction, you encountered a few unforeseen problems. While digging the basement, a water spring was found that had to be capped and routed to a different part of the property. Cost: $8,000. Lumber prices rose 30 percent from the time you started the project. Cost: $12,000. You upgraded the carpeting hoping to make up the difference in other areas. Cost: $9,000. As you neared the end of the project, no matter how hard you tried, you couldn't get the house complete without another $40,000. You've already borrowed as much as you can to get the $150,000. You have no more money of your own. What will you do?

So it is with starting a business. Many well-intentioned entrepreneurs embark on a long journey to prosperity full of hopes and dreams. As they journey along the road, they hit a few "springs," and find that many things cost far more than expected. They make a few mistakes that are expensive to fix, and soon find they didn't budget enough money to get the business off the ground. These people always emerge from the experience learning a golden rule of business: *Know how much money you need and secure the funds before you start.*

How do people find enough capital to start an MLM business, and how much do they need? Finding the necessary funding will take a well-prepared business plan (see below) that is not only reviewed by potential investors or financial institutions, but will also determine the amount of financing needed. No banks or investors will be willing to risk their money without a plan.

Common sources for funding include:

○ *Home equity financing* through banks, savings and loans, etc.

○ *Venture capital* organizations that specialize in helping new businesses. This type of investor or investor group will expect a significant ownership position for taking the risk. Venture capital groups are found by networking with

211

financial planners, accountants, bankers, and specialists in mergers and acquisitions.

○ *Private investors,* including friends, business associates, friends of friends, etc. Find them by networking with everyone you know. Talk to financial planners, accountants, business owners, and others.

○ *Small Business Administration* or other federal and state agencies. These agencies will either loan the money, or guarantee a loan through a bank. In either case, you'll need to be able to pay back the loan on a set schedule.

○ *Local community bond funding.* Some communities, especially those with high unemployment rates, work aggressively with businesses to help them acquire funding for starting or expanding. Contact local county and state agencies to see if programs are available in your area.

○ *General bank financing.* Banks will often lend based on credit history and assets with a personal guarantee of the business owner or another credit-worthy third party.

Don't become impatient and launch the business without the necessary funding! How much funding is necessary will depend on your business plan. Some companies start for as little as $10,000, while others find they require several million dollars.

As my father wisely told me when I started Jenkon, consider every dollar in the beginning as being worth five dollars later on. Save your precious start-up capital as if your life depends on it.

Mistake 2: No Business Plan

The business plan is the blueprint of your success. Companies that are successful without a plan gain their success more by accident and luck than by design and thought. Which type of success do you want? Are you willing to trust luck for your success? A business plan is the "first creation" of the business, just like an architect's blueprint is the first creation of a beautiful home. A good architect will plan out every detail of a home long before the first shovel of earth is moved. So it must be with any MLM business. You must become a business architect before you build the business.

Another aspect of the business plan is that it is often used to attract potential investors, lenders, and vendors. No investors will be willing to risk their hard-earned money on a business venture without a well-designed plan. You shouldn't either! As you establish credit with vendors, they will be more generous granting credit if they can review a well-prepared business plan. Remember that any credit granted by vendors reduces your starting capital requirements; if your manufacturer is willing to extend ninety-day terms up to $100,000 for product, you will need $100,000 less to start.

Key elements of a business plan are:

○ *An overview*—one or two pages describing the business— will help a potential investor become interested in learning more about the opportunity. If an overview is missing, few investors will be interested enough to take the time to read the entire plan. The overview should describe the products or services being sold, the principals involved, funds required to launch, and estimated return on investment, both conservative and potential. This overview is also known as the *Executive Summary.*

○ *Background of principals,* which is a summary résumé of the owners and executives of the company, is a critical part of a business plan that will be read by investors, banks, and other trade creditors.

○ *A mission statement* that clearly identifies what the company is all about should be included. It's been said that *distributors will work for money, but kill for a cause.* Your mission statement should be something you can proudly display in literature or on a wall plaque. A corporate motto might be taken from the mission statement. Most mission statements are expressed in one or two paragraphs. You can find samples of mission statements in annual stockholder reports of many public companies. There are a number of books, such as *The 7 Habits of Highly Effective People,* available that also teach how to write and use a mission statement.

○ *Goals and objectives* should be identified and each should spring from the mission statement. Goals might reflect the level of customer satisfaction, order turnaround, staff efficiency, but most certainly sales and profits.

○ *A market analysis* must be done to determine the potential of the product or service, priced as it is to be priced. The analysis should address market demand, similar products and how they have been accepted and marketed, competition, and so on. This information can be found in libraries and universities, and is provided by other business consulting groups. The Small Business Administration has access to large amounts of information, or people who can get the information for you. Many universities have students who would love to do market research for businesses, often at no charge, for their MBA requirements.

○ *Implementation plans* include answers to questions such as how much office space will you need? How many employees will be needed to handle the expected business volumes? Warehouse space, telephone equipment, initial product orders, printing, distributor kits, videos, and scores of other issues must be addressed in as much detail as possible. This section may be the most important section of all; it is usually the one people try to gloss over. It's more fun to make sales projections than to figure out how much office space is needed. But one major mistake in this area can cost tens (or hundreds) of thousands of dollars. This part of the plan takes time, often several months. Time spent here will pay large dividends in the future.

○ *Profit/loss and cash flow projections* are critical to every business plan. A competent consultant or accountant can assist in this effort by identifying common areas of expenses for start-up businesses. With computer programs like Lotus 1-2-3, Microsoft Excel, and other spreadsheet analysis systems, many different scenarios can be created once an initial spreadsheet format is built. Always prepare a pessimistic worst-case scenario, a middle-of-the-road scenario, and an optimistic (but realistic) best-case version. As you develop your business plan, always plan on the conservative side, but be ready to upscale into the more optimistic version should the need arise. Remember that if potential investors have read the overview, the next thing they'll want to know is how much money is needed. These projections are critical to prospective investors.

○ A *return-on-investment* analysis is also important for those investing into the business. This analysis tells them why they would want to take the risk. Attractive charts and graphs are essential. This section answers the investor's question "What's in it for me?"

○ The *risk analysis study* explains the risks involved. While this section is not intended to turn off a potential investor, most investors will do their own risk analysis anyway—but with only the bits and pieces of information available. This is an opportunity for you to address an investor's potential concerns in a positive and controlled fashion. If you don't need an investor, this section will make your business plan more bulletproof. No plan is viable that hasn't addressed the potential points of failure and risk.

Once the plan is complete, bind it to make an attractive presentation. Include a table of contents, index tabs, and an impressive cover. Don't put the plan on the shelf! Use it in each manager's meeting; refer to it like the corporate bible. Change it when needed, but follow it carefully.

Part of the business plan, of course, is to plan to be a profitable company. It's amazing how many companies fail to plan to be profitable.

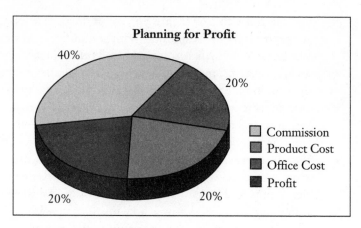

A general rule might be:

40 percent of income for commissions to the field

20 percent of income for cost of goods or products

20 percent of income for administrative expense
(payroll, facilities, utilities, etc.)

20 percent of income for profit

While these numbers are very rough, they have proven to be the target that many successful companies have set.

Mistake 3:
Poor Management and Leadership

No business can rise to the pinnacle of success and sustain it without effective management and leadership. Stephen R. Covey wrote in *The 7 Habits of Highly Effective People:* "Leadership is doing the right things. Management is doing things right." But the graveyard of free enterprise is littered with the bones of companies who were poorly managed or poorly led. Most often, the mismanagement started with an enthusiastic business owner with little or no experience believing that he or she could handle the job. While there are many who launch businesses very successfully, there are few who have the skills to *sustain that success.*

A wise business owner must be honest about his or her own shortcomings and hire talent that makes up the difference. The owner must then empower the hired talent to do their job effectively; don't hire skilled people and then ignore their wisdom and talent!

Once effective managers are empowered to handle the operations, it is the role of the business owner to lead the business. Leadership encompasses planning, reviewing results, promoting, and motivating. Let the managers do their jobs according to the business plan, which becomes the yardstick by which the managers are measured.

Mistake 4: Poor Staff Training

What NBA basketball team would recruit a new player, place him on the floor his first day, and expect him to perform like the rest of the team? Without training with the rest of the team, his performance, at best, would be mediocre. At worst, disastrous, and the game would be lost.

Such it is with any new employee, especially if the whole staff is new, as they often are in a new business launch. Who should train them? What should they be trained to do? How do we know if they have completed their training? Let's address these questions individually.

Who Should Train New Employees?

Don't let the old adage *the blind leading the blind* be used to describe your trainers. If you are a start-up company, find competent people for each department and enlist an experienced general manager to orchestrate the various departments like a symphony. Don't be led into the trap of saving money on inexpensive workers in the beginning; it will cost you far more than it saves.

One critical department that needs to be trained is order processing. This group is charged with taking orders over the phone and receiving orders by mail and fax. They are in constant contact with field distributors and portray an image of your business to everyone they talk to. If you hire educated, warm, and friendly people, your image will be enhanced. If you hire minimum-wage clerks to take orders, they will portray a much less impressive image. These people must be screened during the hiring process for personality traits, patience with frustrated callers, and their ability to think on their toes. They must be trained by others who are of the highest level of competence; don't let them receive training from less experienced peers.

The second most critical department is distributor services. Each person in this department will handle problems, complaints, inquiries, and a thousand other issues that arise. These people must comprise an elite SWAT team with an obsession for customer service excellence. They must be trained by those with a similar obsession for excellence.

Where will you find experienced people to do the training if your company is just starting? Look to consultants, trade organizations such as the MLMIA and the DSA for names, and advertise in industry publications. Working with executive search firms can often be fruitful as well.

What Should They Be Trained to Do?

As an experienced person is hired to supervise a department, his or her first task is to design and document a *system,* or method of operation. For example, to process sales orders, a diagram of how an order must flow through the office could be created. Each exception—and how to proceed—should be noted in a flowchart or diagram. What should an order entry operator do if the credit card is declined while the caller is on the phone? What should a warehouse person do if some of the products ordered are not in stock? Every conceivable problem must be documented in advance with an appropriate solution. Policies need to be documented and organized into a handbook for the staff. They might even be put online on the office computer system for instant lookup. Professional MLM consultants can be an invaluable source to help prepare these flowcharts and documentation.

Once the systems, policies, and procedures are documented, training can begin. With documented systems in place, training proceeds quickly and thoroughly. Without systems, policies, and procedures, training can never be complete, and takes many times longer.

How Do We Know If the Employee Has Been Trained?

An evaluation process should be established that takes a new employee through a sequence of duties and responsibilities. For example, an order entry operator might be required to take ten phone orders with a supervisor at his or her side before being allowed to take an order alone. A distributor services representative might not be allowed to handle commission-related questions until he or she has explained the compensation plan to the department supervisor thoroughly, top to bottom. Each department must also establish a minimum level of competence before allowing employees to perform their assigned tasks alone. Until then, employees should be buddied up with another peer or supervisor. Many companies require employees to take tests that focus on the various objectives of each job. The tests are then scored to determine if an employee has been adequately trained. The best tests focus on the *objectives* rather than on the mechanics of the job.

Mistake 5:
Computer Systems That Don't Work

In the section on training, I addressed the need to have good systems that, if followed, comprise the methods to handle each type of business transaction, whether the transaction is a sales order, a phone inquiry, a complaint, or the return of product for a refund. Computer systems in multilevel marketing companies become the glue that binds the office departments together, a core around which the business is built. No successful MLM company has ever sustained its success without a well-designed computer system. Likewise, there are many MLM companies that have failed due primarily to the lack of a good computer system. Don't let your new venture become another statistic. Choose your software vendor wisely.

There are three major pieces that any MLM/network marketing company's computer system should have:

1. *The equipment, or hardware,* comprises the main processor, which does the "thinking," a disk drive to store the business

information, workstation screens, and printers for reports. Fortunately, the cost of equipment has declined drastically in recent years while the performance, or capacity to process business information, has increased many times.

2. *The operating system software* makes the computer work when you turn it on. It comprises the programming language that the business software is written in, the commands necessary to create a backup tape of data to avoid losing all the information, and many other commands necessary to keep the computer working as conditions change. Without an operating system, the computer is nothing but plastic, metal, chips, and silicon. Operating systems include MS-DOS, UNIX, PICK, VMS, AIX, and scores of others.

3. *The application software* is the most important part of the system because it is the piece that determines how you will run your business. The hardware and the operating system are of little importance compared to the application software. This software provides input screens for order processing, creates your commission checks, prints down-line genealogy reports, and provides lookup information to handle distributor inquiries when they call the office. In short, this software is the core of running your business successfully. It will make or break an MLM business.

The greatest mistake companies make with regard to computer systems is to think they can save money by writing their own software. Not only does this take months or years to do, but it can never include the experience and know-how that packaged MLM software contains. Why reinvent the wheel? Would it be worth the risk of losing the business to poorly designed software that causes incorrect commission checks, errors in tracking a person's down-line records, lost orders, and so forth? Companies that elect to write their own MLM software often find later on that they are vulnerable to the programmer who wrote it. What if he or she moves away, or becomes injured or sick? Never let someone convince you he or she can program an MLM software system in weeks or months. It's never been done successfully before. Why should you believe it could be done now? Companies such as Jenkon have spent many years writing MLM software that works right the first time, every time, and offer it to the public for a small fraction of what it costs to create it. It's the best money you'll ever spend.

So how do you choose a good MLM software package? While this article will not address this subject fully, a few suggestions should be noted:

○ *Choose a reputable vendor.* There are many fly-by-night software companies that make many claims of experience, know-how, and software gadgetry. Unless you are willing to be a guinea pig, choose a vendor that has developed a proven track record. Track records are built over many years of working with MLM companies, not just selling a software package a few times. Indeed, only having a small handful of clients may speak more about a company's persuasive abilities than its actual know how and skill. *Above all, check out at least six of a vendor's references.* Remember that vendors will be eager to provide only their best references. Always get the names of other companies from these first references that you might call. You might be surprised to find a different story when you call companies not included in the reference list.

○ *Visit the software company's office.* When you choose an MLM software package, you not only choose the software, but you also choose the vendor's support services. If the vendor is not able to provide support services in an acceptable manner, what will you do when you need to change your compensation plan, or add a new input field to the order entry screen? Jenkon has serviced more than five hundred MLM companies since 1982 and has yet to find one company that has not needed support services. There is only one constant among all MLM companies: They constantly change things! While at the vendor's office, meet the people who will provide you with general customer service and technical support. What kind of people are they? How long have they worked for the

221

vendor? If you find that they are relatively new, it's likely that the vendor has little experience, is growing rapidly (in which case you may have trouble competing with other clients for good service), or has high staff turnover. All these can mean trouble for you as the vendor may not be able to handle your needs quickly and competently. Be willing to pay for experience and competence. You'll pay far less in the long run. If you think knowledge is expensive, try ignorance!

○ *Avoid very small software companies.* To compete with larger established firms, small software companies must offer software at bargain prices. This often puts them on shaky financial ground during their most critical years. Many MLM companies, trying to save money by purchasing software from these small software houses, find themselves abandoned later on when they need assistance. The problem is that servicing one highly successful client can consume virtually all of the human resources of a small software company, leaving the other clients out in the cold. It can take months (or years) to train competent software technicians on an MLM software package. The more deadly problem, however, is that smaller companies tend to go out of business without warning. The MLM industry is especially brutal on small software companies and has caused a number of firms to close their doors, leaving their clients high and dry. If you value your business, stay away from the small vendors and stick to those with staying power and track records.

○ *Buy a software package that allows you to create your own reports.* Many software packages force you to live only with those reports they put on the menus. Managers must resort to running large reports to answer small questions or concerns instead of being able to run small exception reports on demand. Small exception reports can be reviewed quickly and accurately. Large, general-purpose reports can take hours to review and digest—not a wise use of a manager's time. The computer industry has adopted a standard in modern software engineering that allows nonprogrammers to type free-form queries on a computer terminal. In response, the computer provides specific and focused information according to the query. For example, suppose a manager wants to see a list of all the distributors in Florida with a group volume of $5,000 or more. Most modern software systems would allow the manager to type a relatively simple command sentence to obtain the report.

○ *Make sure the company can program your compensation plan.* Compensation plans are complex and take massive amounts of experience to program properly. When you have your tax return prepared, do you go to an inexperienced person, or do you find the most competent one who is also reasonably priced? Compensation plan programming is not something inexperienced programmers should be doing.

○ *Do you plan to expand internationally someday?* If so, choose a software package that incorporates international issues such as currency conversion, language translation, cross-border sponsoring, value added tax reporting, and foreign address formats.

○ *Buy software that can work on bigger computers and a PC.* While personal computers are terrific for starting a new company, they are not cut out for larger successful MLM operations. Most personal computers allow only one person to use the computer at any given time. Networks allow PCs to be linked together and can grow to become quite powerful and large. Networks are good but expensive. Minicomputers allow less expensive workstations to be connected to more powerful systems, and are usually less complex to manage than networks. Most large MLM companies have either a minicomputer with several hundred workstations attached or larger mainframe computers. In either case, if you expect to be successful, don't limit yourself by choosing software that only runs on PCs. If you do, you will be forced to use networking to expand, which is the most expensive way to connect employees together.

○ *Compare features.* Software is designed to handle specific business issues and often has a great deal of difficulty dealing with matters outside designed limitations. It's difficult to force a software package to do things it was never intended to do. Wise computer buyers compare features and capabilities, side by side, of one package to another. Ask the vendor which features they consider are unique to their package compared to others. A package that is missing an important piece will never be a bargain at any price. As you compare software, use the feature list of the package that has the most to offer, and compare the features of the other packages to it, feature by feature. You'll be quite surprised as to how many holes the other packages have.

Remember that you aren't just buying a computer; you are buying software, expertise, emergency support services, programming services, and starting a long-term relationship. Choose your software vendor wisely. Out of all the aspects of a start-up MLM business, don't be tempted to penny-pinch in the computer area. If you do, you may cripple your chances for success.

Mistake 6: Poor Compensation Plan

A compensation plan that fails to motivate distributors can doom a company as fast as any other factor. Some people believe that a good compensation plan is the key element to success. But having observed many successful companies reach enviable sales volumes with poorly designed compensation plans, I have found this not to be the case. At the heart of the issue is the question "What makes a compensation plan good?" Let's address a few points.

○ *Reasonable compensation percentages.* Most compensation plans of today pay between 30 and 50 percent to field distributors. If a company promotes a plan paying only 25 percent or so, it will have a hard time recruiting and keeping distributors. Real percentage pay-out should fall between 35 and 42 percent, in my opinion. Theoretical pay-out (the percentage the plan would pay if all commissions were paid out in every case) should not be more than 8 percent above actual to avoid disappointing distributors expecting more.

○ *Keep it simple.* Unfortunately, many plans are designed by MLM professionals for MLM professionals. While experience is essential when designing a compensation plan, you must never forget that ordinary people must be motivated by it. The more complex a plan becomes, the fewer people it will motivate. The plan needs to affect the heart of a distributor first, before it can affect his or her pocketbook.

○ *Avoid novelty or fad plans.* Changing a compensation plan is costly in terms of lost momentum and distributor commitment. When a distributor recruits another person, the compensation plan is often a significant part of the selling process. To change it later is, in essence, admitting that the original plan was not very good after all. Some people may perceive the change as a bait-and-switch tactic. By staying within more traditional plans, plans that proved themselves over the years, a new MLM company can still be innovative but know that the plan has staying power. It's often joked that compensation plans are like men's ties: When one plan goes out of vogue, you can count on it coming back a few years later. Stick to more traditional plans that won't need to be changed as new fads come and go.

○ *Don't put too much credence in the impact of your compensation plan.* Many entrepreneurs come to Jenkon convinced that they have the best possible compensation plan imaginable. When asked what product or service they will sell, they say, "We're still looking for the right product." Obviously, these well-intentioned people have focused on only one issue of starting their business, thinking that the compensation plan is the key to their future

225

success. The facts, however, are different. Many companies have gained great success despite poorly designed compensation plans. Put simply, the plan is only *one* part of the puzzle; it isn't the *only* part.

o *Don't change it often.* Those that experiment with the compensation plan are asking for frustrated distributors to join other more stable opportunities. Even good change can be traumatic. Be very reluctant to change the plan.

o *Avoid recruiting "heavy hitters."* These highly successful MLM professionals can bring tremendous short-term success, but they can also be a major cause for failure when they grow bored with your company and join another, often taking thousands of people from their down-line with them. Wise companies always build slowly for the first few years until they have the critical mass to handle changes in business volumes. Don't design your compensation plan to focus on attracting these heavy hitters.

Mistake 7:
Failing to Have the Plan Reviewed Legally

While a compensation plan may motivate distributors, unless it is legal in every state or country where it will be used, it could put the company in jeopardy. There are many legal statutes that must be complied with in order to carry out an MLM business in any state or country. Those that affect multilevel marketing vary, and are well beyond the scope of this article (see Chapter 4, "Compensation Plans," and Chapter 16, "A Legal Primer"). Several major points, however, should be discussed:

o *Nobody should profit by recruiting another person.* Pyramid schemes are illegal and allow distributors to profit simply by recruiting people. Many companies avoid pyramid statutes by paying commissions solely on the sale of product (or services) and stipulating that people are not required to buy any commissionable product in order to join. Never pay commissions on distributor starter kits or other materials purchased as a condition of joining the company.

○ *Have a generous return policy.* "Inventory loading" is a term used to describe a distributor who buys too much product, more than can be sold in a reasonable period of time, to qualify for higher commission percentages. Many states have acted aggressively against this unethical practice. To avoid any association with inventory loading, many companies have instituted generous return policies that allow customers and distributors to return unused product. The Direct Selling Association has recently established a requirement for all company members to offer a twelve-month, 90 percent buy-back policy. Most companies are now adopting this rule and deduct commissions from distributors and their up-lines when products are returned. Incidentally, automatic calculation of commission adjustments for returned product is often considered a major requirement in a software package. Otherwise, it must be done manually, which costs hours of wasted time and leads to embarrassing mistakes.

○ *Sell products and services at a real market price.* If your products or services could not be sold without an MLM compensation plan attached, regulatory agencies will eventually take action. Imagine selling toothpaste for $10 a tube, but paying out $9 in commissions. While some people might be attracted to this scheme, it will most certainly demand the attention of consumer protection agencies as well.

○ *Make no claims of income.* While it's a tremendous temptation to explain the potential income available in your new venture, avoid it at all costs. Regulatory agencies are notorious for videotaping distributor meetings to gather evidence of unsubstantiated claims of income. If you mention any income statistics, then also mention the average income. It is not enough to simply tell the truth in this case. You must also avoid setting unrealistic expectations.

227

It is highly recommended that a new MLM company retain a well-seasoned attorney who specializes in MLM law to review their compensation plan.

Mistake 8: Poor Customer Service

Many companies enter the industry thinking they sell business opportunities and their products. They soon learn that they sell a third product, one of immense power: *customer service.* Distributors are fickle and seem to join the company that appears to offer the most compensation. One great discovery of our age, however, is that people love to be served well, and their loyalty is placed on those who service them best. Some MLM companies find that their average distributor stays active only six months. Others find it is several years. What's the difference between them? It's not the compensation plan. It's not the products they sell. Instead, it is how well the distributor is served.

Excellent customer service does not come by accident. It is the result of well-thought-out plans and hard work. It starts by having a very committed distributor services manager empowered to implement the necessary systems, policies, and procedures to achieve excellence. Your Customer Service Excellence system must comprise at least four areas:

o Customer information database

o Follow-up systems

o Satisfaction measurement

o Workload monitoring

Customer Information Database

In today's business world, customers have very high expectations for service. When a distributor calls the home office to ask for information, they expect to receive an answer immediately, not an hour later. With a customer information database, service reps on the phone can instantly access information that would otherwise take minutes or hours to find.

The goal of any customer information database is to know everything possible about the distributor that might be the source of a question. From order status to commission problems, the customer service software must provide instant answers to distributors as they call the office.

Follow-up Systems

If one thousand distributors were recruited this month, and ten thousand distributors had already joined, how many phone calls would they place with the home office? Statistically, well over one thousand phone calls would need to be answered by professional, courteous, and competent office staff during the month. Of the one thousand calls, how many would require a callback? It depends entirely on the quality extent of the customer information database. The better the online information, the fewer callbacks necessary. The goal of a good customer service system should be to have less than 5 percent of the calls requiring a callback. If 30 percent of the calls required callbacks, there would be at least three hundred opportunities for not following up and finishing the call.

Any customer service system that strives for excellence has a means of tracking each phone call to completion. Open calls can be tracked and aged with priority given to the oldest calls, or to the most important distributors. Such a system, often called an Event Management System, becomes the hub of any professional customer service system. In essence, it tracks each inbound phone call from the field and makes sure that every call is answered in a timely fashion. It provides the department manager with the reports needed to avoid having a call "open" too long.

Satisfaction Measurement

If you don't know how well your customer service people are doing, then you don't know what your company's future will be. If they are doing poorly, the company is doomed to failure. If the distributors rave about the excellent service they receive, you can be assured of future success. A customer service system must include the ability to track satisfaction levels. How is this done?

When a distributor phone call is logged and closed, a follow-up call is placed, or a survey letter is mailed to the distributor asking:

o Was your call answered in a timely manner?

o Was the customer service representative courteous and professional?

o Was your question answered to your satisfaction?

Questions such as these, when answered by field distributors, become invaluable in reaching the goal of customer service excellence. The best software packages today incorporate Customer Service Excellence Systems to make your obsession with excellence become a reality.

Workload Monitoring

No customer service department can survive increasing workloads for long without burnout. If you track the number of calls received each day, with the length of time it takes to handle the average call, expansion plans can be put in motion before workloads become critical. Distributors cannot be serviced with excellence if there are too few people to do the work. Once again, the task of measuring workload will require an excellent MLM software system.

Let customer service be your secret weapon for success. It takes planning, commitment, and hard work to achieve the excellence a successful company seeks.

Mistake 9: No Corporate Marketing Personality on the Road

What businessperson would start a new company and stay in the office waiting by the phone for customers to call? Time after time, the most successful MLM companies have proved the effectiveness of having corporate marketing people hold meetings on the road. Distributors need contact with corporate people for motivation, training, and especially, to help them recruit. There is no substitute for being in the field. Your success will be greatly enhanced by putting highly motivated corporate personalities on the road.

Complement an on-the-road campaign with effective videotapes that motivate, sell, and train. While nothing can substitute for meeting face to face, a videotape is the next best thing.

Mistake 10: Growing Too Fast

While most businesses would give their right arms to grow at exponential rates, MLM has a track record of just that. Unfortunately, this kind of growth has often been a major cause of the demise of many otherwise successful ventures. Success is wonderful, but it can bury you.

New businesses have new staff, new computer systems, new facilities, but they are short on the experience required to handle business efficiently. An office can only handle a certain volume of business. What if that volume is exceeded? Something must give. Many companies go on a spending spree, throwing money at their problems. At this stage cash seems to be unlimited. This too is a false security, for as surely as the growth came, it will level out, and eventually go downward for periods of time. It is far better to limit growth temporarily than to succumb to its demands.

Here are some ways you can control your MLM company's growth:

o Start locally by not accepting distributor applications from everywhere. Distributors who seek to join from unopened regions are simply given a courteous thank-you letter. Let them know how much you want to have them join, but that the opportunity isn't available yet in their area. Notify them when they can join.

o Don't sponsor road trips by corporate or field promoters right away. First take advantage of the less expensive local opportunities. Meetings can be held locally every night of the week for the cost of one meeting on the road.

o Don't recruit professional MLM promoters or heavy hitters. If they want to join, then they must join as any other distributor. Don't, however, go out of your way to recruit them.

o By controlling growth, a business plan can become a real guide to making the business profitable. Use the plan to make success become a reality.

Conclusion

Multilevel marketing offers incredible opportunities, but it also has a vast assortment of pitfalls and traps. By following these simple guidelines, your potential for success will improve dramatically. Those who have money to burn can ignore these rules. Those who must be careful and hit profit projections must give heed to these ten mistakes most often made by other MLM companies.

Life is too short to learn every lesson by ourselves. We are far wiser to observe others, and let their experiences teach us a better way.

The Success Formula

While this chapter explores the ten most common mistakes in MLM and tells you what to avoid, its principles should be reviewed as part of your overall thought process and education. Part of the Success Formula includes avoiding these common mistakes. Knowing what not to do can save you time and money, which is important to your success.

A LEGAL PRIMER

Objective

IN THIS CHAPTER, you will learn the basics about legal issues surrounding the operation of a multilevel or network marketing company. These sections are not intended to teach you everything about the law, but rather to give you topline information about some hot issues that can cause big problems if they're not considered. The primer is contributed by attorneys Kevin Grimes and Spencer Reese, partners in the premier law firm Grimes & Reese. The firm services a comprehensive list of companies in the multilevel/network marketing industry.

The firm's practice includes representing and advising multilevel marketing companies on all aspects of their business, including consumer protection, advertising law, litigation, contracts, marketing plan design, regulatory compliance,

233

trademark law, FDA law, policy development, and distributor compliance. Grimes & Reese is a supplier-member of the Direct Selling Association and the Professional Association of Network Marketers.

Both Kevin and Spencer have extensive knowledge of the laws governing the industry. Both are highly regarded experts by their numerous clients, and I personally think they are two of the finest human beings on Earth.

Legal Principles of Multilevel Marketing
By Kevin Grimes and Spencer Reese

Multilevel Marketing/Pyramids

Federal and state multilevel marketing and anti-pyramid statutes are components of a comprehensive consumer protection umbrella. These laws are designed to protect individuals from being defrauded through illegitimate programs that lure participants with the promise of easy money by compensating them from the investments of additional participants rather than from legitimate product sales. These programs have been called "Ponzi schemes," "airplane plans," "pyramids," "chain letters," and many other names. Although known in the United States only during the twentieth century, such programs have cost their participants hundreds of millions of dollars. Federal and state regulatory agencies have sought to proscribe such illegal activity in multiple ways, including the use of anti-pyramid, mail fraud, business opportunity, franchise, lottery, and securities laws. (Each of these areas will be discussed below.)

Whether a program is a legitimate multilevel marketing plan or an illegal pyramid depends principally on 1) the method by which the products or services are sold and 2) the manner in which participants are compensated. Essentially, if a marketing plan compensates participants for sales by their "enrollees," "recruits," and/or their down-line enrollees and recruits, that plan is multilevel. If a program compensates participants merely for the introduction or enrollment of other participants into the program, it is a pyramid.

Legislative Intent and Judicial Interpretation

As a practical matter, it is impossible for legislators to anticipate the infinite creativity of individuals who devise, implement, and promote legal and illegal marketing programs. Accordingly, anti-pyramid and multilevel statutes—like most consumer protection legislation—are drafted and interpreted very broadly so that they might encompass all of the possible permutations of an illegitimate scheme, and thus have a jurisdictional basis for regulating and eliminating them.

Is Your Program Multilevel?

Multilevel marketing companies must guard against being classified as pyramids on both the state and federal levels. Most states statutorily regulate multilevel activity. Federal regulation, on the other hand, is primarily a function of administrative and judicial decisions that arise from a series of private-party and Federal Trade Commission litigation.

State Statutory Approaches With regard to pyramids and multilevel marketing plans, state statutes have taken two distinct approaches. A sophisticated minority of state laws specifically define and regulate multilevel marketing plans. Georgia's statute provides a typical definition of a multilevel marketing company:

> "Multilevel distribution company" means any person, firm, corporation, or other business entity which sells, distributes, or supplies for a valuable consideration goods or services through independent agents, contractors, or distributors at different levels wherein such participants may recruit other participants and wherein commissions, cross-commissions, bonuses, refunds, discounts, dividends, or

other considerations in the program are or may be paid as a result of the sale of such goods or services or the recruitment, actions, or performances of additional participants.[1]

The definitions of a multilevel company or multilevel marketing plan in the other states that specifically define multilevel marketing are identical or very similar to Georgia's.

Broken into individual components, the elements that must be met to establish a multilevel company or multilevel marketing plan include those listed in Table 16.1.

Table 16.1 Elements of a Multilevel Compensation Plan

DOES YOUR PROGRAM MEET THESE ELEMENTS?

1) A person, firm, corporation or other business entity

2) which

   a) sells;

   b) distributes; or

   c) supplies[2]

3) for consideration

4) goods or services

5) through independent agents, contractors, or distributors

6) at different levels

7) participants may recruit other participants

8) compensation to participants is paid as a result of

   a) the sale of such goods or services; or

   b) the recruitment,[3] actions or performance of other participants

Is Your Program a Pyramid?

The vast majority of states utilize an indirect approach by defining a *pyramid, chain distributor scheme,* or *endless-chain scheme* and proscribing such programs. Regardless of the name used by the statutes, their intent is to prohibit plans or programs that reward participants on the basis of the recruitment or enrollment of other participants rather than compensating participants for sales of products or services to end consumers. For example, North Carolina defines a pyramid as:

> Any program utilizing a pyramid or chain process by which a participant gives a valuable consideration for the opportunity to receive compensation or things of value in return for inducing other persons to become participants in the program.[4]

New York's definition of a chain distributor scheme is more precise, but nevertheless representative of anti-pyramid statutes:

> [A] "chain distributor scheme" is a sales device whereby a person, upon condition that he make an investment, is granted a license or right to solicit or recruit for profit or economic gain one or more additional persons who are also granted such license or right upon condition of making an investment and may further perpetuate the chain of persons who are granted such license or right upon such condition. A limitation as to the number of persons who may participate, or the presence of additional conditions affecting eligibility for such license or right to recruit or solicit or the receipt of profits therefrom, does not change the identity of the scheme as a chain distributor scheme. As used herein, "investment" means any acquisition, for a consideration other than personal services, of property, tangible or intangible, and includes without limitation, franchises, business opportunities and services, and any other means, medium, form or channel for the transferring of funds, whether or not related to the production or distribution of goods or services. It does not include sales demonstration

equipment and materials furnished at cost for use in making sales and not for resale.[5]

Texas law contains a similar definition for endless chain schemes:

"Endless chain" means any scheme for the disposal or distribution of property whereby a participant pays a valuable consideration for the chance to receive compensation for introducing one or more additional persons into participation in the scheme or for the chance to receive compensation when a person introduced by the participant introduces a new participant.[6]

Anti-pyramid statutes provide that pyramids, endless chain schemes, or chain referral schemes are illegal. Thus, as long as a multilevel compensation plan does not fit within the parameters of the prohibited activities, it is permissible (as regards anti-pyramid laws).

Table 16.2 Elements of a Pyramid

DOES YOUR PROGRAM MEET THESE ELEMENTS?
1) A scheme, plan, or program;
2) for which a participant renders consideration to join;
3) for the right or chance to receive compensation or other things of value;
4) which is contingent upon the introduction of additional participants into the scheme, plan or program.

As long as your program does not satisfy the elements listed in Table 16.2, your program does not violate state anti-pyramid legislation.

Federal Administrative and Judicial Decisions There is no federal anti-pyramid statute in the United States.[7] Nevertheless, decisions of the Federal Trade Commission and the federal courts—more so than legislation from any individual state—have largely supplied the legal framework upon which multilevel marketing companies have developed their programs. The most often cited definition of a pyramid scheme is found in the Federal Trade Commission's decision in *In the Matter of Koscot Interplanetary, Inc.*[8] Therein the FTC held that entrepreneurial chains are characterized by "the payment by participants of money to the company in return for which they [the participants] receive 1) the right to sell a product and 2) the right to receive in return for recruiting other participants into the program rewards which are unrelated to sale of the product to ultimate users."

Table 16.3 Elements of a Pyramid (Federal Decisions)

DOES YOUR PROGRAM MEET THESE ELEMENTS?
1) Payment of money to the company;
2) the participant receives the right to sell a product (or service);
3) the participant receives compensation for recruiting others into the program;
4) the compensation is unrelated to the sale of products (or services) to the ultimate user.

Important Issues

The previous discussion and tables are representative of the pyramiding issues facing the multilevel marketing industry. Companies should be careful when developing their marketing plans to stay within the parameters of these laws. However, designing a program that strictly adheres to the literal terms of the law will not guarantee that the program will overcome all legal challenges. There are variables among the states in the definition of a pyramid scheme that may result in a program being entirely legal in one state but illegal in a neighboring state. In addition, judicial interpretation of a statute or a prior decision may result in a decision that is seemingly inconsistent with its literal terms. And finally, the law always looks to substance over form. If a program uses all of the right buzzwords in its marketing literature, but fails to enforce its policies that guard against pyramiding dangers, the program faces the same risks as a program that does not incorporate appropriate safeguards into its plan.

Although the inconsistencies among the states and federal law pose difficulties for companies designing a marketing plan, there are factors that both federal and state forums consider when conducting a pyramid analysis. Although these criteria are typically not specified by statute, they are taken into account because they provide evidence that the dangers posed by a pyramid scheme are mitigated.

Substantiatable Sales of Products to End Users Again, a program that compensates its participants for the mere act of recruiting or enrolling others into the program is a pyramid. Unscrupulous promoters have attempted to circumvent the traditional definition of a pyramid through a practice called *inventory loading*. Although participants in an inventory loading scenario are technically compensated for the sales of products, the sale is in actuality a subterfuge.

Under an inventory loading scenario, new recruits are required or pressured to purchase large quantities of products (often unconscionably overpriced and nonrefundable). This, in turn, produces a large "commission" for up-line participants. The emphasis in such a program is not on the sale of products, but rather on recruiting of new participants with the goal of "loading" them with as much inventory as possible. In addition, there is usually a substantial improbability that the average distributor would either use or be able to resell the quantity of goods that are involved in an inventory loading setting. Because of these factors, courts have consistently held that notwithstanding the "sale of products," such transactions are tantamount to a head-hunting or recruiting bonus, and thus constitute a pyramid. Accordingly, it is important that sales to distributors be reasonable in amount and price, and documented to reflect this.

Sales to "Ultimate Users" Many multilevel marketing companies wish to set up their programs so that distributors can receive commissions based on the purchase and consumption of products by members of their down-line, rather than based on retail sales to third parties. This is a logical approach, since one of the greatest deterrents to enrolling in a program stems from the general public reluctance to engage in sales. Moreover, under a literal interpretation of the *Koscot* definition of a pyramid, personal consumption satisfies the second element of the test because distributors can be classified as ultimate users if they personally consume the products they purchase.

Despite the literal language of the *Koscot* test, courts have interpreted the term *ultimate users* to mean persons who are not participants in the program. The most recent federal decision on this issue was rendered by the Ninth Circuit Court of Appeals on March 4, 1996. In *Webster v. Omnitrition International, Inc.*[9] the court found that personal consumption by a distributor's down-line does not satisfy the *Koscot* requirement that sales be to the ultimate user. Therefore, when designing a multilevel marketing plan, the approach that presents the least risk is to institute and enforce a rule that at least 70 percent of a distributor's purchases result in true retail sales to persons who do not participate in the program.

Inventory Repurchase Requirements The more sophisticated multilevel jurisdictions of Georgia, Louisiana, Massachusetts, Maryland, Puerto Rico, and Wyoming require multilevel companies to repurchase inventory that is returned by their distributors.[10] Additionally, these states mandate that written notice of the policy must be given to distributors in the distributor agreement. The rationale underlying buy-back requirements is that they tend to prevent or substantially reduce inventory loading as well as the chances that a participant will lose substantial sums of money when he or she is saddled with a large inventory of products that he or she cannot sell.

Under some statutes, the requirements are only triggered when a distributor terminates his or her relationship with the company. In other jurisdictions, like Maryland and Puerto Rico, the company must repurchase returned inventory simply if the distributor was unable to sell it within three months of its receipt. These statutes require multilevel companies to repurchase *resaleable* products from their distributors for not less than 90 percent of the products' original purchase price. Any commissions or bonuses that have been paid that are *attributable to the product being returned* (as opposed to commissions being paid due to down-line sales) may be deducted from the repurchase price. Some statutes, like Georgia's, also mandate that a multilevel company repurchase goods that are *no longer marketed* if they are returned to the company within one year from the date the company discontinued marketing the goods.[11]

A 90 percent (or higher) repurchase policy is strongly recommended. Such a buy-back policy is probably the single best way to avert the cookie-cutter class-action lawsuits that have plagued direct selling companies during the last four years. (These lawsuits will be discussed later.) Additionally, a repurchase policy should provide that commissions previously paid to up-line distributors be "recaptured" or deducted from their respective future commission payments to further reduce the incentive for inventory loading.

Buying Clubs

Buying clubs are regulated by a significant majority of states. In general, the term means any business organization that holds itself out as offering discounted prices to members by virtue of its "buying clout." A buying club need not possess any specific set of business or operational characteristics. Whether or not a business organization is a buying club is simply a function of the claims it makes. More precisely, the mere acts of an organization 1) claiming to offer discounted merchandise, 2) as a consequence of its size or other similar attribute, and 3) allowing only "members"[12] to purchase such merchandise, result in that organization being a "buying club." In Minnesota, a buying club is defined as:

> [A]ny corporation, partnership, unincorporated association or other business enterprise organized for profit with the primary purpose of providing benefits to members from the cooperative purchase of services or merchandise.[13]

Other states define buying clubs identically or similarly.[14]

Table 16.4 Elements of a Buying Club

Does Your Program Meet These Elements?
1) Is the organization a corporation?   Partnership?   Unincorporated association?   Other business enterprise?
2) Is the enterprise organized "for profit"?
3) Does the enterprise have "members"?
4) Is the *primary* purpose of the enterprise to provide benefits to members (i.e., discounted goods or services)?
5) Do these benefits result from, or are they promoted as stemming from, the cooperative purchases of goods or services?

The absence of any one of these elements allows an organization to avoid buying club classification.

If a business enterprise is a buying club, several onerous impediments to doing business exist. Buying club status triggers several requirements, including 1) registration with the state (usually the attorney general),[15] 2) the payment of a registration fee,[16] 3) the posting of a bond, 4) a right of cancellation,[17] and 5) notice of the right of cancellation on the membership agreement.[18] Additionally, other states make even more burdensome demands. For example, Florida requires that if a buying club (or any of its agents—arguably members) represents orally or in writing that use of its services will result in savings to its members, the buying club must disclose in writing in the contract that:

All savings claims made by the buying club are based on price comparisons with retailers doing business in the trade area in which the claims are made if the same or comparable items are offered for sale in the trade area and with prices at which the merchandise is actually sold or offered for sale.[19]

Some states limit the maximum duration of members' contracts, although most allow for their extension after an introductory period of usually six months. Other states require additional written disclosures, such as the fact that goods can only be bought through catalogs with no opportunity to inspect samples, if such is the case. Certain statutes mandate that the membership agreement must be approved by the state prior to use, while others impose record keeping requirements that include the right of inspection of corporate books and records by the state.

The legal requirements spanning the country are myriad, inconsistent, and arduous. If a buying club fails to meet each requirement, it is subject to enforcement action by the state, which may take the form of injunctive action to prevent the organization from conducting business (or simply shutting it down), and possibly civil penalties.[20] In Minnesota, each civil penalty may be as high as $25,000. For all of these reasons, companies are strongly urged to avoid buying club status. This can be accomplished quite easily, mainly by eliminating references to buying clubs and discounts due to membership in your company.

Business Opportunity Statutes

Many states have enacted *business opportunity* statutes. The intent behind such legislation is to provide consumers certain protection from large investments for income-producing opportunities. Historically, such "opportunities" have ranged from ostrich farms to vending machine businesses. The protection includes disclosure of information about the opportunity and its promoters, contract rescission rights, bonding, and state registration. As a practical matter, *business opportu-*

nity statutes encompass most business activities for which the promoter asserts that a certain amount of income may be earned. A business opportunity is essentially defined as a sale or lease of any products, equipment, supplies, or services for which the seller represents that: 1) the purchaser may or will derive income that exceeds the price paid for the opportunity or 2) it will provide a sales or marketing program to enable the purchaser to derive income that exceeds the price paid for the opportunity.

Table 16.5 Elements of a Business Opportunity

DOES YOUR PROGRAM MEET THESE ELEMENTS?

---

1) Is there a sale or lease or offer to sell or lease any goods or services?

2) To a purchaser?

3) That are to be used by the purchaser in beginning or operating a business?

4) Involves an initial payment by the purchaser of more than $200?

5) Involves a solicitation of purchasers in which the seller represents that:

   a) the purchaser will provide a sales or marketing plan pursuant to which the purchaser may or will earn an amount in excess of the initial payment as a result of the investment;

   b) a market exists for any goods to be made or services to be rendered by the purchaser;

   c) the seller may buy from the purchaser any goods to be made or services to rendered by the purchaser;

   d) the seller or a person referred by the seller to the purchaser may or will sell, lease, or distribute the goods made or services rendered by the purchaser; or

   e) the seller may or will pay to the purchaser the difference between the initial payment and the purchaser's earnings from the investment?

As with buying clubs, the impact of business opportunity statutes is manifold and burdensome. Generally, business opportunities must be registered with the state (usually the attorney general). Significant personal disclosures about the promoters, the promoters' backgrounds, and the promoters' personal finances are mandatory. In addition, substantial factual and financial disclosures, much like a stock prospectus, must be provided to potential purchasers regarding the opportunity. The rationale behind such disclosures is to afford prospective purchasers the ability to make a fully informed decision regarding the opportunity. Purchasers enjoy expansive rights to rescind their contracts. Further, bonding is typically required in each state in which the opportunity is offered. Some states require that business opportunities establish an escrow account into which all or a significant portion of the purchase price must be placed until the goods are received by the purchaser.

Fortunately, the intent behind such legislation is to protect consumers from large swindles. To that end, and because the risks substantially decline below a minimum investment level, statutes defining business opportunities contain minimum initial investment threshold exemptions. However, to make matters awkward, the minimum threshold differs among states and the Federal Trade Commission's Franchise and Business Opportunity Rule.[21] Under the FTC rule, as well as in a majority of the states, the minimum threshold is $500. The threshold in some states however, such as Maryland, is as low as $200.[22]

It is important to note that business opportunity statutes are concerned only with the initial investments *that are required to become a distributor.* Under various statutory schemes, these costs often extend beyond those initially needed to "acquire the opportunity." Again, the states and FTC differ on what constitutes an initial investment. The FTC and majority rule is that any required purchases within the first six months of joining a program comprise part of the initial investment. Other states specify that the initial investment extends for the duration of the term of the contract governing the parties' relationship. Still others fail to define the term altogether. Other states vary the exemption slightly by mandating that the required sale be not only below the threshold, but also "at cost." For example, under Indiana's business opportunity statute, a business opportunity excludes only "*not-for-profit* sale of sales demonstration equipment, materials, or samples for a total price of five hundred dollars ($500) or less."[23]

Referral Sales

A *referral sale* is typically defined as the provision or offer to provide a customer a prize, discount, rebate, or other compensation as an inducement for a sale that requires the prospective customer to give names of other prospective customers to the seller, if earning the prize, discount, rebate, or other compensation is contingent upon a sale to one of the "referred" customers.[24] To the surprise of most people, particularly salespeople, this type of referral sale is illegal throughout the United States.

Table 16.6 Elements of a Referral Sale

DOES YOUR PROGRAM MEET THESE ELEMENTS?

1) Does the seller offer or promise to a prospective buyer a
   a) price reduction;
   b) rebate;
   c) commission;
   d) credit;
   e) any other consideration?
2) Is the promise or offer an inducement for a sale or lease?
3) Must the purchaser provide the seller names of other potential customers?
4) Is the offer or promise contingent upon the seller's ability to make a sale to one of the potential customers?

As discussed above, referral sales are illegal in all states. Accordingly, companies are strongly encouraged not to make any references to referral sales or referral marketing, or to offer incentives contingent upon the company's successful sale to, or enrollment of, a person referred by participants.

Securities

Although most people would not think of a pyramid as a *security*, the federal Securities and Exchange Commission has used its statutory mechanisms to prosecute pyramids. In some cases, the SEC has been able to show that a pyramid was an "investment contract," and thus, a security.[25] Once it overcame this hurdle, it was relatively easy to show that the promoters were unlicensed securities brokers engaged in selling unregistered securities.

The Securities Act of 1933, the Securities and Exchange Act of 1934, and most state securities acts (Blue Sky laws) include the term investment contract within the definition of a security. None of these statutes, however, defines the term. Thus, the U.S. Supreme Court, in *Securities and Exchange Commission v. W. J. Howey Company*,[26] set forth the following three-prong test to determine if an instrument constitutes an investment contract:

> An investment contract for purposes of the Securities Act means a contract, transaction or scheme whereby a person invests his money in a common enterprise and is led to expect profits solely from the efforts of the promoter or a third party.

Table 16.7 Elements of a Security

DOES YOUR PROGRAM MEET THESE ELEMENTS?
1) Has there been an investment of money?

2) Does a *common enterprise* exist?
     a) A horizontal commonality?
     b) A vertical commonality?

3) Are persons led to expect profits from the efforts of the promoter or a third party?

An Investment of Money

The fact that an application fee must be paid lends itself to an argument that *an investment* is required to become a distributor. Indeed, if the fee is excessive, it will be classified as an investment. However, if the application fee is low and only covers the company's cost of producing sales and training literature and materials necessary for a person to become a distributor, a company may avoid having its application fee categorized as an investment.

It is also helpful in avoiding classification as an investment for companies to refund application fees to distributors who elect to terminate their relationship with the company.[27] With such a policy in place, payment of the fee presents minimal risk of loss to a distributor, and therefore mitigates the potential that it will be deemed an investment. Consequently, multilevel marketing companies should ensure that their Policies and Procedures provide that application fees will be refunded if a distributor terminates his or her agreement with the company within a finite time (for example, thirty days, six months, or one year). Companies are further urged to sell their enrollment kits at cost to keep the initial charge as low as possible.[28]

Commonality

The second prong of the *Howey* test requires that a *common enterprise* exist between a promoter and an investor. A common enterprise is defined as:

> [An enterprise] in which the fortunes of the investor are interwoven with and dependent upon the efforts and success of those seeking the investment or of third parties.[29]

A common enterprise requires evidence of either *horizontal commonality* or *vertical commonality.*[30] Horizontal commonality requires a pooling of investors' funds into a common fund, and pro rata distribution of profits from that fund.[31] In order for horizontal commonality to exist, 1) the participants pool their assets, 2) they give up any claim to profits or losses attributable to their particular investments, 3) in return for a pro rata share of the profits of the enterprise, and 4) they make their collective fortunes dependent on the success of a single common enterprise.[32] Typically, however, there is no horizontal commonality between the company and its distributors because there is no pooling of assets between them. Secondly, distributors usually do not give up claims to profits attributable to their individual efforts in return for a pro rata share of the profits of a single enterprise. Each distributor's commission is earned when sales are generated within his or her sales organization, and is paid regardless of whether the company has positive or negative earnings for the month. Moreover, the company's corporate earnings are not distributed to distributors. Because the profits earned by distributors and the company are derived and distributed from completely different sources, horizontal commonality seldom exists. Nevertheless, companies should be extremely careful not to offer bonuses or commissions that are related in any way to company revenues or profits.

Vertical commonality, on the other hand, requires that the "investor and the promoter be involved in some common venture without mandating that other investors also be involved in that venture."[33] In order to find the existence of vertical commonality sufficient to establish a common enterprise between a promoter and investor, a direct relation must exist between the success or failure of the promoter and the individual investor. Vertical commonality usually does not exist in a multilevel marketing program because the success of a member's business is independent of the success or failure of the company.

Expectation of Profits Solely from the Efforts of Others

The third prong of the *Howey* test requires that the investor "is led to expect profits solely from the efforts of the promoter or a third party." Interpretation of the word *solely* has generated considerable debate among the courts. This debate has ultimately led to a more expansive application of the test than the literal definition would allow. In *Securities and Exchange Commission v. Glenn W. Turner Enterprises, Inc.*, 474 F.2d 476 (9th Cir. 1973), the Ninth Circuit Court of Appeals refined the third prong of the test by holding:

> We adopt a more realistic test, whether the efforts made by those other than the investor are the undeniably significant ones, those essentially managerial efforts which affect the failure or success of the enterprise.[34]

A properly developed multilevel marketing program should not meet this third prong of the *Howey* test for two reasons. First, the essential managerial efforts that affect the failure or success of a direct sales business are the generation of sales and enrollments, and these functions should be performed exclusively by distributors—not by company employees. This is a critical issue. Companies have frequently advised distributors simply to get people to attend company-sponsored meetings. Once the recruits get to the meeting, company employees will do all of the work by presenting the sales plan, signing up the recruits, and making the sales. In such situations, the company is engaged in the essential managerial efforts that make the program operate, and the risk that a court will find the third prong of the *Howey* test satisfied is substantial.

Secondly, a properly developed and presented program should avoid violating the third prong of the *Howey* test by emphasizing to new distributors that their success is dependent on their own efforts and abilities. Distributors should not be advised to rely on the managerial efforts of their upline or anyone else to build their businesses. It is for this important reason that companies take action to ensure that their sales force does not promote the program with the all-too-common representation: "Just get in and I will put people in for you."

A particular word of caution is also urged upon companies in relation to the third prong of the *Howey* test. It is this element that the courts have focused on in determining whether a multilevel program constitutes an investment contract security. Although the test calls for a three-part analysis, some courts have glossed over the first two elements (or avoided addressing them altogether) when handling MLM cases. For this reason, companies should take extreme care to avoid any indication that distributors may rely on the efforts of the company, their distributors, or any other third party for their success.

Lotteries

The majority of states have laws that proscribe the operation of a lottery. Lottery laws were not designed to regulate pyramids, but rather to prevent illegal gambling. Although lottery laws have been used to prosecute pyramids, more appropriate vehicles, namely anti-pyramid and multilevel laws, are now used. Consequently, the application of lottery laws to pyramids and multilevel companies rarely occurs in regulatory proceedings.[35]

A lottery consists of a disposition of property, on contingency determined by chance, to a person who has paid valuable consideration for the chance of winning the prize. California Penal Code § 319 defines a *lottery* as:

> [A]ny scheme for the disposal or distribution of property by chance, among persons who have paid or promised to pay any valuable consideration for the chance of obtaining such property or a portion of it, or for any share or any interest in such property, upon any agreement, understanding, or expectation that it is to be distributed or disposed of by lot or chance, whether called a lottery, raffle, or gift enterprise, or by whatever name the same may be known.

Each of three elements must be present to constitute a lottery, namely a prize, distribution of the prize by chance, and consideration for the opportunity to win the prize.

As applied to pyramids, if the element of chance, rather than skill, determines the receipt of "the prize," such plans have been held to be lotteries. The most notable case illustrative of this is *U.S. Postal Service v. Unimax, Inc.*[36] In *Unimax*, the administrative law judge determined that a participant's compensation was beyond his control, and thus, determined by chance. Rather than allowing its distributors to place their down-line distributors where they desired in their organization, Unimax *assigned* distributors to positions in the down-line organization. This resulted in a matrix of unrelated distributors who were spread throughout the country and were thus less controllable.[37] The judge determined that the compensation received by Unimax distributors was based "principally on the exertions of others over whom they have no control and no substantial connection (and that) success of such marketers is determined by chance."

Under a legitimate multilevel marketing program, a distributor's compensation (the prize) is earned (won) not by chance, but rather by his skill and efforts in building and maintaining a down-line organization. In a lottery analysis, a member's efforts in building his or her organization would constitute "consideration." However, this is of no consequence because the element of "chance" remains absent. Thus, a proper multilevel program is not a lottery.

Two other similar programs, contests and sweepstakes, are perfectly legal. Each combines only two of the three lottery elements. For example, a contest combines the elements of prize and consideration, but the element of chance is absent. In a contest, the prize is awarded on the basis of skill rather than luck (for example, the person who sells the most cars or reaches a certain goal faster than her competitors). A sweepstakes combines the elements of prize and chance, but lacks the element of consideration. A sweepstakes awards its prize solely on the basis of luck, but a participant need not provide "consideration" (anything of value, frequently money or effort). The most common examples of sweepstakes are magazine sweepstakes. Although they welcome your purchase, none is necessary to participate.

Recent Litigation

In recent years, several direct selling companies have been systematically targeted by plaintiffs' securities and class-action law firms. The first class action was filed in 1991 by a plaintiffs' firm from San Francisco against NuSkin International, Inc., of Provo, Utah. The complaint alleged three counts of securities laws violations, three counts of the Racketeering Influence and Corrupt Organizations Act (RICO), and three counts of common law fraud. NuSkin settled the case in less than ten months. The exact amount that the settlement cost NuSkin is confidential and unavailable to the public. The success of the San Francisco firm enticed it to file an identical class-action complaint later in 1991 against a second direct selling company, Nikken, Inc. Nikken is a U.S. subsidiary of a Japanese direct selling organization. Nikken settled its case even faster than NuSkin did. Neither NuSkin nor Nikken had, at the time of the lawsuits, a 90 percent inventory repurchase policy. Interestingly, the remedy fashioned by the parties simply involved allowing distributors to return resaleable products for 90 percent of their purchase price, less any commissions or bonuses that had been paid to them. It is widely suspected throughout the direct selling industry that these settlements cost their respective companies many millions of dollars.

The San Francisco firm and another plaintiffs' securities firm out of Boston quickly filed multiple cookie-cutter complaints against several medium-size and larger U.S. direct selling companies. Although each company has handled its defense differently, those that have been careful to structure a legitimate multilevel marketing plan that includes the protections enumerated in this analysis, have been able to successfully defeat the pyramiding, securities, RICO, and fraud claims. The significance of these cases underscores the paramount importance of ensuring that a direct selling company's marketing/compensation plan is well within the bounds of federal and state legal constraints.

It is equally important that direct sellers also include reasonable mechanisms in their plans to prevent the risks of pyramiding, securities violations, lotteries, business opportunities, and other legal maladies. This requires the implementation of procedures to enforce policies and procedures intended to ensure the legitimacy of the program. Indeed, in the *Omnitrition* decision discussed above, one of the reasons the Ninth Circuit Court of Appeals rejected the defendant's arguments that its plan was not a pyramid was based on the finding that the company failed to provide sufficient evidence that it actually enforced its policies. Although the company had policies in place identical to those implemented by Amway, the court stated that the mere existence of policies, without evidence of enforcement, renders the policies nugatory. Multilevel companies are therefore well advised that "staying legal" requires much more than developing a program that meets state and federal requirements. Rather, it is an ongoing process that calls for vigilance and action to ensure that distributors stay within the rules.

The Personal Consumption Dilemma: Messages from *Webster v. Omnitrition*

By Spencer M. Reese

The event having the greatest impact on the course of the multilevel marketing industry in the last decade was the Ninth Circuit Court of Appeals' decision in *Webster v. Omnitrition International, Inc.*[38] The restrictions placed on the industry are, in some cases, groundbreaking. Other limitations are simply a restatement of well established principles that have governed the industry for the last twenty years. This article will discuss the Ninth Circuit's decision, how it impacts your business, and explore measures that can be taken to meet the standards it sets.

The Omnitrition Program

Omnitrition marketed nutritional supplements through a multilevel marketing program. Its distributors could purchase products at a 20 percent discount from suggested retail and sell them at retail. At the lowest distributor level there was no obligation to purchase or sell products. However, the lowest-level distributors were not entitled to receive commissions on the sales of their down-line. To receive commissions on down-line sales, a distributor was required to become a "supervisor." The lowest level supervisor position (the "bronze" level) required the distributor to purchase $2,000 in merchandise in one month or $1,000 in two consecutive months.

Procedural History

In 1992 various Omnitrition distributors filed a class-action lawsuit against the company, its principals, and its outside attorneys. The complaint alleged that Omnitrition operated a pyramid scheme, violated federal securities laws, the civil Racketeering Influence and Corrupt Organizations (RICO) Act statute, and state fraud laws through the creation, promotion, and marketing of Omnitrition distributorships. In 1994 the trial court dismissed the case against Omnitrition. The plaintiffs appealed the trial court's decision to the U.S. Ninth Circuit Court of Appeals. On appeal, the Ninth Circuit found that numerous factual questions existed that should be resolved by a jury, and therefore reversed the trial court's dismissal and remanded the case back to the trial court.

"Pyramid" Is Not Redefined

The starting point for the Ninth Circuit's pyramid analysis of the Omnitrition marketing program was a review and adoption of the longstanding definition of a pyramid contained in the FTC's decision in *Koscot Interplanetary, Inc.*[39] Therein the FTC defined a pyramid as:

> Characterized by the payment by participants of money to the company in return for which they receive 1) the right to sell a product and 2) the right to receive in return for recruiting other participants into the program rewards which are unrelated to sale of the product to ultimate users.

The *Koscot* pyramid test does not break new ground. It has been on the books for more than twenty years and has been cited in numerous pyramid cases. However, in applying the test to the Omnitrition program, the Ninth Circuit set new implementation standards that must be met by MLMs if they are to avoid operating as a pyramid.

Retail Sales Must Drive MLM Programs

The Ninth Circuit made it painfully clear that commissions paid to distributors must be directly tied to retail sales. The court stated: "The key to any anti-pyramiding rule where the basic structure serves to reward recruitment more than retailing, is that the rule must serve to tie recruitment bonuses to actual retail sales in some way."[40] This appears to be a straightforward requirement, but the court threw several obstacles in the way of traditional methods of tying commissions to retail sales.

What Qualifies as a Retail Sale?

The court stated that *sales to persons who are participants in the company's compensation program* do not qualify as *retail sales* for purposes of satisfying the *Koscot* test.[41] This interpretation of the *Koscot* test precludes companies from paying commissions on products sold to distributors for personal consumption. This is contrary to the foundation of many MLM programs, where personal consumption by distributors is the driving force powering sales. The court's reason for requiring that commissions be based on sales to nondistributors rests on its belief that mandatory minimum distributor purchases foist inventory on people who may not want the products or be able to sell them. Rather, the real reason for the purchase is simply to participate in the compensation plan. The facts of the Omnitrition case presented the court with compelling evidence that enrollments rather than sales were the driving force behind the program. A key factor on which the court focused was evidence that under the Omnitrition program distributors were encouraged to buy large amounts of merchandise ($2,000 per month) and simply "give them away" in order to participate in Omnitrition's "proven plan of success." The message in this practice is that the product is irrelevant—all that matters is getting people enrolled. Once enrolled, new distributors will make their required purchases whether they can sell the merchandise or not. These mandatory sales drive the compensation plan. In the Ninth Circuit's view, companies operating under this scenario are promoting inventory loading. Although there is a sale of a legitimate product involved, the court will regard the product as nothing more than a facade to camouflage a pyramid scheme.

Inventory Loading—A New Standard?

Inventory loading is the principal evil that anti-pyramid laws seek to prevent. The danger presented by inventory loading is that companies may saddle distributors with large quantities of expensive inventory that they cannot resell or return for a refund. For the last eighteen years, the multilevel marketing industry has operated under the FTC's definition of inventory loading, which was handed down in *In the Matter of Amway Corporation, Inc.*[42] In the *Amway* decision, the FTC defined inventory loading as a practice that "[requires] a person seeking to become a distributor to pay a large sum of money . . . for the purchase of a large amount of nonreturnable inventory."

One of the key terms in the definition of inventory loading is the word *nonreturnable*. Companies have traditionally avoided inventory loading by implementing inventory repurchase policies for distributors who elect to cancel their distributorship agreements. Inventory repurchase policies (sometimes called buy-back policies) ensure that distributors can recover much or all of their inventory and sales aid expenditures if the business does not meet their expectations. Therefore, the financial risk associated with participating in a multilevel marketing program is minimal.

However, the *Omnitrition* court issued a new definition of inventory loading that completely changes the direction companies must take to avoid inventory loading. The Ninth Circuit's new definition provides that:

> "Inventory loading" occurs when distributors make the minimum required purchases to receive recruitment-based bonuses without reselling the products to consumers.[43]

The court provided no basis for this definition. In fact, it omits all reference to the *Amway* decision's definition of inventory loading. Rather, the court placed this definition in a footnote, seemingly as an afterthought. However, the court's new definition has a dramatic impact on the MLM industry. First, it arguably removes an inventory repurchase policy as a defense to an inventory loading allegation. Secondly, it places in jeopardy those MLM programs that require distributors to produce minimum sales volumes to qualify for commissions. Unless the distributors resell the products, the company is engaged in inventory loading, even if the quantity of required purchases is small enough that it can easily be personally consumed by the distributor.

Calculation of Commissions Based on Actual Sales

It is common for companies to calculate commissions to their distributors based on the volume of merchandise purchased by their down-line organizations, whether at wholesale, suggested retail, or on a point basis. Companies can track these figures and calculate commissions with relative ease. The *Omnitrition* court determined that such a practice does not sufficiently tie commissions to retail sales. The court stated that payment of compensation based on the volume of merchandise ordered by a distributor *is facially unrelated* to the sale of product to ultimate users.[44]

Prohibiting commissions from being calculated on purchases made by distributors creates enormous operational difficulties for companies. With the right software, tracking a distributor's purchases is a relatively simple process. On the other hand, few if any companies have an infrastructure that allows them to determine how much product has been sold to retail customers versus how much has been personally consumed by the distributor. Most companies simply rely on distributors' certifications that they have resold 70 percent of their prior order before ordering more merchandise.

Traditional Safeguards Are No Longer Guaranteed

Most MLMs incorporate some form of the traditional "Amway safeguards" into their programs under the belief that these policies will protect them from operating as a pyramid. These safeguards are: 1) distributors must sell to ten retail customers each month, 2) distributors must resell 70 percent of the product they purchase every month, and 3) if a distributor elects to cancel his or her distributorship, the company will repurchase the distributor's remaining inventory at 90 percent of the cost paid by the distributor. Omnitrition incorporated these safeguards into its program, but the court nevertheless found that the mere existence of these safeguards did not deter inventory loading and promote retail sales to the degree necessary to insulate the company from operating as a pyramid.

The Ten-Customer Rule Omnitrition required its distributors to sell to ten customers per month to qualify for commissions. To ensure compliance with this rule, the company would randomly survey members of its distributor force and inquire about retail sales. The court found that this rule, even though enforced, was insufficient to tie commissions to retail sales. The basis for the court's analysis was the fact that Omnitrition required its distributors to purchase "thousands of dollars" worth of merchandise per month to qualify for upper-level (supervisor level) commissions. The court held "that [just because] some amount of product was sold by each supervisor to only ten customers each month does not insure that overrides are being paid as a result of actual retail sales."[45]

One of the messages in the court's ruling is that the number of retail customers that a company requires its distributors to service each month must be proportionate to the amount of inventory required to be purchased. For example, by requiring distributors to purchase $2,000 of inventory per month, and selling to only ten customers, each customer would have to buy an average of $200 worth of nutritional supplements. This is an unrealistic assumption. If however, a company requires its distributors to purchase $200 worth of inventory per month, and sell to a minimum of five customers, for an average sale of $40 per customer, a far more realistic scenario exists.

A minimum customer rule that has a rational relationship to the amount of required inventory purchases, although an important step, is not in and of itself sufficient to actually deter inventory loading and to promote retail sales. The second Amway safeguard, the 70 percent rule, must be implemented to ensure that regardless of the number of customers, the majority of the inventory is being resold to retail customers and is not gathering dust in distributors' basements and garages.

The 70 Percent Rule Omnitrition required its distributors to "certify" that they sold 70 percent of the merchandise they had previously purchased before becoming eligible to receive commissions. The court held that Omnitrition failed to present evidence that it enforced the rule or that the rule actually served to deter inventory loading. In fact, the court emphasized two points that made it unlikely that the 70 percent rule tied commissions to retail sales: 1) The requirement could be satisfied by sales to the distributor's down-line, and 2) the requirement could be satisfied by distributors' personal consumption of the merchandise they purchased from Omnitrition.[46]

The court's analysis of Omnitrition's application of the 70 percent rule is one of the strongest statements in the decision that sales to distributors do not qualify as a sale to the ultimate user. On this point, the court held that:

> [P]laintiffs have produced evidence that the 70% rule can be satisfied by a distributor's personal use of the products. If *Koscot* is to have any teeth, such a sale cannot satisfy the requirement that sales be to "ultimate users" of a product.[47]

To further drive home the point that distributors are not the ultimate users (retail customers) of Omnitrition's products, the court pointed out that the company does not treat distributors the same as true retail customers. Under Omnitrition's product-satisfaction guarantee, retail customers are entitled to return the products within thirty days for a refund. This same offer was not extended to distributors who purchased Omnitrition products for personal consumption.[48]

Inventory Repurchase Rule In attacking Omnitrition's inventory repurchase rule, the court again stated that Omnitrition presented no evidence that it actually repurchased excess inventory from distributors who elected to cancel their distributorships. Fortunately for the multilevel marketing industry, enforcement of an inventory repurchase policy does not present a major problem. Indeed, if a company has a buy-back policy, but does not honor it, there are few industry members who will sympathize with the company because such conduct gives the entire industry a bad reputation.[49]

What is more disturbing about the court's analysis of the inventory repurchase rule is that it focused on two points that it asserted made Omnitrition's buy-back policy weaker than the Amway policy. First, the court focused on the fact that Omnitrition only refunded 90 percent of the price of the product returned. This is problematic because 90 percent is the standard refund rate for inventory repurchases in the MLM industry. This is not by coincidence, as all six jurisdictions that statutorily regulate MLMs uniformly specify that a

90 percent refund is acceptable.[50] Although the Ninth Circuit did not specifically hold that a 100 percent inventory repurchase is required, subsequent courts can certainly make this inference now that the Ninth Circuit has questioned whether a 90 percent rate is adequate. Moreover, the court's position potentially creates an inconsistency between state and federal law that companies can only reconcile if they have a 100 percent inventory repurchase policy.

The second reason the court stated that Omnitrition's inventory repurchase policy was weaker than the Amway policy, and therefore does not deter the possibility of inventory loading, is that under the Omnitrition policy, the company will only repurchase consumable products if they are less than three months old. On this point, the court observed:

> Omnitrition will only repurchase consumable products (the majority of what it sells) if they are less than three months old. The latter fact is very significant. The buy-back rule is only effective if it can reduce or eliminate the possibility of inventory loading by insuring that program participants do not find themselves saddled with thousands of dollars' worth of unsaleable products. Omnitrition's rule potentially would not achieve this goal for any person who participated in the program for more than three months.[51]

Although Omnitrition's three month buy-back policy is on the shorter end of policies adopted by most industry members, it is not totally lacking in support. Maryland specifies in its MLM statute that buy-back provisions must last at least three months, and Puerto Rico requires a buy-back provision be held open for ninety days.[52] The Ninth Circuit's analysis, however, brings into question how long a buy-back period must remain open, but fails to provide any meaningful guidance on what length of time it would consider adequate. The few jurisdictions that have statutes that address the issue are not uniform, and the Ninth Circuit has added an additional layer of confusion to the issue.

What Do We Do Now?

The Ninth Circuit's decision is already having a dramatic impact on the MLM industry. It is often cited by attorneys general in negotiating settlements with companies allegedly violating pyramid laws. The die is cast, and it is now incumbent upon companies in the industry to design and implement their programs to operate within the strictures dictated by the court if they wish to avoid pyramid violations and the securities, RICO, and state fraud violations associated with the operation of a pyramid. Following are recommendations that, if implemented, will minimize the risks associated with operating as a pyramid.

Focus on Retail Sales, Then Promote Recruiting

Too often multilevel marketing companies exclusively emphasize the importance of recruiting new distributors. Others emphasize sales, but only secondarily to recruiting. *What is necessary is a paradigm shift from a primary emphasis on recruiting to a primary emphasis on retail sales.* It is certainly acceptable to promote recruitment of new distributors, for this is an essential element to growing a business. However, the emphasis on recruitment must be of secondary importance; distributors must be taught that the primary emphasis is on the development of retail sales. This will be difficult for many companies because it removes the inducement to purchase offered by a lucrative compensation plan and forces them to compete with retail brand products based on price, quality, convenience, and uniqueness.

Offer Direct Customer Programs A very effective means of promoting retail sales is through a direct customer program. Under these programs, distributors recruit individuals who wish to purchase merchandise directly from the company, but who do not wish to participate in the compensation plan. Customers are assigned an identification number and are placed in the recruiting distributor's down-line. When the customer wishes to purchase products, he or she contacts the company, places an order, and it is directly shipped to the customer. These programs can be easily marketed to customers by promoting their convenience because the distributor need not handle the inventory, and the customer need not be bothered by repeated sales calls from the distributor. All a customer needs to do is call the company and order more product. In fact, if a company institutes an autoship program for customers, even the hassle associated with making repeat orders disappears. However, the distributor (and his or her up-line) who recruited the customer is entitled to a commission based on the purchases of the customer.

Direct customer plans represent true retail sales since the customers, no matter how much they spend, do not receive commissions. Moreover, since distributors do not handle any inventory, they avoid problems associated with inventory loading. They are also advantageous because companies can track retail sales with relative ease, and therefore determine if a sale is commissionable under the *Omnitrition* ruling. Moreover, satisfied customers are a warm market for potential future distributors. If an individual is familiar with a company's products through months or years of personal use, they will be more receptive to selling the product themselves.

Competitive Price Strategies Products sold through multilevel marketing programs are historically priced higher than retail store brands. Most MLMs recognize that they will not be able to compete on a price basis with mass production and merchandising machines like the Proctor & Gambles and Wal-marts of the world. Therefore, MLMs tend to focus on niche markets by producing and selling higher-quality products than the mass merchandisers offer. In addition, although MLMs do not have the high advertising costs associated with mass marketing, there are many layers of commission that are paid on the sale of each product. These two factors tend to drive up the price of goods sold by MLMs.

Although MLMs' production and commission expenses are higher than those of mass marketed goods, MLMs must not ignore the realities of supply and demand if they are going to compete for legitimate retail sales. To reasonably attract customers, competitive pricing is essential. In order to advance retail sales, companies must price their products competitively with other goods competing for the same niche. Thus, for example, if a company positions a product as a high-end hair care system, it should at a minimum be priced competitively with similar high-end salon and designer products.

Implement Safeguards against Inventory Loading

Although Omnitrition had the traditional Amway safeguards in place, the court was not willing to rule as a matter of law that these policies effectively deterred or prevented inventory loading. This ruling *does not* mean that the Amway safeguards are no longer valid anti-inventory loading policies. Rather, the court ruled against Omnitrition because *it lacked sufficient evidence that the policies were enforced* and that they effectively safeguarded against inventory loading. The clear message is that companies must implement effective anti-inventory loading policies, and they must enforce the policies. *Without enforcement, even the most sound policy will not provide a defense.*

The following discussion presents policies that can be utilized to guard against inventory loading. Bear in mind, however, that because a lack of retail sales is so closely tied to inventory loading under the *Omnitrition* definition of inventory loading, implementing a solid retail sales program is the most critical safeguard against inventory loading.

The Amway Safeguards Despite the fact that Omnitrition did not win on appeal with the Amway defense, the Amway safeguards are nevertheless a good starting point for most companies that sell tangible goods.[53] A review of numerous 1996 settlements between state attorneys general and multi-level marketing companies reveals that a five-customer rule (rather than ten customers as in the Amway case) and a 70 percent resale requirement are very common components in the agreements. Additionally, an inventory repurchase policy that requires refunding 90 percent of a terminating distributor's net cost for returned merchandise is not only common in settlements, it is mandated in six jurisdictions (Georgia, Louisiana, Maryland, Massachusetts, Puerto Rico, and Wyoming).

The Ninth Circuit questioned whether Omnitrition's three month, 90 percent inventory repurchase policy adequately prevented inventory loading. Despite the court's position, 90 percent still represents the industry standard. Although a company may receive incrementally more protection by incorporating a 100 percent refund policy, the fact that various jurisdictions have enacted legislation specifying a 90 percent rate is strong evidence that a 90 percent refund rate remains satisfactory.

The duration of the buy-back period is also a critical question. Although two jurisdictions require as little as three months or ninety days (Maryland and Puerto Rico, respectively), it is highly advisable to extend the policy to one year or longer (in some states the repurchase policy may have to be extended even further). The most generous inventory repurchase policy will take back all inventory, regardless of when purchased, with no questions asked. Although this policy offers the greatest protection, it also opens the company up to abusive practices by distributors. A policy that balances consumer protection concerns and the company's interests is more practicable. An example of such a policy is to allow a refund as long as the merchandise remains currently marketed by the company and is returned in resaleable condition. Four states—Louisiana, Wyoming, Massachusetts, and Georgia—have open-ended statutes (Louisiana utilizes an administrative rule) requiring companies to take back products as long as the goods are resaleable.

Central to the effectiveness of any inventory repurchase policy is the company's ability to *prove* that its refund policy is honored. This requires that companies keep detailed records of the returned merchandise that they have taken back and the refunds that have been issued. Companies should maintain a monthly refund report so that if their programs are challenged, they can provide the court with compelling evidence that distributors are not saddled with unwanted inventory if they elect to cancel their participation in the program.

Many MLMs have adopted the Amway safeguards under the misunderstanding that they are the *only* viable inventory loading safeguards and are therefore mandatory, or that they constitute a complete defense to an inventory loading charge. In fact, the FTC decision merely found that the safeguards were effective in preventing inventory loading *in that case.* Thus, the door is open to other creative measures, which, *if enforced,* can assist in preventing inventory loading and should be considered.

Other Disincentives to Inventory Loading Some companies limit the quantity of merchandise that a distributor can purchase unless the distributor presents invoices or other evidence that he or she has presold orders exceeding the limit. Other companies limit commissionable purchases to the first $100 or $200 per month in product orders, with no commissions being paid on purchases over that amount. These policies can be very useful under the traditional definition of inventory loading as stated in the *Amway* decision (inventory loading requires that "a person seeking to become a distributor . . . pay a large sum of money" for the purchase of a large amount of nonreturnable inventory). These policies do not, however, satisfy the *Omnitrition* court's new definition of inventory loading. Under the *Omnitrition* definition, a distributor is engaging in inventory loading if he or she makes the minimum required purchases to receive recruitment-based bonuses without reselling the products to consumers. Thus, under this definition, a distributor must sell the product that they purchase to avoid inventory loading.

Despite the *Omnitrition* court's definition of inventory loading, disincentives to excess inventory purchases, such as maximum purchases and limiting commissions and bonuses to the first $100 or $200 of purchases, are a recommended practice. Such policies put the company in a good position to avoid inventory loading under the traditional definition. Furthermore, the *Omnitrition* court's definition of inventory loading lacks legal foundation. Rather, the court's definition is a statement representing the individual views of the author of the opinion, and should not be binding in subsequent cases (in legalese, such a statement of opinion is known as *dicta*). Certainly, regulatory bodies will seize upon the language and use it to their advantage at every opportunity, but industry members must be aggressive in fighting this definition; otherwise it could become an accepted definition.

Allow Personal Production Quotas to Be Satisfied by Retail Sales As discussed above, many programs require their distributors to purchase a minimum amount of product each month. In theory, distributors must retail the majority of the products (typically 70 percent of their inventory) before qualifying for a commission. In reality, distributors often meet their quotas by personally consuming most or all of the products they purchase. To reduce the personal consumption of distributors and to promote the development of retail sales, companies should allow the distributors to satisfy their monthly minimum volumes through purchases made by their personally enrolled direct customers. This option will move the company one step closer to satisfying the retail sales requirements set forth by the Ninth Circuit.

Low Minimum Qualifications If a company requires minimum monthly purchases of its distributors, the minimums should be kept low. There is no bright line test as to what constitutes a high or a low purchase requirement, but a strong dose of common sense should be used. Set minimum quotas low enough so that the products can realistically be sold at retail before the distributor must purchase the next month's inventory. Without question, Omnitrition's $2,000 per month quota caught the court's attention, and would certainly catch the attention of any regulatory body investigating a company.

Conclusion

The multilevel marketing industry is currently operating in an atmosphere of extreme regulatory scrutiny. The *Omnitrition* decision makes doing business even more challenging. However, by paying attention to the lessons contained in the decision, companies can chart a course that will allow them to operate legitimately and profitably.

At the very least, there are two lessons the multilevel marketing industry must take from the *Omnitrition* decision. First, companies must place their primary emphasis on retail sales rather than recruiting. It is certainly possible for companies to grow and prosper with programs that are driven by sales to retail customers. These programs will not emerge without some resistance, but the innovative companies that are able to make this paradigm shift will be the ones that emerge as the future success stories.

The second message, which must echo loud and long, is that *enforcement* of policies that deter inventory loading and encourage retail sales are of paramount importance. Without enforcement, even the most perfectly drafted policy is useless. It is therefore critical that companies proactively monitor their sales forces to ensure that retail sales requirements are satisfied and that their programs are properly presented to emphasize retail sales ahead of recruitment.

The Success Formula

In order to build a successful network marketing company, you must follow the rules. Legal issues are extensive, and it takes time and money to do things right. It is important to consult with reputable legal counsel at start-up and throughout the expansion of your company. If you decide to take shortcuts on the legal aspects of your business, don't plan to be around in the long run, or expect to pay dearly for your shortsightedness. The essential Success Formula ingredient here is to abide by the laws, and understand that you do not know this specialized area, so seek appropriate guidance.

Notes

1. Georgia Code § 10–1–410.

2. Statutes do not define the terms *supply* or *distribute.*

3. This should not be interpreted to mean that payment of compensation simply for recruiting others is proper. Exactly the opposite is true. Commissions must be paid based on the sale of products or services, not for recruiting others.

4. North Carolina Statutes § 14–291.2(b).

5. New York Gen. Bus § 359–fff.

6. V.T.C.A. Penal Code § 32.48.

7. Unlike the United States, Canada has passed federal anti-pyramid legislation. See Section 55 of the Competition Act.

8. 86 FTC 1106, 1180 (1975).

9. 79 F.3d 776 (1996).

10. For example, Section 10–1–415(d) of the Georgia Code provides:

    (1) If the participant has purchased products or paid for administrative services while the contract of participation was in effect, the seller shall repurchase all unencumbered products, sales aids, literature, and promotional items which are in a reasonably resalable or reusable condition and which were acquired by the participant from the seller; *such repurchase shall be at a price not less than 90 percent of the original net cost to the participant of the goods being returned* . . .

    (Emphasis added.) The 90 percent buy-back requirement is also a condition of membership in the Direct Selling Association.

11. There is some protection afforded to multilevel companies. In certain circumstances, goods that are no longer marketed by a multilevel company need not be repurchased if they were sold to participants as nonreturnable, discontinued, or seasonal items and the nonreturnable, discontinued, or seasonal nature of the goods was clearly disclosed to the participant seeking to return the goods prior to the purchase of the goods by the participant.

12. *Member* means a status by which any natural person is entitled to any of the benefits of a club (Minnesota Statute, Chapter 325G.23., Subd. 7).

13. Minn. Stat., Chapter 325G.23., Subd. 6.

14. The definitions of a buying club in Kentucky, New Hampshire, South Dakota, and Tennessee, to name but a few, are identical to Minnesota's. In Florida, a "buying service," "buying club," or "club" means "any corporation, nonprofit corporation, partnership, unincorporated association, cooperative association, or other business enterprise which is organized with the primary purpose of providing benefits to members from the cooperative purchase of service or merchandise and which desires to effect such purpose through direct solicitation or other business activity" (Florida Statutes Annotated § 559.3902). North Carolina defines a "discount buying club" as "any person, firm or corporation, which in exchange for any valuable consideration offers to sell or to arrange the sale of goods or

271

services to its customers at prices represented to be lower than are generally available" (General Statutes of North Carolina § 66–131).

15. Every buying, health, or social referral club doing business in this state shall register with the attorney general and provide all information requested on forms the attorney general provides. The person shall furnish the full name and address of each business location where the club's memberships are sold as well as any other registration information the attorney general considers appropriate [Minn. Stat., Chapter 325G.27., Subd 1(a)].

16. The Minnesota Statute, Chapter 325G.27., Subd 1(b) states:

The initial registration fee in Minnesota is $250. For each year thereafter, the fee is $150. [Minn. Stat., Chapter 325G.27., Subd 1(b).] Registration fees should be paid in each state in which your company is doing business.

17. Minn. Stat., Chapter 325G.24. states:

Any person who has elected to become a member of a club may cancel such membership by giving written notice of cancellation any time before midnight of the third business day following the date on which membership was attained. Notice of cancellation may be given personally or by mail. If given by mail, the notice is effective upon deposit in a mailbox, properly addressed and postage prepaid. Notice of cancellation need not take a particular form and is sufficient if it indicates, by any form of written expression, the intention of the member not to be bound by the contract. Cancellation shall be without liability on the part of the member and the member shall be entitled to a refund, within ten days after notice of cancellation is given, of the entire consideration paid for the contract. Rights of cancellation may not be waived or otherwise surrendered.

18. Minn. Stat., Chapter 325G.25. provides:

A copy of every contract shall be delivered to the member at the time the contract is signed. Every contract must be in writing, must be signed by the member, must designate the date on which the member signed the contract and must state, clearly and conspicuously in bold face type of a minimum size of fourteen points, the following:

"MEMBERS' RIGHT TO CANCEL"

"If you wish to cancel this contract, you may cancel by delivering or mailing a written notice to the club. The notice must say that you do not wish to be bound by the contract and must be delivered or mailed before midnight of the third business day after you sign this contract. The notice must be delivered or mailed to: (Insert name and mailing address of club). If you cancel, the club will return, within ten days of the date on which you give notice of cancellation, any payments you have made."

If the contract does not contain this notice, it may be canceled by the member *at any time* by giving notice of cancellation *by any means.*

19. Florida Statutes Annotated, § 559.3904.

20. Minn. Stat., Chapter 325G.28. requires the attorney general to investigate and prosecute violations of the buying club statutes.

Subdivision 1. The attorney general shall investigate violations of sections 325G.23 to 325G.28, and when from information in his possession he has reasonable ground to believe that any person has violated or is about to violate any provision of sections 325G.23 to 325G.28, or that any club is insolvent, he shall be entitled on behalf of the state

(a) to sue for and have injunctive relief in any court of competent jurisdiction against any such violation or threatened violation without abridging the penalties provided by law;

(b) to sue for and recover for the state, from any person who is found to have violated any provision of sections 325G.23 to 325G.28, a civil penalty, in an amount to be determined by the court, not in excess of $25,000; and in case the club has failed to maintain the bond required by sections 325G.23 to 325G.28, or is insolvent or in imminent danger of insolvency, to sue for and have an order appointing a receiver to wind up its affairs. All civil penalties recovered under this subdivision shall be deposited in the general fund of the state treasury.

21. See 16 C.F.R. § 436.

22. MD Bus. Reg. § 14-103.

23. Indiana Revised Statute §24–5–8–1.

24. Minn. Stat., Section 325F.69., Subd. 2. provides:

Referral and chain referral selling prohibited. (1) With respect to any sale or lease the seller or lessor may not give or offer a rebate or discount or otherwise pay or offer to pay value to the buyer or lessee as an inducement for a sale or lease in consideration of the buyer's or lessee's giving to the seller or lessor the names of prospective purchasers or lessees, or otherwise aiding the seller or lessor in making a sale or lease to another person, if the earning of the rebate, discount or other value is contingent upon the occurrence of an event subsequent to the time the buyer or lessee agrees to buy or lease.

25. See *SEC v. Glenn W. Turner Enterprises, Inc.*, 348 F. Supp. 766 (D. Ore. 1972), aff'd 474 F.2d 476 (9th Cir. 1973), *cert. denied* 414 U.S. 821 (1973).

26. 328 U.S. 293, 66 S.Ct. 1100, 90 L.Ed. 1244 (1946).

27. In a comprehensive securities and pyramiding analysis, the Federal Trade Commission analyzed the Amway marketing plan in *In the Matter of Amway Corporation, Inc.* (93 FTC 618 [1979]). The FTC carefully considered Amway's requirement that an individual purchase a $15.60 sales literature kit to become a distributor in order to determine if the purchase constituted an investment sufficient to warrant a finding that the Amway plan constituted an illegal pyramid and an unregistered security. The FTC's initial decision held that there was no investment involved in the purchase of the sales kit:

The Amway system does not involve an "investment" in inventory by a new distributor. (Finding 61) A kit of sales literature costing only $15.60 is the only requisite. (Finding 34) And that amount will be returned if the distributor decides to leave Amway. (Finding 37) (93 FTC at 700)

28. It is important that sales kits be sold "at cost" for purposes of avoiding pyramid classification as well as securities investment classification. If profits are made on the sale of starter kits, it can be deemed an initiation or headhunting fee under a pyramid analysis.

29. *Brodt v. Bache & Co., Inc.*, 595 F.2d 459, 460 (9th Cir. 1978), quoting *SEC v. Glenn W. Turner Enterprises, Inc.*, 474 F.2d 476, 482 n. 7 (9th Cir. 1973).

30. *Hocking v. Dubois*, 885 F.2d 1449, 1455 (9th Cir. 1989).

31. *Brodt*, 595 F.2d at 460.

32. *Hocking v. Dubois, supra*, 885 F.2d at 1459.

33. *Brodt*, 595 F.2d at 461.

34. 474 F.2d at 482.

35. Although violation of anti-lottery laws is not a primary focus in most regulatory actions, it is commonly included as a cause of action in civil actions brought by private-party plaintiffs against multilevel companies. Multilevel companies are therefore advised to be cognizant of lottery issues, particularly when developing promotional programs and sales contests for their distributors.

36. P.S. Docket No. 28/77, June 10, 1988.

37. Also of significance was the lack of any training or supervisory requirement for up-line distributors.

38. 79 F.3d 776 (1996).

39. 86 FTC 1106, 1181 (1975).

40. 79 F.3d at 783.

41. 79 F.3d Id. at 783.

42. 93 FTC 618, 715 (1979).

43. 79 F.3d at 783, note 3.

44. 79 F.3d Id. at 782.

45. 79 F.3d Id. at 783.

46. 79 F.3d Id. at 783.

47. 79 F.3d Id. at 783.

48. 79 F.3d Id. at 783.

49. This statement is not intended to imply that Omnitrition was not honoring its buy-back policy. The Court of Appeals only stated that the company did not present any evidence in support of its summary judgment motion that the buy-back policy was enforced. The court left it to the trial court to determine if Omnitrition actually enforced the policy.

50. Georgia: GC §10–1–415; Maryland: MD Bus. Reg. §14–302; Massachusetts: M.G.L.A. 93 § 69; Puerto Rico: 10 L.P.R.A. §997b; Wyoming: W.S. §40–3–105; Louisiana: L.A.C. §16:III, 503B. In addition, the Direct Selling Association provides for a 90 percent repurchase policy in its Code of Ethics.

51. *Id.* at 784.

52. MD Bus. Reg. §14–302; 10 L.P.R.A. §997b.

53. Companies that offer services can easily avoid inventory loading situations. Distributors for long-distance telephone services, for example, cannot inventory load because there is no merchandise to hold in inventory; commissions are paid based on actual usage by their customers and down-line distributors rather than inventory purchases. Service companies must nevertheless ensure that they have sufficient retail sales to ensure that commissions are properly payable.

THE SUCCESS FORMULA REVISITED

Objective

T HROUGHOUT THE BOOK, I have developed a checklist of the factors necessary for success in the network marketing industry. They have unfolded as the Success Formula. Following is a recap of these factors. This recap can serve as a checklist for start-ups to follow, for existing companies to see how they measure up, and for prospective distributors or investors to determine if the company they are reviewing qualifies as a winner.

Delivering on the Promise of Success

The Success Formula requires that each company involved in network marketing take responsibility for delivering on the promise of success to its distributors. Components of the formula include: unique, safe, quality products; an attractive opportunity and compensation plan; an easy-to-replicate recruiting process; and systems that make it all work together. Additionally, some of the "magic" ingredients include a company mission or higher purpose, recognition that makes people feel good, and strong personal relationships between the company leadership and the field sales force.

Creating Your Company

To create and maintain a successful company, you must know who you are, what you sell, and what you stand for. Once you establish your mission, your story, your culture, and your image, you must maintain its integrity. The best way to build your brand and franchise is by sending a consistent message through product line choices, your logo, your literature, the look and feel developed at events, and the warmth your executives show distributors and customers.

You must also be vigilant about maintaining a balance of emphasis on both your product line and your Opportunity. If emphasis is placed strictly on product, your "franchise" of stores or distributor count will not grow as fast as you would like. If the emphasis is strictly on the Opportunity, with no demand being created for the product, the chances for long-term success are minimal. The best approach is to maintain a balance between the two, respecting the source of sales from each effort. You can't have product sales without distributors, and you won't keep distributors without excellent products.

Selecting a Product

The product you select and offer for sale is a crucial ingredient in the Success Formula. It will mean the difference between success and failure for your company in the long run. The products in your line must be unique and consumable, have a compelling story behind them, offer a value to customers, and be of the highest quality to support a money-back guarantee. If you can also offer one or two high-impact products to make distributors' jobs easier and more successful, you are one step ahead on the road to success.

Choosing a Compensation Plan

Indeed, the compensation plan plays a major role in the Success Formula. It is, however, not the end-all ingredient many make it out to be. As long as it is fair, competitive, and legal, it will serve you well. If you can make it simple, too, that will be a miracle.

The attractiveness of the entire "franchise package" is what's the most important. You can have a great product and a fair compensation plan and have great success. On the other hand, if you have a marginal or poor product, even with a great compensation plan, you will not succeed.

Marketing Your Opportunity

Because the Opportunity is an extremely important product, make sure you devote sufficient financial and human resources to this factor. Many companies fall short here. They simply forget that they need promotional dollars and a full-time person to focus on and be responsible for creating the ongoing support the sales group needs to have a truly contemporary and attractive Opportunity/Franchise product to market. Having a good performer in the position of brand manager for the Opportunity may mean the difference between success or failure, or slow growth and rapid growth. Part of the Opportunity brand manager's role is to create a *duplicatable* (the word used in network marketing to mean the ability to imitate over and over) recruiting process and recruiting strategy. The combination of a dynamic Opportunity brand manager and a duplicatable recruiting process is definitely a key ingredient in the Success Formula.

The Sales Personality or Rainmaker

The importance of having a rainmaker to lead the recruiting effort cannot be underestimated. In order to jump-start, gain momentum, and sustain the growth of your MLM sales organization—which in turn translates to business growth—a key ingredient of the Success Formula is the sales personality/ rainmaker. Sometimes it is a person from the corporate office, other times it is a top distributor or group of distributors in the field.

Field Support

While basic field support like toll-free telephone ordering and company publications is essential, companies that take advantage of the plethora of other high-tech and high touch vehicles to support their field definitely have an edge. Advanced supports that effectively and positively impact recruiting efforts are the ones that are most important to the Success Formula.

Recognition

Recognition is vital. The more sophisticated and efficient you can be in executing your recognition programs, the more powerful this factor will be in your success. Everyone loves to be recognized, and the effort expended and resources you allocate to allow people to participate will pay off with huge rewards. Recognition and incentive trips cement relationships with your company. Effective recognition is what gives network marketing companies a competitive advantage in drawing people in from the corporate world and from lives that often lack appreciation.

Events vs. Meetings

Events play a big part in the Success Formula. If done well, they give a company instant credibility and help distributors get the big picture and vision of greatness. Events are a big step up from meetings. Events also serve as a bonding experience that will pay back big dividends in the area of distributor retention. Once you get distributors to attend a well-orchestrated major company event, they will generally stay with you for years to come.

Customer Service

Customer service is an integral part of the Success Formula, and specifically important when it comes to retention of distributors and customers. The two most critical elements of customer service in the Success Formula are 1) *always* make sure your distributors' checks go out on time, and 2) avoid merchandise shortages. In addition, one of the secrets to enjoying a competitive advantage is to set the amazing service standard, and establish a daily meeting with an accompanying system to monitor your performance.

The Home Office Team

Having the right team or talent pool at the home office is definitely a component in the Success Formula. If competent resources exist, regardless of the size of the team, they will have a positive impact on success. Even at first, when you cannot employ separate expert individuals to perform each function required, someone with appropriate cross-functional skills must be available and assigned responsibility for each function. If you cannot afford even this level of full-time staffing, utilize a consultant who brings the skills you need to bridge the gap. It may feel like you can't afford one, but if you choose a consultant wisely, the money you spend will save you thousands of dollars in mistakes you may make without proper guidance.

Capitalizing on the Channel

The area of distributor benefits is not of significant importance as an ingredient in the Success Formula at start-up. However, as your company grows and more of the competition offers these services, you need to be aware that business supports and other distributor benefits will become important both as an additional source of income and as retention support. Since retention is a vital success factor and important at all times, the best thing to start with early on is a TLC call. The next step would be to offer a limited logo merchandise line. Later, significant supports and benefits that help distributors in the efficient execution of their duties are the best choice.

Listen to Those Who Know

Important aspects of the Success Formula as suggested by CEOs, presidents, and other executives who have been there include: Listen to your sales force, remember that your distributors are your customers, develop a compelling and crystallized story and tell it often, make product king, have lots of capital, and build on relationships to grow the business.

The Value of Education

Education is significant to the Success Formula. Because there are so many entities and individuals who may have misconceptions about the industry, it is important that everyone involved helps to educate others to ensure a better understanding of what we have to offer. Also, joining the Direct Selling Association and contributing to the Direct Selling Education Foundation, as well as participating in their educational seminars, serves as a way to keep yourself updated on industry-wide issues. Because executives of member companies are open to sharing ideas with one another, and new members are assigned an executive mentor from an established company, you can also pick up inside tips to apply to your business and help accelerate its success.

Avoid Common Mistakes

Dan Jensen has observed a pattern of pitfalls that companies in the network marketing industry can get into. He identified the ten things that weaken new companies—and can take them to the point of tragic failure. You need to be sure to make this list a guideline of what *not* to do—and how to avoid doing it. The mistakes to avoid are:

- Inadequate funding
- No business plan
- Poor management
- Poor staff training
- Computer systems that don't work
- Failing to have the compensation plan reviewed legally
- Poor customer service

- O   No corporate marketing personality on the road
- O   Growing too fast

Understanding and avoiding these ten mistakes are part of the overall Success Formula application.

Play by the Rules

In order to build a successful network marketing company, you must follow the rules. Legal issues are extensive, and it takes time and money to do things right. It is important to consult with reputable legal counsel at start-up and throughout the expansion of your company. If you decide to take shortcuts on the legal aspects of your business, don't plan to be around in the long run, or expect to pay dearly for your short-sightedness. The essential Success Formula ingredient here is to abide by the laws, and understand that you do not know this specialized area, so seek appropriate guidance.

Conclusions

Congratulations. By taking this journey with me, you have a huge head start on successfully launching or enhancing your business. Equipped with this knowledge, you can focus on the specific elements needed to get your business energized and moving ahead. I trust you have gained some valuable insights into what makes successful network marketing companies tick. It's a phenomenal industry, and I hope you decide to make it part of your life. It has added a lot of joy to mine. Thank you for letting me share what I've learned.

If you would like more information about building a successful network marketing/MLM company, following is a list of resources to contact. All firms specialize in the network marketing, direct selling, and multilevel marketing industry.

Associations

The Direct Selling Association
or the Direct Selling Education Foundation
1666 K St., NW, Suite 1010
Washington, DC 20006
Phone: (202) 293-5760
Web site: www.dsa.org

Consulting Services/Strategy Development

Angela L. Moore
Your Partner in Success
P. O. Box 2814
Coppell, TX 75019
Phone: (208) 528-2886
and
P. O. Box 2084
Idaho Falls, ID 83403
E-mail: angelam@ida.net

Educator

Raymond W. "Buddy" LaForge
Brown-Forman Professor of Marketing
University of Louisville
College of Business and Public Administration
Louisville, KY 40292
Phone: (502) 852-4849

Executive Search

Al Wakefield
Wakefield Talabisco International
Mendon Meadows
Suite 8, Route 4
Mendon, VT 05701
Phone: (802)747-5901

Legal Services

Kevin Grimes and Spencer Reese
Grimes & Reese
1270 S. Woodruff Ave.
Idaho Falls, ID 83404
Phone: (208) 524-0699
Web site: www.mlmlaw.com

Recruiting Systems
and Marketing Communications

Kirsten Park
Mark Communications
307 West 200 South
Salt Lake City, UT 84101
Phone: (801) 531-9808

Sales Force Compensation Plan
Development

Doug Cloward
Salesforce Development Services
851 E. 1100 So.
Spanish Fork, UT 84660
Phone: (801) 798-0909

Software Systems

Jenkon International
Contact: Jerry York
7600 N. E. 41st St.,Suite 350
Vancouver, WA 98662
Phone: (360) 256-4400
Web site: www.jenkon.com

Glossary

FOLLOWING ARE SOME terms that are used in the network marketing/MLM and direct selling industry. While they may each have slightly different meanings, often these terms are used generically or interchangeably. I suggest you read through them all to get a basic understanding of the terms. For more in-depth details about any term, check the index to see where it's covered, or refer to the chapter on that topic.

BV (bonus volume), QV (qualifying volume), BP (bonus points), PV (personal volume), sales volume, average order, volume.

These are various terms reflecting measures that are assigned as point values to reward individual or group sales achievements. There are varying relationships to dollar values; some have a one-to-one relationship, while others are a variable percent of the dollar amount. Points translate into earnings or status (pay-out or position) in the compensation plan. They are like an internal currency or standard that gets exchanged into dollars based on a formula.

Compensation plan, commission plan, pay plan, levels of compensation, marketing plan, coded bonuses, commission, leadership bonus, and training bonus.

These are all labels for the ways compensation or dollars are paid out by companies to distributors for their sales and leadership efforts.

Core product or main product.

The core product is the category, categories, or main product line that supports the company mission, and is sold by the sales force to ultimate consumers for standard commissions and points in the compensation plan. The core product is distinguished from a noncommissioned sales aid, or other sideline benefit product or service that is outside the normal pay plan structure.

Distributor, sales representative, marketing representative, marketing executive, independent representative, customer of the Opportunity.

These are names used to identify all individuals who sell to ultimate consumers for a company and/or recruit and train others to do the same. They are not employed by the company, but have an independent contractor status in a network marketing company.

Distributor benefits, sideline businesses.

These are items that are sold or bought by your field sales force that are not part of your core product line. They can be services that help distributors in the execution of their duties, and they can add to the richness of the compensation plan. They are not the core product line such as personal care or nutritional supplements. Often they are only offered to the sales force, and they are other business aids or supplemental beneficial items. Examples of these are company-branded credit cards, long-distance telephone services, a travel agency or club, or health insurance. They are referred to as sideline businesses because, if structured properly, they can add to the profitability of both the company and its distributors.

Duplicatable.

A term used in conjunction with the recruiting and sponsoring function. It is used to mean a process that can be imitated and duplicated over and over again, with similar success.

Events, meetings, special events, conventions, rallies, training meetings, corporate sponsored meetings.

These are identifiers for various events held in locations including the company's headquarters city, and other key cities where large numbers of distributors are. The purpose of the gatherings is to train and motivate the sales organization, and to bond the distributors to the people and culture of the company they represent.

Field support, sales support, sales operations.

This is the group and function of the corporate office that supports the functions of the field sales force, and often plans training and other corporate functions. They also create, manage, and track recognition and incentive programs.

Network marketing, direct selling, and multilevel marketing.

While all of these terms actually have specific meanings, they are often used interchangeably in the industry. For purposes of giving a brief explanation here, suffice it to say that *network marketing* encompasses the practice of person-to-person selling using a marketing approach where individuals directly introduce someone within their circle of influence to a company and product line. That person serves their acquaintance as the main link and primary source of connection between the company and its customers. *Direct selling* refers to the person-to-person aspect of the selling approach. *Network marketing* refers to the chain of relationships between the seller and his or her customers; that is his or her personal network. *Multilevel* describes not only the compensation plan structure, but also the appearance of steps on a ladder joining individuals on different levels of a distributor's organization to the company. This stepladder effect also produces the terms "up-line" and "down-line," describing a position on the ladder above (closer to the company) or below an individual's own status.

Opportunity, business opportunity, business presentation, opportunity presentation, opportunity night.

These terms refer to the business an individual gets into once he or she decides to contract with a company to represent it and earn money doing so. In order to solicit individuals and tell them about the program and business, it is a general practice to provide a business opportunity presentation for the current sales force to use to entice others into the business. Sometimes open meetings are held to inform a group of individuals about the company and its plan. These are known as business presentations or opportunity nights.

Prospect, recruit, potential distributor.

These are terms used to describe individuals who are eligible and should be targeted for a business presentation, or anyone not currently representing a company. It is the body of people available to target or recruit for future growth of the company by getting the message of the company and its products to them.

Recognition, incentives.

Recognition and incentives are programs and processes designed to reward achievement. They produce desired results by providing a valuable benefit for the accomplishment of select behavior. Most often, these are in the form of "You do, you get." For instance, "Reach X cumulative volume in sales this month and achieve status level Y and lapel pin Z."

Up-line, down-line, organization, field sales organization.

All of these terms describe a unit of people who hold positions in the compensation plan, which, overall, translates into the entire field sales force.

Index